RECIPES OF NOTE

FOR ENTERTAINING

ROCHESTER
CIVIC MUSIC
GUILD

ROCHESTER, MINNESOTA

All proceeds from the sale of this cookbook
will be donated to Rochester Civic Music.

For additional copies, use order blanks
at the back of the book or write to:

Recipes of Note for Entertaining
Rochester Civic Music Guild
P.O. Box 5802
Rochester, MN 55903

First Printing 1994
ISBN 0-9621066-1-5

Cover Design by Ads & Arts, Rochester MN
Cover Photograph by Curt Sanders, M. Photog., Cr., CPP

Stoyles Graphic Services
204 N. Second Avenue W.
Lake Mills, Iowa 50450

TABLE OF CONTENTS

FOREWORD

The Rochester Civic Music Guild, formed in 1963, was first called the Rochester Symphony Guild. The original purposes of the organization were to promote interest in the Rochester Civic Music program, to award music scholarships to Rochester area young musicians, and to further public understanding and appreciation of music through programs and projects. When the city's music program expanded, the group changed its name in 1974 to Rochester Civic Music Guild. Today the Guild is an organization of over 200 women and men who work for the enhancement and financial support of Rochester Civic Music. The Guild arranges concert previews, hosts post-concert receptions, provides ushers, decorates for the pops concerts, volunteers in the music office, coordinates the Yule-Fest Matinee family concert, sponsors a scholarship competition for young musicians, plans monthly Lunch and Learn programs and raises money for Rochester Civic Music through several fund-raising projects.

In 1988 the Rochester Civic Music Guild published its first cookbook, **Recipes of Note**. It sold out, and a second printing was required. Because of the success with this first endeavor, the Guild decided to publish a second cookbook. Two years in the making, **Recipes of Note for Entertaining** is sure to please you. Filled with excellent recipes that have been contributed by Guild members, their families, and friends, this cookbook also has a special section with menus to help you with your entertaining. You will still find, however, the same quality of recipes and clear directions that made the first cookbook so successful.

We are proud to present **Recipes of Note for Entertaining.** We hope it will give you many hours of cooking pleasure!

Georgia Hurley, Renda Meloy
Co-Chairs

COOKBOOK COMMITTEE

Georgia Hurley, Renda Meloy
Co-Chairs

Nancy Brubaker   Ann Jost
Kay Love-Caskey   Carolyn Rorie
Margo Stich   Nina Sudor

TYPING

Ann Jost, Becky Brey
Jeanette Howe, Laura Meloy
Carolyn Rorie

MUSIC SELECTIONS

Jere Lantz
Music Director and Conductor
Rochester Symphony Orchestra

WINE SUGGESTIONS

Staff of Andy's Crossroads Liquor
Rochester, MN

TECHNICAL COMPUTER ASSISTANCE

Anne Hammond, Scott Stiving

INDEX

Georgia Hurley, Margo Stich

TESTING

Sheila Kramer, Sandra Weissler

MARKETING

Bari Amadio, Chair
Beverly Spittell-Lehman, Lisa Rodysill
Ann Northcutt, Linda Van Straaten

Thank you to the many people who tested and tasted recipes—Guild members, friends, husbands, families. Your interest, enthusiasm, and tasting expertise were greatly appreciated!

CONTRIBUTORS

The following people generously contributed their favorite recipes for this project. Without them this cookbook would not have been possible.

Jane Aughenbaugh	Renee Jacobson	Carolyn Rorie
Judi Bolander	Kathy Johnstone	Alice Schiefen
Becky Brey	Ann Jost	Ina Chase Sherman
Nancy Brubaker	Mary Jo Kelly	Pam Smoldt
Chuck Canfield	Lois Kennel	Margo Stich
Ellen Cascino	Judy King	Lisa and Scott Stiving
Dora Ann Chase	Peggy King	Maren Stocke
Mary Creel	Ramona Kisrow	Nina Sudor
Suzanne Dinusson	Marion Kleinberg	Lois Swanson
Nan Douglas	Sheila Kramer	Cathy Tiegs
Sally Duffy	Mim Kurland	Kathleen Tomjack
Janet Engels	Kristina Lantz	Rebecca Torgerson
Jim Eppard	Julie Larson	Phyllis Tracy
LouAnn Eppard	Kay Love-Caskey	Cindy Ullman
Laurie Fulgham	Rhoda Logan	Mary Urquhart
Connie Gambini	Kathleen Lowery	Vicki Valente
Lorene Geidel	Mary-Jean Martens	Zola Vantaggi
Eleni George	Lois Martin	Faye Waldo
Sonia Gisvold	Marilyn McKeehen	Loren Walters
Ann Groover	Margaret McVay	Giuseppi's Olive
Phyllis Hammes	Judy Mellinger	Grove Restaurant
Jeannette Hansen	Renda Meloy	Holiday Inn
Sally Hanson	Tom Meloy	Downtown
Dorothy Hartman	Cherie Miles	Amy Waugh
Joan Hinds	Lois Milner	Betsy Ogle Weitz
Colleen Hodges	Diane Nippoldt	Celia Weitz
Jeanette Howe	Bev Olander	Lily Weinshilboum
Julie Huettner	Margaret O'Sullivan	Almyra Whitehead
Dan Hurley	Karen Petitt	Marion Williams
Diane Hurley	Karen Porayko	Jennie Wilson
Ellen Hurley	Mona Price	Marilee Wood
Georgia Hurley	Marilyn Riederer	Barbara Young
Philip Hurley	Lisa Rodysill	Bunny Young
Bob Jacobson	Julie Roenigk	

RECIPE FOR A VOLUNTEER

Cream together one part spare time with desire
to help others.

Add slowly, series of indoctrination and
orientation courses.

Add dash of enthusiasm, courage, and
originality for flavor.

Combine thoroughly, steadily beating in many
hours of service.

Then add large quantities of well-sifted patience
and equal amounts of milk of human kindness.

Pour into a warm heart, bake well in a pan of
experience.

When done—top with three "D's": Discipline,
Drill, Dependability.

Serve in generous portions.

Author Unknown

GUIDELINES FOR RECIPE
SELECTION AND FORMAT

This collection of recipes represents a cross-section of the several hundred we received. As we were unable to include every recipe, we attempted to select a variety based on ingredients, flavor, appearance and ease of preparation. When similar recipes were submitted by more than one person, we acknowledged each contributor and noted a variation if differences significantly changed the final product. According to the wishes of some contributors, individual names are not given for every recipe.

The recipes in this cookbook were edited to follow a similar format whenever possible. We hope the cook will find this consistency helpful when preparing recipes from this collection.

Guidelines to note:

— no abbreviations

— ingredients listed in order of use

— measured amounts designated before or after ingredient as appropriate

e.g.: 1 cup walnuts, chopped or 1 cup chopped walnuts
1 cup rice, cooked or 1 cup cooked rice

— all purpose enriched flour used unless otherwise indicated

— vegetable oil used unless otherwise indicated

— when measuring brown sugar, it should be packed, unless otherwise indicated

— pan preparation followed by pan size

— baking or cooking temperatures followed by time

— temperature given in degrees Fahrenheit

— oven should be preheated unless otherwise indicated

— directions given as one continuous paragraph

— ♪ recipe included in book

We hope **Recipes of Note for Entertaining** will become a favorite in your cookbook collection.

The Cookbook Committee

MENUS

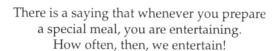

There is a saying that whenever you prepare
a special meal, you are entertaining.
How often, then, we entertain!

The menus in this chapter have been
carefully selected for you to entertain
family and friends.
They have been arranged with an eye toward
color, texture, taste, balance and season of the year.

The wines suggested with each menu
were chosen to accent the meal.
Be sure, however, to provide
sparkling water with lemon or lime slices
for those who prefer a non-alcoholic drink.

The musical selections were personally
recommended by Maestro Jere Lantz,
Music Director and Conductor
of the Rochester Symphony Orchestra.
We hope the music will enhance your
entertaining and add a special touch
to your dining experience.

A SYMPHONY PRELUDE

Let's make a night of it!
Before I have to conduct a concert,
I eat little, keep to myself, move with energy-conserving
deliberation and focus on the intricacies
of the music to come.
But that's hardly appropriate for anyone else!
There's nothing like a sumptuous meal before
a concert, and a sumptuous meal needs a
sumptuous accompaniment.
Still, we don't want to overshadow the main musical
event. This is the time for music that relaxes and
focuses the mind. Nothing emotional or dramatic,
just gently stimulating.

Jere Lantz

MUSIC

Bach: The Well-Tempered Clavier
Goldberg Variations
English or French Suites
Handel: Concerto Grosso from Op. 3 or Op. 6
Haydn: Symphony 6 (Morning), 7 (Noon), 8 (Evening)
"Sixteen-hundred Renaissance Hits"
Dances by Josquin des Prez, Hassler, Lasso and Weelkes

Scallops Mornay♪
Champagne

———

Pineapple Sorbet ♪

———

Spinach Salad with Honey and Mustard Dressing♪
Assorted breads or rolls

———

Filet of Beef in Phyllo Pastry with Madeira Sauce♪
Glazed Baby Carrots ♪

Chateau Graville-Lacoste
White Graves

———

Bete Noire ♪
Coffee and Tea

DINNER AT SEVEN

Truly a Minnesota meal! The George S. Kaufman/
Edna Ferber play was titled "Dinner at Eight," but that
was New York. We're on Central Time, so here it's
Dinner at Seven.

One advantage of being American is our diverse
heritage. As in our society, so it is in our cuisine. Dinner at
Seven celebrates true culinary diversity and introduces
us to a variety of national specialties within one menu.

J. L.

MUSIC

Gregorian chant
Kings Singers (ancient or modern)
Whiffenpoofs (if you have them)

Grieg: Suites from Peer Gynt
Debussy: Prelude to the Afternoon of a Faun
Ravel: Pavane or Mother Goose Suite

Jazz: Gershwin: Concerto in F
Ellington: The River
Bernstein: On the Town
or your favorite jazz artists

Copland: Appalachian Spring or Our Town
Something oriental: Japanese koto or samisen,
Balinese gamelan

Sally's Baked Brie

Chicken Breasts Supreme ♪
Mushroom Herb Rice ♪
Italian Beans with Water Chestnuts and Almonds ♪
Orange and Red Salad ♪
Dinner Rolls

Italian White Wine
Frascati
Pinot Grigio

Triple Chocolate Torte ♪
Coffee and Tea

OCTOBERFEST

What a wonderful idea for a meal!
Reminiscent of the traditional fall festival in Bavaria,
this menu is just the thing for those cool,
crisp days of autumn—
a time for friends to gather together again
and enjoy the pleasures
of good food and good company.
N. B.

MUSIC

Polkas, schottisches, etc., with
an accordion or folk band, or
the many such dances by the Strauss family

Contredanses and German Dances by
Haydn, Mozart and Beethoven

Any recording by a German male chorus

Brahms' Liebeslieder Waltzes or Choral Folksongs

Wagner's opera Die Meistersinger
(nearly four hours worth!)

Camembert and Brie Cheese with Grapes
Melon Wrapped in Black Forest Ham ♪
Herring with Assorted Crackers

German Beer and Wine
Apple Cider

Rouladen ♪
Bratwurst and Buns
Blaukraut (Red Cabbage) ♪
Sauerkraut ♪
Kartoffelsalat (Potato Salad) ♪
Spatzle ♪
Brotchen (Rolls)
Rye Bread
Mustard
Pickles

German Mosel
Kabinett

Schwarzwalder Kirschtorte (Black Forest Cherry Torte) ♪
Hazelnut Torte ♪
Obstorte (Fruit Flan) ♪

Frangelico Liqueur
Coffee and Tea

UNE SOIRÉE ELEGANTE

(An Elegant Evening)

A hint of spice,
a touch of garlic,
a crisp baguette,
an aromatic mousse:

all conjure up the sun of southern France.
So, a bouquet of French composers
in their southern leanings.

J. L.

MUSIC

Bizet: L'Arlesienne Suites Nos. 1 & 2
Chabrier: Espana
Debussy: Iberia
Ravel: Rapsodie Espagnol
Ibert: Ports of Call

Cherry Tomatoes with Roasted Garlic Filling ♪
Scallop Puffs ♪

Muscadet

————

Cream of Lentil Soup with Grilled Shrimp ♪

————

Trio of Salads ♪
French Bread

————

Game Hens with Honey Sauternes Sauce,
Spinach and Pearl Onions ♪

Alsace Riesling

————

Chocolate and Grand Marnier Mousse ♪
Coffee and Tea

HARVEST GATHERING

There's a nip in the air.
We need food to keep us warm, to stick to our ribs.
A real meat-and-potatoes, apple pie dinner
that will keep us full till at least lunch tomorrow.
Is there meat-and-potatoes music, too? Absolutely!

J. L.

MUSIC

Beethoven: Symphony No. 5
Brahms: Symphony No. 4
Bruckner: Any symphony (try No. 3 for starters)
Tchaikovsky: March Slav
Brahms: Piano Quintet in F Minor, Op. 34

Hot Mushroom Dillweed Dip ♪

———————

Smoked Brisket ♪
Hash Brown Potatoes ♪
Colleen's Baked Beans ♪
Fresh Fruit

Iced Tea

———————

English Apple Pie ♪
Creme de Menthe Brownies ♪
Coffee and Tea

CHRISTMAS BREAKFAST

The joy of Christmas finds a special place in the
hearts and lives of many, year after year.
As time goes on, we continue to treasure
holiday memories from the past.

One way to preserve those memories is with traditions.
Small things—
a particular carol sung by the family on Christmas Eve,
a special menu for Christmas dinner,
a poem, grace or scripture passage
read by the oldest member of the family—
these small things grow in our hearts through the years.

Many families celebrate Christmas morning
with breakfast in the living room while presents are opened.
Christmas breakfast can be a full meal or
just a bite between presents,
with muffins that go on forever and tea,
always hot beneath the lacy cozy.
It's informal and it's fun,
and it keeps parents going on a day
when morning always seems to come too soon!

MUSIC

Carols on an old music box (Rita Ford's and other albums)

Fred Waring and the Pennsylvanians:
"The Sounds of Christmas"
Philadelphia Orchestra: "The Glorious Sound of Christmas"
Kings College Choir: "Carols for Choirs"

Live recordings of YULE-FEST
with the Rochester Symphony Orchestra and Chorale

Marinellis Sparkling Cider

———

Christmas Morning Frittata ♪
Toasted English Muffins with Spiced Honey ♪
Fruit Cup

———

English Breakfast Tea

YULE-FEST BUFFET

A traditional holiday meal
calls for traditional holiday carols,
and no one does them better
than the English choirs
from the great colleges of
Oxford and Cambridge.

J. L.

MUSIC

Kings College Festivals of Lessons and Carols

Carols from St. John's

Carols from Magdalen College, Oxford

"Christmas Eve at the Cathedral of St. John the Divine"
Vienna Boys Choir

Winter Cider ♪
Stuffed Cornets with Ginger Cream ♪
Baked Cheddar Olives ♪
Cranberry Glazed Brie ♪
Crackers
Spiced Nuts ♪

Curried Carrot and Parsnip Soup ♪

Crown Roast of Pork with Spiced Fruit Chutney ♪
Beef Tenderloin ♪
Potato Gratin with Boursin Cheese ♪
Mixed Greens with Raspberry Vinaigrette and Roasted Pecans ♪
Assorted Relish Platter
Dinner Rolls

Guigal Cotes-du-Rhone
Columbia Crest Merlot

Candy Cane Cheesecake ♪
Buche de Noel with Meringue Mushrooms ♪
Coffee and Tea

NEW YEAR'S EVE DINNER

There are two ways to celebrate New Year's Eve:
crying over last year or rioting over next.

This meal clearly opts for celebration,
so let the music celebrate too!

J. L.

MUSIC

Zwilich: Celebration
Beethoven: Symphony No. 4
Tchaikovsky: Symphony No. 4 (last two movements)
Glinka: Overture to Russlan and Ludmilla
Dvorak: Carnival Overture
Shostakovich: A Festival Overture
Ginastera: Estancia Suite

Shrimp Mousse ♪
Baked Brie en Croute ♪
Champagne

Sliced Avocado Vinaigrette ♪

Cornish Game Hen with
Sausage and Wild Rice Stuffing ♪
Tomatoes Baked with Spinach and Feta ♪
Norwegian Lefse

Caramel Custard ♪
Coffee and Tea

MIDWESTERN WINTER SOUPFEST

Winter in Minnesota is often a mixed blessing.
The scenery can be spectacular—anything from a
light dusting of white flakes to shoulder-high
mounds of heavy snow—with bright blue skies,
puffy white clouds and crisp, fresh air.

But when the temperature plummets below zero,
what better way to fend off the chill than with this
Midwestern Soupfest Menu? Assorted cookies of the
season allow sweet flavors to linger on the palate,
a nice complement to the warm feelings inspired by
the season. So, pass the ladle and enjoy!
M. S.

MUSIC

Vivaldi: "Winter" from The Four Seasons
(Listen closely: it's really icy with a cuddly
slow movement.)

Tchaikovsky: Symphony No. 1: "Winter Dreams"
(Especially the first two movements: "Dreams of a
Winter Journey" and "Land of Gloom, Land of Mists")

Rutter: Cantata: "When Icicles Hang"

Wassail ♪

Beer Cheese and Bacon Soup ♪
Italian Tomato Soup ♪
"Creamless" Creamy Wild Rice Soup ♪

Grapefruit Pomegranate Medley ♪
Assorted Breads and Cracker Tray

Italian Soave

Butter Pecan Turtle Bars ♪
Assorted Christmas Cookies and Peppermint Ice Cream
Coffee and Tea

COMPANY IS COMING

With company coming, we want to show our best:
our best china, silver, manners,
menu,
and musical taste.
Why not make it Mozart?
A classic meal with THE classical composer,
whose popularity has never been so high
as in the last decade.

J. L.

MUSIC

Mozart:

Eine kleine Nachtmusik (A Little Night Music)

Overtures: The Marriage of Figaro, The Magic Flute,
Don Giovanni, Cosi fan tutte, The Abduction from the Seraglio

Symphonies: Nos. 29 in A, 40 in G Minor, 41 ("Jupiter")
Divertimenti for Strings: K. 136, 137, 138
Violin Concertos

German Spatlese

Apricot Stuffed Chicken Breasts
with Sauce Supreme ♪
Wild Rice
Carrot and Parsnip Medley ♪
Mixed Green Salad

American Johannisberg Riesling
White Zinfandel

Poached Winter Pears ♪
Coffee and Tea

SPRING BRUNCH

For those of us who feel as if
we've been snowed in since December,
the arrival of spring
brings a sense of new hope and rejuvenation
to our hearts.

Here's a spring brunch,
combining the twin ambrosias of
French toast and cream cheese with
the nectar of delectable fresh fruit.

G.J.H./A.J.

MUSIC

Vivaldi: "Spring" from The Four Seasons or,
for comparable vernal effervescence,

Vivaldi: Any flute concerto ("Il Gardellino" is great) or
combine "Spring" with flute in James Galway's
dazzling version

Schumann: Symphony No. 1 ("Spring")

but avoid

Grieg: Last Spring
(a nostalgic lament, gorgeous but sad)
Stravinsky: Rite of Spring
(great music but poor for digestion)

Mock Pink Champagne

———————

Mixed Fruit with Honey Rum Dressing ♪
Spinach and Ham Frittata ♪
Cream Cheese Stuffed Cinnamon French Toast ♪
Assorted Fresh Baked Muffins

———————

Coffee and Tea

AN EVENING WITH FRIENDS

If you ask us what our favorite social event is,
it's simply an evening at home with friends.
Such evenings are becoming too rare.
So, they are most satisfying when they are long and slow
with plenty of time to savor each course,
and plenty of time between
simply to talk.

J. L.

MUSIC

An evening with favorite friends ought to have music
by favorite friends. Since it's a long evening, make a
long tape of the music that feels comfortable and
familiar. Contrast between selections, as between
courses, keeps the evening interesting.
(A word of note: Keep the lively tunes well
separated by quieter strains so as not to strain
digestion.) Some of our favorites:

Beethoven: Choral Fantasy, Violin Concerto, Quartet Op. 127
Bach: Orchestral Suites, Partitas for Unaccompanied Violin
Schubert: Die Schoene Muellerin, Moments Musicaux
Chopin: Preludes and Nocturnes
Dvorak: Symphony No. 8, Slavonic Dances
Brahms: Academic Festival Overture, Quintet Op. 34
Tchaikovsky: Romeo and Juliet, Capriccio Italien
Debussy: Nocturnes, Piano Preludes
Stravinsky: Pulcinella Suite, Suites for Small Orchestra
Walton: Henry V Suite and other film music

Cherry Tomatoes with Roasted Garlic Filling ♪
Chicken Leek Rolls ♪

White Sangria
Gin and Tonic
Flavored Mineral Water

———

Red Bell Pepper Terrine with Asparagus Vinaigrette ♪
Mixed Green Salad with Raspberries, Dijon Dressing
and Brie Toasts ♪

———

Fruit Sorbet

———

Grilled Salmon Fillets with Avocado Citrus Salsa ♪
Steamed Carrot and Zucchini Julienne ♪
Rosemary Potatoes ♪

California Chardonnay

———

Blueberry and Buttermilk Tart ♪
Mocha Almond Ice Cream Pie ♪
Coffee and Tea

DINNER WITH VIVALDI

Vivaldi came to music early. Brought up under the vast vaults of the Cathedral of Saint Mark, Vivaldi knew the greatest composers of Venice. He quickly surpassed his father, a barber cum musician, on the violin but forsook music to take holy orders in 1703. Fortunately for us, the rigors of clerical life were too much for Vivaldi, whose asthmatic lungs kept him from saying a complete mass.

So he became music master at the "Ospedale della Pieta," an orphanage for girls. Concerts by his students soon became all the rage—the best musical entertainment in Venice. For his students, Vivaldi created some 450 concertos for every possible combination of instruments, plus sonatas, solo pieces, chamber music and nearly 50 operas.

Though he died in poverty in 1741, Vivaldi left one of the most popular musical legacies in the history of music. The "red priest," as he was called because of the color of his hair, brought a great deal of music to life—and breathed much of his life into music.

This menu lends itself to dining al fresco, though its mood can be savored indoors as well. An added touch would be a string quartet performing a preprandial concert in the garden—with music by Vivaldi, of course!!

K. L. C./J. L.

MUSIC

Vivaldi:
The Four Seasons, Opus 8
Concerto Grosso in A minor, Opus 3, No. 8
Concerto in D Minor for Flute, Violin and Piano
Pastorale for Flute, Cello and Piano
Sonata in G Minor for Oboe, Violin, Cello and Piano

Vivaldi Cocktails ♪
Shrimp in Lemon and Olive Oil ♪

Italian Stuffed Beef Tenderloin
with Roasted Red Peppers and Garlic Sauce ♪
Polenta Notes ♪
Tossed Fresh Greens with Cumin Vinaigrette ♪
Crusty Rolls with Italian Herbs ♪

Cantina Traduttori San Michele
Chardonnay, Alto Adige
Fossi Fiesole Chianti Classico

Ricotta Tart ♪
Zuccotto ♪

Chateau Ste. Michelle Muscat Canelli
Coffee and Tea

SUMMER SEAFOOD FEAST

The sun is broiling—
time to head to the beach.
As the heat and humidity wilt us,
we look to the water for refreshment.
And the water yields back a rich harvest of tasty food
while inspiring a flood of great music.

J. L.

Music

Schumann: Symphony No. 3 (Rhenish)
Debussy: La Mer
Handel: Water Music
Respighi: The Fountains of Rome
Britten: Four Sea Interludes from "Peter Grimes"
Smetana: The Moldau
Thomson: The River Suite

Paddler's Passion ♪
Curried Crab in Endive Spears ♪

Grilled Swordfish with Ginger Butter ♪
Barbecued Garlic Shrimp♪
Marinated Tricolor Bell Pepper and Mushroom Salad ♪
New Potatoes
Crusty French Bread

California Sauvignon Blanc

Margarita Charlotte ♪
or
Triple Berry Tart ♪
Coffee and Tea

AN ORCHESTRAL FINALE

A stimulating concert can stimulate the appetite—
it always seems to for musicians and conductors.
What do we need?
A bit of this and that:
some sweet, some tart, some tangy with
a sip of dessert wine to bring out the flavors.

Dessert deserves dessert—musical dessert.
Now is the time for the sinfully sweet music we really love.
Strauss waltzes, Tchaikovsky ballets,
Offenbach or Suppe overtures,
Gilbert & Sullivan,
Victor Herbert, Sigmund Romberg, or
if it's your cup of cappuccino, New Age.
My sweet sin is Swing, maybe Count Basie backing
the mellow voice of Joe Williams or Arthur Prysock.

But whatever it is, sample a variety.
Let the music circulate, as old and new friends drift
among conversations and the evening slowly winds down.

Indulgence is the key!
For this evening, at least,
your work—and mine—is done.

Jere Lantz

Fine German Auslese

———

Chocolate Hazelnut Cake ♪
Kathryn's Cheesecake ♪

Assorted Fruits
Dessert Cheeses
Crackers

———

Coffee and Tea
Muscat

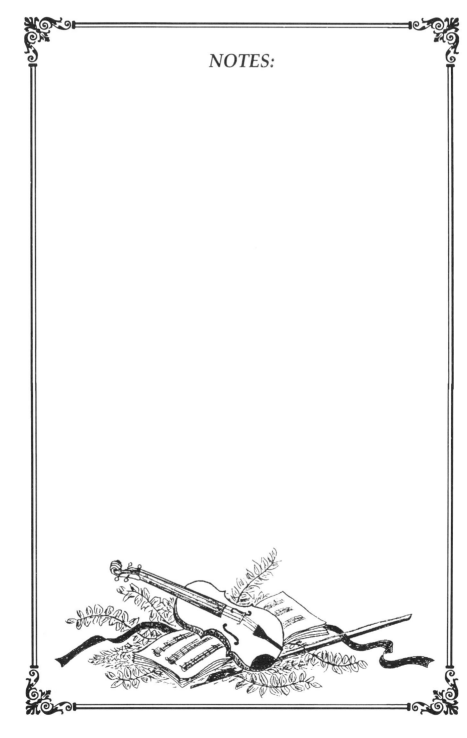

NOTES:

A Victorian Tea

The ritual of having tea has brought joy and memories for more than a century. Many of us remember our first experience as children, fascinated with the small cups and saucers, thrilled with tiny sandwiches and other goodies. It was a moment of politeness and gentility.

Teas became popular during Queen Victoria's reign (1837 - 1901). She had a passion for sweets and loved her tea. Teatime became the main attraction for an afternoon of socializing. It was a delicate affair, loved for the company as well as the meal it provided. It was a wonderful reason to extend an invitation or to make a visit.

Although tea at the palace was always served from the Queen's ornate silver tea service, many preferred a china or crockery teapot. And as Queen Victoria was Empress of India and Ceylon, there was no question as to what kind of tea would be brewed.

Today, a tea creates an opportunity to leave the cares of the day behind and enter a graceful, relaxing moment. Use a white damask tablecloth or any heavy lace to create a Victorian atmosphere. Mix and match china patterns, as the Queen loved seeing pattern upon pattern. The raw sugar of today, with the large crystals of brownish color, is reminiscent of the Demerara sugar which was used to sweeten tea years ago. And last, but not least, have a pitcher of milk for the tea standing by.

Turn the page to begin an extravagant journey into a royal Victorian Tea. Your guests will delight in these dainty sandwiches and sweets.

MUSIC

Arthur Sullivan:	Overtures to Operettas with W. S. Gilbert
Edward Elgar:	Serenade for Strings Cockaigne (In London Town)
Ralph Vaughan Williams:	Fantasia on "Greensleeves" Serenade to Music The Lark Ascending
Eric Coates:	London Every Day Suites I and II
Frederick Delius:	On Hearing a Cuckoo in Spring Summer Night on the River Deux Aquarelles Prelude to Irmelin
Percy Grainger:	Shepherds' Hey Irish Tune from County Derry

THE QUEEN'S TEA

Punch
Sherry
Spiced Nuts

Assorted Sandwiches:
Pinwheels
Asparagus Whirls
Salmon, Watercress and Cucumber
Cucumber-Shrimp
Potted Shrimp
Tomato-Egg
Curried Tuna Hearts
Curried Chicken and Chutney

Victorian Cheese Dainties
Scones with Clotted Cream and Jam

Assorted Sweets:
Gingerbread Husbands
Petticoat Tails
Trilbys
Ratafias
Miniature Chocolate Eclairs
Cupid's Love Wells
Victorian Tea Cakes
Apricot Sugar Plums
Lemon and Cherry Tarts
Battenberg Cake with Marzipan
Bonbons

Ceylon Black Tea/Milk
Coffee/Cream
Coarse Brown Sugar

SPARKLING CATAWBA PUNCH

½ (46-ounce) can
   unsweetened pineapple
   juice, chilled
1 quart gingerale, chilled
1 quart sparkling white
   Catawba juice, chilled
2 (6-ounce) cans lemonade
   concentrate, thawed, but
   cold

Grenadine, to taste and for
   color
Ice ring for garnish

Mix chilled juices together in a large
punch bowl just before serving
time. Stir in grenadine. Add ice ring
as desired.

Yield: 42 (4-ounce) servings.

Kay Love-Caskey

SPICED NUTS

1 egg white
1 teaspoon water
1 cup almonds, blanched
1 cup pecan halves
½ cup sugar
½ teaspoon salt
1 teaspoon cinnamon
½ teaspoon nutmeg
½ teaspoon ground ginger

Beat egg white with water until
frothy. Add nuts and stir until nuts
are well coated; set aside. Mix
sugar, salt, cinnamon, nutmeg and
ginger in another bowl. Toss nuts in
sugar and spice mixture and mix
well. Spread nuts on a large baking
sheet. Bake at 225° for 1 hour,
stirring mixture every 15 minutes.
Remove nuts from pan and shake
off loose sugar. Cool.

Yield: 2 cups nuts

Nina Sudor

Pinwheel Sandwiches

1 unsliced sandwich loaf,
  brown bread
1 unsliced sandwich loaf,
  white bread
Butter, softened

Salmon Filling:
1 (7 ½-ounce) can salmon,
  drained
1 (8-ounce) package cream
  cheese, softened
1 tablespoon chopped
  fresh dill

Watercress Filling:
1 (8-ounce) package cream
  cheese
½ cup watercress, packed
⅓ cup parsley, packed
2 tablespoons chopped
  chives

Have the baker slice the loaves lengthwise. Discard crusts. Flatten bread with a rolling pin. Spread slices lightly with butter. *For salmon filling,* combine salmon and cream cheese in a food processor; process until smooth. Blend in dill. *For watercress filling,* combine all ingredients in a food processor and blend until mixture is smooth and green. Spread fillings over buttered bread. Roll up each slice from the short end (like a jelly roll). Wrap in plastic wrap and chill before cutting into ½-inch pinwheels.

Yield: 30 to 40

Nina Sudor

Asparagus Whirls

1 loaf day-old unsliced
  white or whole wheat
  bread
1 (3-ounce) package cream
  cheese, softened
⅓ cup butter, softened
1 (15-ounce) can whole
  asparagus spears, drained
1 (2-ounce) jar sliced
  pimientos, drained

Have baker slice bread horizontally into 6 slices. Remove crusts from bread. Flatten each slice lightly with rolling pin. In a small bowl, whip cream cheese and butter together. Spread evenly on slices of bread. Starting at short end of each slice, place 2 spears of asparagus and a few strips of pimiento. Roll jelly-roll fashion from short end. Wrap in waxed paper or plastic wrap. Refrigerate until ready to serve. *To serve,* remove wrap and slice each roll into 4 to 5 pinwheels.

Yield: 24 to 30

Marion Kleinberg

ASSORTED TEA SANDWICHES

Salmon sandwiches:
¼ pound thinly sliced
   smoked salmon
½ (8-ounce) package cream
   cheese, softened
1 tablespoon chopped fresh
   dill
8 thin slices large square
   Pumpernickel bread

Watercress sandwiches:
⅓ cup watercress sprigs
¼ cup fresh parsley leaves
¼ cup (½ stick) butter or
   margarine, softened
½ (8-ounce) package cream
   cheese, softened
2 tablespoons finely
   chopped chives
Salt and ground black
   pepper to taste
8 slices large firm white
   bread, crusts removed

Cucumber sandwiches:
2 small cucumbers, peeled
¼ teaspoon salt
8 slices large firm whole-
   wheat bread, crusts
   removed
¼ cup light or reduced-
   calorie mayonnaise
1 teaspoon distilled white
   vinegar
Ground white pepper to
   taste

Fresh dill sprigs or
   watercress (optional)

For salmon sandwiches, combine salmon and cream cheese in a food processor; process with chopping blade until smooth. Fold in dill with a spatula until well mixed. Spread salmon mixture evenly over half the bread slices and top with remaining slices. Cut each sandwich diagonally into 4 triangles. Place on a tray or plate; cover with slightly damp paper towel and plastic wrap. Refrigerate until serving time. *For watercress sandwiches,* combine watercress and parsley in a food processor; process with chopping blade until finely chopped. Add butter, cream cheese, chives, salt and pepper; process until mixture turns green. Spread watercress mixture on half the bread slices and top with remaining slices. Cut each sandwich diagonally into 4 triangles. Place on a tray or plate; cover with slightly damp paper towel and plastic wrap. Refrigerate until serving time. *For cucumber sandwiches,* cut cucumbers lengthwise in half; remove and discard seeds. Cut cucumber halves crosswise into paper-thin slices. In a bowl, toss cucumbers with salt; let sit for 15 minutes. Meanwhile, spread each bread slice with mayonnaise on one side. Drain cucumbers on paper towels; return to bowl and toss with vinegar and pepper. Arrange cucumbers over half the bread slices. Top with remaining bread slices, mayonnaise-side down. Cut each sandwich into 4 squares. Place on a tray or plate; cover with slightly damp paper towel and plastic wrap. Refrigerate until serving time. *To serve,* arrange an assortment of the sandwiches on a serving platter. Garnish with fresh dill sprigs or watercress, if desired.

Yield: 48 tea sandwiches

Kay Love-Caskey

"These dainty sandwiches are perfect to counteract the sweets at teatime."

CUCUMBER-SHRIMP TEA SANDWICHES

1 loaf white bread, sliced thin
1 (8-ounce) package cream cheese, softened
2 tablespoons milk
1 medium cucumber
3 tablespoons wine vinegar
1 tablespoon sugar
2 teaspoons dill weed
1 (4 ¼-ounce) can medium shrimp, drained and rinsed

Cut 2½-inch circles from bread; cover and set aside. Blend cream cheese and milk together until smooth. Slice cucumber in thin slices (peel if desired). With a small round canapé cutter, cut cucumber seeds from the center of each slice and discard; place slices in a bowl. Combine vinegar, sugar and dill weed. Pour over cucumbers and marinate for at least 1 hour in refrigerator. Drain cucumbers on paper towels. Spread bread rounds with cream cheese. Place a cucumber round in the center and place one shrimp in the cut out cucumber slice. Place sandwiches on a baking sheet, cover with plastic wrap and refrigerate until ready to serve.

Yield: 24 to 30

Nina Sudor

POTTED SHRIMP SANDWICHES

½ pound cooked shrimp,
   peeled and deveined
¼ cup butter, softened
1 tablespoon lemon juice
2 teaspoons sherry
½ teaspoon dry mustard
⅛ teaspoon salt
Dash of mace
12 slices thin-sliced white
   bread, crusts removed
Fresh parsley sprigs for
   garnish

Process shrimp in an electric blender until coarsely ground. Combine ground shrimp and butter; stir well. Add lemon juice, sherry, mustard, salt and mace; mix well. Chill. Roll bread slices flat with a rolling pin. Spread shrimp paste on each bread slice and roll up jellyroll fashion. Cover with plastic wrap and chill. *To serve,* cut rolls into 3 equal portions. Tuck a sprig of parsley into one end of each rolled section.

Yield: 3 dozen

Kay Love-Caskey

TOMATO-EGG SANDWICHES

12 slices rye bread
1 cup mayonnaise
4 hard-cooked eggs, sliced
   (use small eggs)
8 cherry tomatoes, sliced
Fresh parsley sprigs for
   garnish

Cut bread into 24 rounds, using a 2-inch biscuit cutter. Spread each round with a small amount of mayonnaise. Spoon remaining mayonnaise into a pastry bag fitted with a small star tip; set aside. Top each bread round with a slice of hard-cooked egg and a slice of cherry tomato. Pipe reserved mayonnaise on tops, and garnish each with fresh parsley. Cover and chill until ready to serve.

Yield: 2 dozen

Kay Love-Caskey

CURRIED TUNA HEARTS

Tuna:
1 (7-ounce) can solid white tuna in water, drained, flaked
½ cup salad dressing or mayonnaise
1 teaspoon lemon juice
¼ teaspoon curry powder
¼ teaspoon prepared horseradish
½ teaspoon salt

Gelatin:
1 teaspoon unflavored gelatin
1 tablespoon cold water
⅔ cup salad dressing or mayonnaise
6 tablespoons half and half

12 slices white bread
Lemon leaves for garnish
Radish roses for garnish

Combine tuna, salad dressing, lemon juice, curry, horseradish and salt in a small bowl. Cover and refrigerate until ready to assemble. *For gelatin mixture,* sprinkle gelatin over cold water in a small heat-proof container. Place container with gelatin mixture in small saucepan of boiling water. Heat over low heat, stirring constantly, until gelatin dissolves. Remove from heat and stir gelatin into salad dressing in a small bowl. Gradually add half and half to gelatin mixture, stirring to mix thoroughly. Cut out 12 hearts from bread slices. *To assemble,* spread about 1 tablespoon tuna mixture on each heart. Spread gelatin mixture evenly on top of the tuna mixture. Refrigerate, covered, until set, at least 1 hour. Serve on a plate lined with lemon leaves. Garnish with radish roses.

Yield: 12 heart sandwiches

Kay Love-Caskey

CURRIED CHICKEN AND CHUTNEY SANDWICHES

1 cup diced cooked chicken
½ cup chopped almonds
¼ cup chutney
¼ cup celery
¼ to ½ cup mayonnaise
2 tablespoons plus 2
  teaspoons half and half
¼ teaspoon salt
¼ teaspoon pepper
¼ teaspoon curry

24 slices white bread, crust
  removed
2 tablespoons butter,
  softened

Combine first nine ingredients together in a bowl, mixing well. Adjust seasonings to taste. Cut bread into an even number of matching shapes. Spread chicken mixture evenly on half of the bread shapes. Butter remaining bread shapes and then place on top to make sandwiches.

Yield: 2 dozen

Kay Love-Caskey

VICTORIAN CHEESE DAINTIES

2 ¼ cups flour
⅛ teaspoon salt
½ teaspoon red pepper
Dash of paprika
¾ cup butter or margarine
2 cups (8-ounces) shredded
  sharp Cheddar cheese

Sift together flour, salt, red pepper and paprika in a large mixing bowl; cut in butter with a pastry blender until mixture resembles coarse meal. Stir in cheese. Turn dough out onto a floured surface and knead lightly 3 to 4 times. Shape dough into a ball; cover and chill for at least 1 hour. Work with ¼ of the dough at a time, keeping remaining dough chilled. Shape dough into small crescents, using 1 tablespoon dough for each crescent. Place on a lightly greased baking sheet and bake at 400° for 8 minutes or until lightly browned. Cool slightly on baking sheets; remove to wire racks to cool completely.

Yield: About 6 dozen

Kay Love-Caskey

CREAM SCONES

2 cups flour
2 teaspoons double-acting
   baking powder or
   4 teaspoons tartrate-type
   baking powder
2 teaspoons sugar
½ teaspoon salt
¼ cup butter
2 eggs
½ cup cream or milk
1 teaspoon water
Sugar

Sift flour, baking powder, sugar and salt together in a mixing bowl. Using fingertips, a pastry mixer or fork, work in butter. Break eggs in a small bowl, reserving a small amount of the egg white for the topping. Beat eggs. Add eggs to flour mixture along with cream or milk. Add a little more cream or milk if needed to make dough firm enough to handle but still soft. Turn dough out onto a floured board. Knead for 30 seconds. Pat and roll into an oblong shape, ¾-inch thick. Cut into diamonds by making diagonal cuts with a long sharp knife. Dilute reserved egg white with water. Brush on dough to glaze. Sprinkle with sugar. Bake at 450° for 15 minutes.

Yield: 12 plus

Kay Love-Caskey

"Serve with Homemade 'Devonshire' Cream ♪ and a good quality jam."

HOMEMADE "DEVONSHIRE" CREAM

1 (8-ounce) package cream
   cheese, softened
½ cup sour cream
2 tablespoons powdered
   sugar

In a small bowl, with an electric mixer, beat cream cheese until fluffy. Add sour cream and powdered sugar, beating until well mixed. Spoon into a serving bowl. Cover and refrigerate until time to serve.

Yield: About 1 ⅓ cups

Kay Love-Caskey

"Serve with scones. Clotted cream may be substituted if it can be found."

GINGERBREAD HUSBANDS

1 cup dark molasses
1 cup brown sugar
1 cup butter, cut into
    1/2-inch pieces
2 large eggs, beaten
5 to 5 1/2 cups flour, divided
1 tablespoon ginger
1 1/2 teaspoons baking soda
1 teaspoon cinnamon
1/2 teaspoon cloves

Currants

Icing:
1 cup powdered sugar
Few drops of lemon juice

Heat molasses and sugar to boiling in a small saucepan. Place butter in a large bowl; add hot molasses and stir until butter melts and mixture is warm to the touch. Whisk in eggs until blended. Sift 4 cups flour, soda and spices together over batter and stir until smooth. Gradually stir in remaining flour until dough comes together. Shape dough in a thick disc with floured hands. Wrap in plastic wrap and refrigerate for 2 to 3 hours. Divide dough into quarters. Work with one quarter of dough at a time while remaining dough is in the refrigerator. On a lightly floured pastry cloth with a stocking-covered rolling pin, roll out dough to 1/8-inch thickness. Cut out shapes with a gingerbread man cutter. Press currants in for eyes and buttons. Place on a greased baking sheet. Bake at 350° for 8 to 10 minutes. Cool slightly on sheet, then remove to wire rack to cool completely. Continue rolling and baking remaining dough. *For icing,* mix powdered sugar and just enough lemon juice to blend together. With a skewer, apply icing to make eye brows, a smile, lapels and a bow tie.

Yield: 5 dozen (depending on size of
      cookie cutter)

Nina Sudor

PETTICOAT TAILS

5 cups flour
1 cup powdered sugar
2 cups butter

Sift together flour and sugar in a large mixing bowl. Cut in butter with a pastry blender until mixture resembles coarse meal. Shape mixture into a roll, 2 inches in diameter. Wrap in waxed paper and chill for 30 minutes. Remove wax paper and cut into ¼-inch slices. Place on ungreased baking sheets. Press the floured tines of a fork around edge of each cookie. Bake at 350° for 8 to 10 minutes.

Yield: About 9 dozen

Kay Love-Caskey

TRILBYS

⅓ cup butter, softened
½ cup sugar
1 egg
1 teaspoon vanilla
2 scant cups flour
½ teaspoon baking powder
¼ teaspoon baking soda
⅓ cup sour cream
Raspberry jam

Cream butter and sugar together until light. Beat in egg and vanilla. Sift dry ingredients together. Add to butter mixture, alternating with sour cream; blend well. Divide dough in two and wrap in plastic wrap. Chill at least 3 hours. As dough is soft, alternate working with the portions, keeping one refrigerated while working with the other. Roll dough to ¼-inch thickness. Cut out 2½-inch circles. Place half the circles on a greased baking sheet, and spread each with ½ teaspoon jam. Cut out a small circle in the center of the remaining circles (or make an X in the center of each, spreading it open when in place to expose the jam). Place remaining circles on top of "jam" circles. Press edges to seal. Bake at 350° for 15 minutes, until edges begin to color. Cool on rack.

Yield: 2 dozen

Nina Sudor

Ratafias

Meringue:
4 large egg whites
¼ teaspoon salt
¼ teaspoon cream of tartar
1 cup sugar
1 teaspoon vanilla
6 (or more) almond slivers

Chocolate Mousse:
1 (1-ounce) square
    unsweetened chocolate
2 tablespoons instant
    espresso powder
½ cup (1 stick) unsalted
    butter, cut into pieces
½ cup sugar
1 teaspoon vanilla
2 large eggs

or

Lemon Curd Filling:
3 eggs plus 1 egg yolk,
    beaten
1 cup sugar
½ cup lemon juice
1 tablespoon lemon zest
½ cup butter

Whipped Cream:
1 cup heavy cream
1 tablespoon powdered
    sugar
1 teaspoon vanilla

Butter and flour a baking sheet. Using an electric mixer, beat egg whites with salt and cream of tartar to soft peaks. Add sugar 1 tablespoon at a time and beat until stiff and shiny. Beat in vanilla. Immediately spoon into a pastry bag fitted with a ⅜ to ½ -inch tip. Pipe a 4½ x 2½ -inch oval on the prepared sheet. Pipe meringue in center to fill completely. Pipe three layers of meringue atop the outer edge of the oval. Repeat process 5 more times to make six swan bodies. Pipe at least 6 question marks for swan heads and necks (more in case of breakage). Set almond into each head for a beak. Bake at 225° for about 1½ hours, until meringues are dry and crisp but still white. Reduce oven temperature if they begin to color. Using spatula, loosen meringues; do not remove from sheet. Let cool in the oven with the door slightly ajar for about 30 minutes. Remove from baking sheet and store in an airtight container until ready to use. (Can be prepared 3 days ahead.) *For mousse*, melt chocolate with espresso powder in a double boiler over gently simmering water; stir until smooth. Cool completely. Using an electric mixer, beat butter until smooth. Gradually beat in sugar. Add melted chocolate and mix well. Blend in vanilla. Add eggs, one at a time, beating 5 minutes after each addition. Cover and refrigerate until well chilled. (Can be prepared 2 days ahead.) *For lemon curd filling*, stir beaten eggs and sugar together in the top of a double boiler. Add lemon juice, zest and butter. Cook over gently boiling water, stirring constantly until mixture is thick. Remove from heat and cool. Refrigerate (keeps for 2 weeks in the refrigerator). *For whipped cream,* beat cream until peaks form. Blend in powdered sugar and vanilla. *To assemble,* place meringue ovals on plates. Fill with mousse or lemon curd filling. Pipe or spoon on whipped cream to fill completely. (Can be prepared 3 hours ahead. Cover and refrigerate.) Just before serving, place meringue neck-and-head piece in mousse or lemon curd to attach.

Yield: 6

Kay Love-Caskey

Note: This recipe calls for uncooked eggs.

MINIATURE CHOCOLATE ECLAIRS

1 cup water
½ cup (1 stick) butter or
   margarine, cut in pieces
¼ teaspoon salt
1 cup unsifted flour
4 large eggs

Chocolate Mousse Filling:
1 cup milk
½ cup sugar
2 large egg yolks
1 tablespoon flour
1 envelope unflavored
   gelatin
⅛ teaspoon salt
2 (1-ounce) squares
   unsweetened chocolate,
   finely grated
1 teaspoon vanilla
½ cup heavy cream,
   whipped

Fresh strawberry blossoms
   and leaves (optional)

Grease 2 large baking sheets. In a 2-quart saucepan, heat water, butter and salt to boiling. With a wooden spoon or hand-held electric mixer, beat in flour until the mixture forms a ball and pulls away from the side of the pan. Remove pan from heat. Add eggs, one at a time, beating after each addition until mixture is smooth and shiny. Place dough into a large pastry bag, fitted with a large round pastry tip. Pipe 24, 2 x 1-inch oblong, eclairs onto greased baking sheets, leaving 1 inch between eclairs. Bake at 425° for 10 minutes. Reduce heat to 375° and bake 10 minutes longer. Turn off oven. With a fork, pierce eclairs once to allow steam to escape. Leave eclairs in turned-off oven for 15 minutes longer. Remove from oven and let eclairs cool on wire racks. *For chocolate mousse filling,* combine milk, sugar, egg yolks, flour, gelatin and salt in a 2-quart saucepan. Beat with a wire whisk until smooth. Heat mixture over medium heat until thick enough to coat the back of a spoon, about 4 minutes (do not boil or it will curdle!). Pour mixture into a medium-size bowl. With wire whisk, beat in chocolate and vanilla. Cool mixture for 15 minutes in refrigerator (do not allow to cool longer or gelatin will stiffen). Fold in whipped cream. Cover filling tightly and refrigerate for 30 minutes or until it sets. When eclairs are cooled, spoon filling into pastry bag, fitted with a star-shaped tip. Pipe some of the filling into both small ends of each eclair, filling the center and leaving a star design on each end. Refrigerate on a tray until serving time. Just before serving, arrange eclairs on serving plate and garnish with blossoms and leaves, if desired.

Yield: 24 eclairs

Kay Love-Caskey

"These tiny cream-puff pastries, filled with a light, fluffy chocolate mousse, are an elegant teatime treat."

Note: This recipe calls for uncooked eggs.

CUPID'S LOVE WELLS

8 ounces puff pastry
Water
Yolk of 1 egg
Sugar
Cherry jam (that contains whole cherries) or 1 (21-ounce) can cherry pie filling

Roll pastry to ⅛-inch thickness. With a 1½-inch fluted cutter, cut about 18 circles. Place circles on a baking sheet that has been rinsed with water. With a 1-inch cutter, cut another 18 circles. Cut the centers of these out with a very small (½-inch) cutter or very sharp knife. Brush circles with water and lay these rings on top. Press with fingers. Brush egg yolk over top. Sprinkle with sugar. Bake at 375° about 20 to 25 minutes, or until golden and puffed. Remove from oven and cool on racks. Before serving, fill with jam or pie filling.

Yield: 18

Nina Sudor

VICTORIAN TEA CAKES

1 cup butter, softened
2 cups sugar
3 cups flour
2 teaspoons baking powder
¼ teaspoon salt
1 cup ice water
1 teaspoon almond extract
6 egg whites, room
     temperature
1 cup apricot jam

Icing:
7 cups sifted powdered
     sugar
½ cup plus 3 tablespoons
     water
3 tablespoons light corn
     syrup
1 teaspoon almond extract
Paste food coloring

Grease a 13 x 9-inch baking pan, and line with parchment paper. Lightly grease paper; set aside. Cream butter in a large bowl with electric mixer. Gradually add sugar, beating until light and fluffy. Sift together flour, baking powder and salt. Add flour to creamed mixture alternately with ice water; mix well. Stir in almond extract. In a separate bowl, beat egg whites until soft peaks form; fold into creamed mixture. Pour batter into prepared pan. Bake at 325° for 50 minutes or until a wooden pick inserted in center comes out clean. Remove from oven and cool in pan for 10 minutes. Remove cake from pan to a wire rack; discard paper, and cool completely. Wrap cake in aluminum foil. Freeze until firm. *To make tea cakes,* slice cake horizontally, separating layers. Heat jam over low heat, stirring frequently, until jam melts. Spread on the bottom layer of the cake. Replace top layer. Cut cake into assorted shapes, using 1¾-inch cookie cutters. Place cakes 2 inches apart on a wire rack; place rack in shallow pan. *For icing,* combine all ingredients in a saucepan. Cook over low heat, stirring constantly, until icing reaches pouring consistency (about 110°). Use white icing before tinting remaining icing with desired colors. Quickly pour warm icing over cakes, covering the top and sides. Spoon up all icing that drips through rack, and reheat to 110°; add a small amount of water, if necessary, to maintain original consistency. Continue pouring and reheating until cakes are smoothly and evenly coated. (This may take 2 to 3 coatings.) Allow icing to dry. Place cakes on a cutting board; using a sharp knife, trim any surplus icing. Using a little stiffer icing, tint to desired color; spoon into pastry bag fitted with a No. 2 or 3 round tip. Pipe simple designs on cakes, as desired. (The more proficient cake decorator may choose Royal Icing for designs.)

Yield: About 2 ½ dozen

Kay Love-Caskey

APRICOT SUGAR PLUMS

¾ cup sweet butter,
  softened
½ cup milk
1 cup sugar
2 eggs
1 teaspoon baking powder
3 ¾ cups flour, divided
1 teaspoon vanilla
⅔ cup apricot jam
2 tablespoons chopped
  peppermint leaves
¼ cup chocolate pieces,
  melted and cooled
⅓ cup ground pecans
2 teaspoons rum or sherry
¼ cup water
⅓ cup red sugar
⅔ cup yellow-orange sugar
Whole candied mint leaves
  for garnish

In a large bowl with an electric mixer, combine butter, milk, sugar, eggs, baking powder and 2 cups flour. Blend 1 minute on low speed, scraping the bowl constantly, then beat 1 minute on medium speed while continuing to scrape the bowl. Stir in remaining flour and vanilla. The dough will be smooth and soft. Shape the dough into smooth ¾ -inch balls. Place balls 1 inch apart on an ungreased baking sheet. Bake at 325°, with baking sheet on center shelf of oven, for 15 to 20 minutes or until cookies are lightly browned on the bottom. Cool cookies completely on wire rack. *To make sugar plums,* place the tip of a small knife in the center of the flat side of each cookie and carefully rotate to make a hollow, reserving the crumbs. In a small saucepan over low heat, warm jam with chopped mint leaves. Mix minted jam with 1½ cups of reserved crumbs, chocolate, pecans and rum. Fill hollowed-out cookies with this mixture. Assemble the 'plums' by putting the flat side of two cookies together and pressing gently. Brush each 'plum' lightly with water, and immediately roll one side in red sugar for the blush. Sprinkle yellow-orange sugar over, covering 'the plum' completely. Put a candied mint leaf in the crack at the top. Set on a rack to dry.

Yield: About 2 dozen

Kay Love-Caskey

LEMON AND CHERRY TARTS

Pate Brisee:
1 cup flour
¼ cup sugar
½ cup (1 stick) butter
1 egg yolk
2 tablespoons ground
    blanched almonds
½ teaspoon almond extract

Lemon Curd Filling:
3 eggs plus 1 egg yolk,
    beaten
1 cup sugar
½ cup lemon juice
1 tablespoon lemon zest
½ cup (1 stick) butter

Cherry Filling:
1 (21-ounce) can cherry pie
    filling

Combine flour and sugar in a bowl. Cut slightly softened butter into flour mixture until it resembles coarse crumbs. Add egg yolk, almonds and extract; stir with fork until blended. Press 1 teaspoon of dough into 1¾-inch fluted tart tins. Arrange on a baking sheet. Place in the freezer for 15 minutes. Bake at 400° for 8 to 10 minutes. Let cool 5 minutes, then carefully turn out onto cooling rack. *For lemon curd filling,* stir beaten eggs and sugar together in the top of a double boiler. Add lemon juice, zest and butter. Cook over gently boiling water, stirring constantly until mixture is thick. Remove from heat and cool. Refrigerate (keeps for 2 weeks in the refrigerator). Fill shells just before serving. *For cherry tarts,* fill the baked tart shells with canned cherry pie filling before serving.

Yield: About 3 ½ dozen tarts
    1 pint lemon curd filling

Nina Sudor

BATTENBERG CAKE

½ cup butter
1 cup sugar
4 eggs
1 teaspoon vanilla
2 cups flour
2 teaspoons baking powder
Red and yellow food
   coloring
½ cup apricot jam

Marzipan:
1 cup almonds, blanched
1 cup powdered sugar
1 tablespoon water
½ teaspoon almond extract
1 egg white
Yellow food coloring

Use heavy-duty foil to divide an 8-inch square baking pan in half. Fold foil several times to create a divider the length and height of the pan. It will be supported by the stiff dough, pink on one side and yellow on the other. Butter pan bottom well. Have all ingredients at room temperature before starting. Cream together butter and sugar until light and fluffy. Gradually beat in eggs. Add vanilla and 4 drops of yellow food coloring. Sift flour with baking powder and gently fold into mixture. Divide mixture in half. To one portion add 5 or 6 drops of red food coloring to tint it a pale pink. (Color deepens during baking.) With spatula, smooth batters into divided pan, yellow on one side, pink on the other. Bake at 375° for 30 minutes or until cake tester inserted in center comes out dry. Cool for 5 minutes before turning cake out onto rack. When completely cool, slice each cake lengthwise down the center. Trim away crusts remaining on tops and sides. Warm apricot jam and strain it. Place a yellow cake strip next to a pink strip. Use a pastry brush to spread apricot jam generously to join the two strips. Repeat with the remaining two strips. Spread the top of one joined cake with jam and place the second joined cake on top, placing pink on yellow and yellow on pink. Save remaining jam to spread on outside of cake later. Wrap cake tightly in plastic wrap and place in refrigerator while preparing marzipan. *For marzipan,* grind almonds and sugar in a processor or blender, until powdered. Add water, almond extract, egg white and a drop or two of yellow food coloring. Blend until a soft paste is formed. Refrigerate until paste firms. Measure the length, sides and top of the cake. Roll out marzipan to cake dimensions. Dust rolling pin and board with powdered sugar if paste is sticky. Coat top and two long sides of the cake with warmed apricot jam. Drape marzipan over and press on. Trim both ends. Refrigerate until serving time.

Yield: 12 or more slices
  1 cup marzipan

Kay Love-Caskey

"Marzipan was originally called marchpane. This ground almond and sugar comfit was a court favorite."

Note: The marzipan recipe calls for an uncooked egg.

BONBONS

1 (12-ounce) package semi-
    sweet chocolate chips
¼ cup butter or margarine
1 (14-ounce) can sweetened
    condensed milk
2 cups flour
½ cup finely chopped nuts
    (optional)
1 teaspoon vanilla
60 milk chocolate candy
    kisses or white and
    chocolate-striped candy
    kisses, unwrapped

Glaze:
2 ounces white baking bar
    or vanilla-flavored candy
    coating
1 teaspoon shortening

In a medium saucepan, melt chocolate chips and butter together over low heat, stirring occasionally, until chips are melted and smooth. Remove from heat and add sweetened condensed milk, mixing well. In a medium heat-proof bowl, combine flour, nuts, chocolate mixture and vanilla; mix well. Shape 1 tablespoonful of dough around each candy kiss, covering completely. Place 1 inch apart on an ungreased baking sheet. Bake at 350° for 6 to 8 minutes. (Dough will be soft and appear shiny but becomes firm when cool. Do not overbake.) Remove from baking sheet to cool completely. In a small saucepan, melt white baking bar and shortening together over low heat, stirring occasionally, until melted and smooth. Drizzle over bonbons. Store in a tightly covered container.
Yield: 5 dozen

Sheila Kramer

"A delightfully decadent sweet!"

APPETIZERS AND
BEVERAGES

BAKED BRIE EN CROUTE

1 sheet puff pastry
1 small wheel (8 ounces)
   Brie cheese
½ cup apricot preserves
¼ cup chopped pecans

Crackers or cocktail bread

Top Brie wheel with apricot preserves and pecans. Encase in puff pastry. Set on baking sheet. Bake at 350° for 25 to 30 minutes, until golden brown. Serve hot with crackers or bread.

Serves: 6 to 8

Eleni George

BRIE TORTE

1 (14-ounce) wheel of Brie
   cheese
½ cup butter, softened
1 large clove garlic, minced
⅓ cup chopped walnuts
⅓ cup chopped black olives
2 tablespoons chopped
   fresh basil leaves (or 2
   teaspoons dried basil)

Assorted crackers

Place cheese in freezer for approximately 30 minutes or until very firm. Cut cheese horizontally in half (you may need the aid of a couple of spatulas); set aside. In a small bowl, cream butter and garlic together. Stir in walnuts, olives and basil. Mix well. Spread mixture on cut side of one Brie half. Top with the other half, cut side down. Press together. Cover with plastic wrap and chill in refrigerator. Bring to room temperature before serving. Serve with assorted crackers.

Serves: 6 to 8

Jane Aughenbaugh

SALLY'S BAKED BRIE

**1 small wheel (8 ounces)
    Brie cheese
Brown sugar
Chopped pecans**

Crackers

Sprinkle Brie with brown sugar.
Bake at 350° for 4 to 5 minutes.
Sprinkle chopped pecans on top
and bake another 2 minutes. Serve
with plain or bland crackers.

Serves: 6

Betsy Ogle Weitz

"Easy, but amazingly good."

BACON CHEESE SNACKS

**2 cups sharp Cheddar
    cheese, shredded
1 cup mayonnaise
2 tablespoons chopped
    onion
1 (4-ounce) can chopped
    black olives, drained
Cocktail rye bread, thinly
    sliced
Real bacon bits**

Mix cheese, mayonnaise, onion and
olives together. Spread on slices of
cocktail rye bread. Top with bacon
bits. Place slices on baking sheet.
Bake at 300° for 10 to 15 minutes.

**Yield: 3 ¾ cups
        about 24 appetizers**

Lisa Rodysill

CHEESE STRIPS

12 slices white bread
1 (8-ounce) package sharp
  Cheddar cheese, grated
6 slices bacon, cooked crisp
  and crumbled
1 small onion, minced
1 cup mayonnaise
Salt and pepper to taste

Cut crusts from bread and place slices on a baking sheet. Bake at 350° for 5 minutes. Combine remaining ingredients in a bowl, mixing well. Spread cheese mixture on top of bread. Cut each slice into three strips. (At this point, you may freeze strips on baking sheet. Once frozen, place in a plastic bag to keep fresh until ready to serve.) *To serve,* place strips on a baking sheet and bake at 350° for 12 to 15 minutes or until bubbly.

Yield: 36 strips

Karen Petitt

SOUTHWESTERN APPETIZER CHEESECAKE

2 (8-ounce) packages cream
  cheese, softened
2 cups shredded Cheddar
  cheese
2 cups sour cream, divided
1 (1.25-ounce) package taco
  seasoning mix
3 eggs
1 (4-ounce) can chopped
  green chilies, drained
⅔ cup salsa

Garnish:
Avocado pieces
Parsley
Chopped black olives
Tomato pieces

Crackers or tortilla chips

Beat together the cream cheese and Cheddar cheese until light. Beat in 1 cup sour cream and taco seasoning mix. Add eggs, beating well. Fold in chilies. Turn mixture into a 9-inch springform pan. Place on baking sheet and bake at 350° for 35 to 40 minutes or until center is almost set. Remove from oven and cool on a rack for 10 minutes. Do not turn oven off. Combine 1 cup sour cream and salsa; spoon over appetizer. Return to oven and bake 5 minutes more. Cool completely. Refrigerate at least 3 hours or until ready to serve, up to 24 hours. To serve, run knife around edge of pan. Remove sides. Garnish top generously with diced avocado, parsley, chopped black olives and diced tomato. Serve with crackers or tortilla chips.

Serves: 8 to 10

Sonia Gisvold

CHICKEN LEEK ROLLS

2 whole chicken breasts
3 tablespoons soy sauce, divided
1 tablespoon dry sherry
¼ teaspoon fresh ginger root, shredded
2 teaspoons sugar
2 leeks
2 tablespoons vegetable oil
½ cup water

Skin and bone chicken breasts. Pound into a thin, even layer with a rolling pin. Divide into 8 equal portions. In a shallow dish, large enough to hold chicken in one layer, stir together 2 tablespoons soy sauce, sherry, ginger root and sugar. Place chicken on top and allow to marinate. Cut roots and some of the green part off leeks. Cut into quarters and wash to remove sand. Do not take leek apart completely. Arrange one leek quarter on each piece of chicken. Wrap chicken around leek, securing with toothpicks as necessary. Return chicken rolls to marinade. Refrigerate 30 minutes, turning occasionally. Heat vegetable oil in a large skillet. Add chicken rolls and brown on all sides. Add remaining 1 tablespoon soy sauce and water. Cover and simmer 10 minutes or until the chicken is tender. Remove from skillet, remove toothpicks, and cut each roll into four even pieces. Serve hot or cold.

Yield: 32 pieces

Sally Duffy

CHINESE CHICKEN WINGS

3 pounds chicken wings
½ cup soy sauce
2 tablespoons honey
3 cloves garlic, crushed
¼ cup sherry
⅓ cup catsup
3 tablespoons peanut butter
⅓ cup granulated sugar
½ teaspoon Chinese 5-spice
  powder

Cut off wing tips and save for stock. Cut each wing into two pieces. Combine remaining ingredients. Add chicken wings, cover and marinate several hours or overnight, turning occasionally. Remove wings from marinade and place in a single layer in shallow baking dish. Bake, covered at 325° for about 15 minutes. Baste with marinade; bake another 15 minutes. Turn over. Bake 10 to 15 minutes more, uncovered.

Yield: About 30 wings

Janet Engels

CURRIED CRAB IN ENDIVE SPEARS

¼ cup mayonnaise
2 tablespoons minced celery
2 tablespoons minced onion
1 teaspoon curry powder
1 cup crabmeat
Fresh pepper to taste

4 heads Belgian endive,
  spears separated
2 tablespoons minced fresh
  cilantro

Combine first four ingredients in a small bowl. Mix in crabmeat. Season to taste with pepper. (Can be prepared early in the day to this point. Cover and refrigerate.) Place 1 heaping teaspoon crab mixture on the base of each endive spear. Sprinkle with cilantro. Arrange on a serving platter. Cover and refrigerate until ready to serve.

Yield: About 24

Julie Roenigk

CRAB ROLLS

½ pound processed
   American cheese
1 pound butter, divided
2 (7-ounce) cans crabmeat
20 slices white bread
2 cups sesame seeds, roasted

Melt cheese and half of butter in double boiler. Cool. Add crabmeat, stirring until mixture is spreadable. Trim crusts from bread and flatten each slice with a rolling pin. Spread crab mixture on bread and roll up. Melt remaining butter. Dip rolls in butter. Roast sesame seeds by spreading on baking sheet and baking at 250° for approximately 5 minutes, stirring several times. After dipping rolls in butter, roll in sesame seeds. Place seam side down in shallow pan. Cover and freeze. *To serve,* thaw slightly and cut into thirds. Bake at 350° for 10 to 15 minutes or until golden.

Yield: 60

Lisa Rodysill

BAKED CRAB DIP

1 (8-ounce) package cream
   cheese, softened
1 (6-ounce) package frozen
   crabmeat, defrosted and
   well-drained
1 tablespoon chopped onion
1 teaspoon milk
2 tablespoons mayonnaise
1 teaspoon horseradish
¼ teaspoon salt
⅛ teaspoon pepper
Crushed almonds (optional)

Assorted crackers

Combine all ingredients except almonds. Place in a greased casserole dish. Bake at 325° for 30 minutes. Top with crushed almonds, if desired. Serve hot with crackers.

Serves: 8

Betsy Ogle Weitz

Hot Crab Dip

1 (8-ounce) package cream
   cheese, softened
1 pound crabmeat, flaked
2 tablespoons finely
   chopped onion
1 tablespoon milk
1 teaspoon creamy
   horseradish
Salt and pepper to taste
Paprika

Assorted crackers or
   cauliflower

Combine all ingredients except
paprika, mixing well. Spoon
mixture into a glass pie plate or
baking dish suitable for serving.
Sprinkle with paprika. Bake at 375°
for 15 minutes. Serve hot with
crackers or crisp cauliflower.

Yield: 2 ½ to 3 cups

Sheila Kramer

Spicy Cranberry Appetizer

2 (8-ounce) packages cream
   cheese, softened
1 cup cranberries, chopped
⅓ cup finely chopped
   onion
¼ teaspoon cayenne pepper

Crackers

Mix cream cheese, cranberries,
onion and cayenne pepper together.
Serve with your favorite crackers.

Yield: 2 ½ to 3 cups

Lois Kennel

GRILLED GRAPEFRUIT WITH KIRSCH

4 grapefruit, halved
1 cup sugar
1 cup kirsch
Maraschino cherries for
  garnish
Mint sprigs for garnish

Cut grapefruit in half. Cut out center and remove seeds from each grapefruit half. Cut around each section with a grapefruit knife, to loosen. Sprinkle each half with 2 tablespoons sugar, then with 2 tablespoons kirsch. Broil, 4 inches from heat, about 5 minutes, or until bubbly and slightly browned. Garnish with maraschino cherries and mint sprigs, if desired.

Serves: 8

Variation: Sprinkle with cinnamon sugar. Broil until bubbly and slightly browned. Serve with a dollop of sour cream.

MELON WITH BLACK FOREST HAM

¼ pound sliced Black
  Forest ham, prosciutto
  (Italian ham) or baked
  Virginia ham
1 (2 ½ -pound) honeydew
  melon, well-chilled
1 lemon
1 lime

Cut ham into 1-inch strips. Cut melon in half; scoop out seeds and fibers. Cut each half into six wedges; remove rind. Roll each melon wedge in a strip of ham. Serve garnished with lemon and lime wedges.

Yield: 6 servings (2 wedges per person)

HOT MUSHROOM-DILLWEED DIP

2 tablespoons oil
4 cups fresh mushrooms, chopped
½ cup onion, finely chopped
1 clove garlic, minced
2 tablespoons flour
1 (8-ounce) package cream cheese, cubed
2 teaspoons Worcestershire sauce
½ teaspoon dillweed, or to taste
½ cup sour cream
Salt and pepper, to taste

Party rye bread

Heat oil in frying pan. Add mushrooms, onions and garlic to pan. Cook until soft and most of the liquid has evaporated. Stir in flour; cook 1 minute. Add cream cheese and Worcestershire sauce. Stir until cheese melts. Add dillweed, sour cream, and salt and pepper to taste. Heat through, but do not boil. Serve warm with tiny party rye slices.

Yield: 2 ½ cups

Margo Stich

"A great appetizer to a beef main course."

SEAFOOD STUFFED MUSHROOMS

Mushroom Caps:
2 tablespoons unsalted butter, plus more if needed
2 tablespoons vegetable oil, plus more if needed
36 large mushroom caps, 1 ½ to 2 inches in diameter, cleaned and patted dry

Filling:
2 tablespoons unsalted butter
6 tablespoons finely chopped shallots
8 ounces tiny bay scallops, ½ to ¾-inch in diameter, rinsed and patted dry
1 cup heavy cream
1 ¾ cups grated Gruyere cheese, divided
½ cup grated Parmesan cheese
¾ cup dry bread crumbs
¼ teaspoon salt, plus more if needed
Freshly ground pepper to taste
Sprigs of watercress for garnish

Heat 2 tablespoons butter and oil in a large heavy skillet over medium heat. Add enough mushroom caps, hollow side up, to fit comfortably in one layer in the pan. Sauté caps for 2 to 3 minutes, then turn them hollow side down and sauté until golden, another 2 minutes. Remove mushrooms from pan and drain on paper towels. Repeat with remaining mushrooms. Add additional butter and oil if needed. *For filling,* melt 2 tablespoons butter in a medium heavy skillet. Add shallots; cook until softened, about 2 minutes. Add scallops; cook 2 minutes more. (Do not overcook, as scallops become tough.) Remove scallops and shallots with a slotted spoon; set aside. In a medium saucepan, heat cream over medium heat until hot. Gradually stir in 1 ½ cups Gruyere cheese and all of the Parmesan cheese until melted. Add scallops and shallots. Stir in bread crumbs and salt. Remove from heat. Salt and pepper the cavities of the mushroom caps. Fill each cap with a tablespoon or more of the filling. (You may have some filling left over.) Place the filled caps on a generously buttered baking dish or pan that can withstand the heat of a broiler. Sprinkle each top with the remaining Gruyere cheese. Cover with plastic wrap and refrigerate until 1 hour before serving. Bring to room temperature. Broil for 2 minutes, or until mushrooms have browned slightly on top and are heated through. Garnish with sprigs of watercress and serve immediately.

Yield: 36

Renda Meloy

"This is an easy appetizer to make, and tastes wonderful!"

OLIVE PESTO

1 (5 ¾ -ounce) can jumbo
   pitted ripe olives
⅓ cup pine nuts
Fresh basil to taste
⅓ cup freshly shredded
   Parmesan cheese
1 tablespoon melted butter
1 clove garlic, chopped
¼ cup olive oil

Foccacia Bread

Combine all ingredients in food processor. Process just until finely chopped. Be careful not to over process; nuts should have an occasional crunch. Serve with fresh foccacia bread.

Yield: 1 cup

Georgia Hurley

"This is a little on the dry side for pesto, but oh so good!"

MUSHROOM PALMIERS

5 tablespoons butter
18 ounces fresh mushrooms,
   finely chopped
1 large onion, finely
   chopped
¾ teaspoon fresh lemon
   juice
2 tablespoons flour
1 ½ teaspoons dried thyme,
   crumbled
Salt and freshly ground
   pepper
3 frozen puff pastry sheets,
   thawed
2 eggs beaten with 4
   teaspoons water (glaze)

Melt butter in heavy large skillet over medium-high heat. Add mushrooms and onions and cook until juices evaporate, stirring occasionally, about 8 minutes. Mix in lemon juice, flour and thyme; stir for 2 minutes. Season with salt and pepper. Cool. Spread ⅓ of mushroom mixture evenly over 1 pastry sheet. Starting from one short side, roll up jelly roll fashion to center. Starting at second short side, roll up to center. Press two sides together and transfer to baking sheet. Repeat with remaining sheets and mushroom mixture. Cover; chill until firm, at least 1 hour or overnight. (Can be prepared 1 week ahead and frozen. Thaw slightly before continuing.) Using a serrated knife, slice pastry into ¼ -inch slices. Arrange cut side down on greased baking sheets, spacing 1 inch apart. (Can be prepared 1 day ahead. Wrap tightly and refrigerate.) Brush with glaze. Bake at 400° until golden brown, about 20 minutes. Serve warm.

Yield: 5 dozen

Renda Meloy

PESTO TORTA

2 (8-ounce) packages cream
   cheese, room temperature
2 cups unsalted butter, room
   temperature

Pesto Sauce:
¼ cup pine nuts
2 cloves garlic, chopped
1 cup fresh spinach, tightly
   packed
1 cup fresh basil, tightly
   packed
½ cup fresh parsley
½ teaspoon salt
½ cup best quality olive oil
¾ cup freshly grated
   Parmesan cheese
3 tablespoons butter, room
   temperature
Sun-dried tomatoes

Assorted crackers

Combine cream cheese and 2 cups butter in a medium bowl. Beat until smoothly blended. Set aside. *For pesto*, roast pine nuts at 325° for 10 minutes. Cool slightly. Using a food processor, puree nuts, garlic, spinach, basil, parsley, and salt together. Add olive oil and blend. Add Parmesan cheese and 3 tablespoons butter, pulsing briefly. Cut an 18-inch square of cheesecloth. Moisten with water, wring dry and line a 6-cup mold, draping excess over the rim. With a spatula, make an even layer with ⅙ of the cream cheese mixture, followed by ⅕ of pesto. Continue to layer, ending with cheese. Fold ends of the cheesecloth over torta. Chill for several hours. *To serve*, invert onto a serving dish. Remove cloth. Cover top with sun dried tomatoes. Serve with crackers.

Serves: 8 to 10

Cherie Miles

"Easy to make and delicious "

PINEAPPLE SORBET

2 (20-ounce) cans chunk
   pineapple

Champagne or white wine

Drain pineapple, reserving juice. Freeze pineapple chunks. After pineapple is frozen, blend in blender (adding small amount of reserved juice as necessary). Scoop into balls. Place on baking sheet and freeze. *To serve,* place frozen balls into sherbet glasses. Pour champagne or white wine over top.

Serves: 6

Peggy King
Julie Huettner

"A pallatizer (after the appetizer) to clear the palate."

ROSÉ SORBET

2 ½ cups medium-dry rosé
   wine
1 cup sugar
1 cup water
2 tablespoons fresh lemon
   juice, or to taste
4 mint sprigs for garnish
   (optional)

In a saucepan, bring wine to a boil; simmer for 5 minutes. Remove from heat and pour wine into a metal bowl set in a larger bowl of ice and cold water. In the same saucepan combine sugar and water. Bring to a boil, stirring until sugar is dissolved. Stir syrup into wine. Let wine mixture stand, stirring occasionally, until cold. Stir in lemon juice. Freeze mixture in an ice-cream freezer according to the manufacturer's instructions. Transfer the sorbet to a freezer container and freeze until firm. (Sorbet may be made 1 week in advance and kept frozen.) *To serve,* scoop sorbet with a small scoop into parfait glasses and garnish with a mint sprig.

Serves: 4

SALMON PATÉ

1 (8-ounce) package cream
 cheese, softened
8 ounces smoked salmon,
 flaked
2 tablespoons drained
 capers
¼ cup finely chopped red
 onion

Crackers

Combine cream cheese, salmon,
capers and onion, mixing well.
Chill. Serve with crackers.

Yield: 2 cups

Sonia Gisvold

SCALLOPS IN GRUYERE CHEESE

½ cup fresh bread crumbs
5 tablespoons butter,
 divided
1 ½ cups (6 ounces)
 shredded processed
 Gruyere cheese
1 cup good quality
 mayonnaise
¼ cup dry white wine
1 tablespoon chopped
 parsley
1 pound scallops, quartered
½ pound sliced mushrooms
½ cup chopped onions

Toss bread crumbs with 1
tablespoon melted butter. Set aside.
Stir together cheese, mayonnaise,
wine and parsley. Set aside. Over
medium heat melt 2 tablespoons
butter and cook scallops until
opaque, stirring frequently. Remove
and drain. Sauté mushrooms and
onion in remaining 2 tablespoons
butter. Combine with cheese
mixture and scallops. Spoon into
individual baking dishes or into a
9 x 9-inch pan. Sprinkle with bread
crumbs. (Can be covered and
refrigerated overnight.) Bake at 325°
for 25 minutes until bubbly and
lightly browned. May be served as
an appetizer or a main course.

Serves: 6 to 8 as an appetizer

Julie Larson

SCALLOPS MORNAY

3 pounds scallops
2 cups dry white wine
1 cup water
3 small onions, chopped,
    divided
¼ cup chopped fresh
    parsley
Salt and pepper
½ cup (1 stick) butter or
    margarine
1 pound fresh whole
    mushrooms
½ cup flour
1 cup milk
4 ounces grated mozzarella
    cheese
Fresh parsley sprigs for
    garnish

In a large pan, combine scallops, wine, water, 1 chopped onion, parsley, salt and pepper. Cook slowly over low heat for 30 minutes. Remove from heat and drain scallops, reserving stock. In a separate saucepan, sauté 2 chopped onions and mushrooms in butter. Add flour. Stir in milk and 2 cups of reserved stock. Stir until thick. Add cheese and scallops. Garnish with parsley and serve.

Serves: 8 to 10

Julie Huettner
Peggy King

SCALLOP PUFFS

½ pound sea scallops
¼ cup mayonnaise
¼ cup freshly grated
  Gruyere cheese
½ teaspoon Dijon-style
  mustard
1 teaspoon fresh lemon
  juice
1 tablespoon finely chopped
  fresh parsley leaves
Salt and pepper to taste
1 large egg white
8 slices homemade-type
  white bread, toasted
  lightly, crusts discarded,
  and each slice cut into 4
  squares

In a saucepan, combine scallops with enough salted water to cover them completely. Bring the water to a simmer; poach scallops for 5 minutes. Drain scallops well, then cut them into ½-inch pieces. In a bowl whisk together mayonnaise, cheese, mustard, lemon juice and parsley. Add scallops. Season with salt and pepper to taste. In a small bowl beat egg white until it just holds stiff peaks. Fold egg white into scallop mixture gently but thoroughly. Top each bread square with a heaping teaspoon of scallop mixture. Arrange puffs about ½ inch apart on baking sheets. Broil puffs under a preheated broiler, about 6 inches from the heat, for 1 to 2 minutes, or until the topping is bubbly and lightly golden (do not allow the edges of the toasts to burn).

Yield: 32 toasts

Julie Larson
Rebecca Torgerson

MARINATED SHRIMP WITH YELLOW BELL PEPPER AND RED ONION

⅓ cup white wine vinegar
2 tablespoons medium dry
  sherry
½ teaspoon dried thyme,
  crumbled
1 teaspoon salt
½ teaspoon sugar
1 teaspoon cracked black
  peppercorns
⅓ cup extra virgin olive oil
1 bay leaf
2 tablespoons bottled
  capers, drained
1 red onion, cut in half and
  thinly sliced
2 yellow bell peppers, cut
  into 2-inch strips
1 ½ pounds medium
  shrimp (about 40)

Garlic Toast Rounds:
1 long loaf of day-old
  French or Italian bread
3 garlic cloves, minced
½ teaspoon salt
⅓ cup olive oil

In a bowl whisk together vinegar, sherry, thyme, salt, sugar and cracked pepper. Add oil in a stream, whisking constantly until mixture is emulsified. Stir in bay leaf, capers, onion and bell peppers until marinade is combined well. In a kettle of boiling salted water, cook shrimp for 1 minute. Drain and shell, adding shrimp to marinade as they are shelled. Toss shrimp with the marinade. Transfer mixture to a sturdy resealable plastic bag. Marinate in the refrigerator for at least 8 hours or overnight. _For garlic toast rounds,_ cut bread into ¼-inch slices. Arrange slices in one layer on baking sheets. Mince and mash garlic with salt until it forms a paste. In a small bowl, whisk together oil and garlic paste. Strain mixture through a fine sieve into a bowl, pressing hard on the solids. Brush oil on bread. Bake at 350° for 10 minutes, or until bread is golden. Let toast rounds cool before serving. (The toast rounds may be made two days in advance and kept in an airtight container.) _To serve,_ drain shrimp and vegetables, discarding bay leaf. Arrange as desired on a platter and serve with garlic toast rounds.

Serves: 12 to 15
  Makes 70 toast rounds

Renda Meloy

Shrimp in Lemon and Olive Oil

Marinade:
¾ cup extra virgin olive oil
½ cup fresh lemon juice
¼ cup chopped fresh
    parsley
2 garlic cloves, lightly
    crushed
½ teaspoon freshly ground
    pepper
½ teaspoon salt

Shrimp:
12 cups water
2 tablespoons fresh lemon
    juice
1 tablespoon plus 1
    teaspoon balsamic or red
    wine vinegar
2 celery stalks, chopped
1 carrot, chopped
1 (2-inch) strip lemon peel
1 bay leaf
2 pounds uncooked
    medium shrimp

Assorted crackers

Combine ingredients for marinade in a large bowl. Set aside. In a large pot, combine water, lemon juice, vinegar, celery, carrot, lemon peel and bay leaf. Bring to a boil. Simmer for 20 minutes. Increase heat to high and add shrimp. Boil until shrimp just turn pink. Remove shrimp with a slotted spoon. Cool slightly. Peel and devein. Add shrimp to marinade. Cover and refrigerate for at least 3 hours. Serve shrimp at room temperature with assorted crackers.

Serves: 8 to 10

Kay Love-Caskey

Shrimp Mousse

1 envelope unflavored
    gelatin
¼ cup water
1 (10 ¾-ounce) can tomato
    soup
3 (3-ounce) packages cream
    cheese, softened
1 cup mayonnaise
¾ cup diced celery
½ to ¾ cup chopped onion
1 (7 ½-ounce) can shrimp
    (or use frozen)

Crackers

In medium saucepan, dissolve gelatin in water and bring to a boil. Remove from heat. Add cream cheese, stirring until smooth. Cool for 5 minutes. Add remaining ingredients except shrimp. Refrigerate for 5 minutes. Break shrimp into pieces and fold into cream cheese mixture. Grease a 4-cup mold with a little mayonnaise. Pour in mousse and chill at least 4 hours until set. Serve with crackers.

Serves: 10 to 12

Eleni George

ANITIA'S SALSA

5 to 7 jalapeno peppers,
  seeded
1 clove garlic
1 teaspoon salt
1 tablespoon lemon juice
1 (16 ounce) can whole
  tomatoes, juice drained
  and reserved
1 to 2 large fresh tomatoes
Cilantro to taste

Tortilla chips

Combine jalapeno peppers, garlic, salt and lemon juice in a blender. Drain juice from canned tomatoes into blender. Blend until well mixed. Add canned and fresh tomatoes and blend for 1 to 2 seconds. Add cilantro, whisking to incorporate. Refrigerate until ready to serve. Garnish with cilantro. Serve with tortilla chips.

Yield: 2 cups

Marilyn Riederer

"Tailor this salsa to your own tastes by adjusting jalapeno peppers. You may also add celery, onion, or avocado."

SHRIMP TOAST

1 pound shrimp, peeled and
  deveined
1 medium onion, peeled
  and chopped
1 ½ -inch slice fresh ginger
  root, peeled and chopped
½ teaspoon salt
Large pinch of freshly
  ground black pepper
2 egg whites
30 strips (1 x 3 inches) firm
  thinly-sliced bread, crusts
  removed
½ cup fine fresh bread
  crumbs (made in a food
  processor from bread
  crusts or trimmings)
Light vegetable oil for
  frying

In a food processor or blender, process shrimp, onion, ginger, salt and pepper until finely chopped. With the motor running, drop the egg whites through the feed tube and process until the mixture is well combined. Spread shrimp mixture, approximately ¼-inch thick, on the strips of bread and dip the mixture-coated side in bread crumbs, covering well. Cover with plastic wrap. Chill on baking sheets, shrimp side up, until ready to cook. To cook, heat oil 1 ½ to 2 inches deep in a large skillet. When oil is hot (360°), fry toast on both sides until golden brown. Drain on paper towels and serve.

Yield: 30

Julie Larson

"Shrimp toast may be frozen, uncooked. Fry in hot oil as directed above, right from the freezer."

CHERRY TOMATOES WITH ROASTED GARLIC FILLING

1 (6-ounce) head of garlic
1 tablespoon olive oil
1 pint cherry tomatoes
  (about 30)
6 ounces cream cheese,
  softened
1 teaspoon fresh lemon
  juice, or to taste
Salt and pepper to taste
Fresh basil leaves,
  shredded, for garnish

Remove outer husk from garlic head and cut ¼ inch off the stem end. Place garlic in a foil-lined baking dish. Drizzle the garlic with the olive oil. Bake, covered loosely with foil, in the middle of a preheated 325° oven for 1 ¼ hours, or until the pulp is very soft. Let it cool until it can be easily handled. Squeeze the pulp from the cloves into a bowl and let it cool. Mash pulp until it is smooth (there should be about ¼ cup puree.) Using a serrated knife, cut a thin slice from the bottom of each tomato so that it stands upright. Cut off a thin slice from each stem end and with a small melon-ball cutter, scoop out the flesh and seeds carefully, forming tomato shells. Sprinkle the insides of the tomato shells with salt. Invert the tomatoes on racks set over paper towels, and let them drain for 30 minutes. In a bowl, whisk together cream cheese, lemon juice, garlic puree, salt and pepper to taste, until filling is smooth. Using a pastry bag fitted with a small star tip, pipe the filling into the tomato shells. Garnish filled shells with fresh basil leaves.

Yield: 30

Sally Duffy
Julie Larson

"Remove tomato pulp with a small melon-ball scoop."

CHERRY TOMATOES STUFFED WITH SPINACH

4 eggs
2 cups herb seasoned
   stuffing mix
1 red onion, finely chopped
½ cup Parmesan cheese
½ teaspoon thyme or
   oregano
½ teaspoon salt
½ teaspoon garlic powder
   or garlic salt
1 teaspoon pepper
2 (10-ounce) packages
   frozen chopped spinach,
   cooked and drained
¾ cup butter, melted
48 cherry tomatoes

In a small bowl, beat eggs; set aside. In a large bowl, combine stuffing mix with onion, cheese and seasonings. Add cooked spinach and eggs. Pour melted butter over and mix thoroughly. Chill for about an hour. Roll into 48 small balls and place on a baking sheet. Bake at 350° for 15 minutes. Let cool. Meanwhile, prepare tomatoes by cutting off the tops and scooping out pulp. Stuff one spinach ball into each cherry tomato. Serve immediately or refrigerate until ready to serve.

Yield: 4 dozen

Julie Huettner

COCKTAIL WIENERS

1 (12-ounce) jar chili sauce
1 (10-ounce) jar grape jelly
2 pounds cocktail wieners

Combine chili sauce and grape jelly in a large saucepan. Add cocktail wieners. Bring to a boil. Reduce heat and simmer on low for several hours.

Serves: 20

FROZEN DAIQUIRI

2 (6-ounce) cans frozen pink
   lemonade
1 (6-ounce) can frozen
   orange juice
1 (8-ounce) bottle lime juice
1 (6-ounce) bottle of cherries
   (including juice)
1 quart light rum
8 cups water

Combine all ingredients together. Pour into plastic container and cover. Freeze until ready to serve. (Note: this does not freeze solid). Remove from freezer 10 to 15 minutes before serving. Stir to mix well before spooning into daiquiri or sherbet glasses.

Yield: 4 quarts

Faye Waldo

"Cheers!"

HOT SPICED CIDER

Whole cloves
1 large orange
8 cups apple juice or cider
3 tablespoons lemon juice
4 cinnamon sticks

Insert cloves about $1/2$ inch apart into orange. Place in shallow pan; bake at 350° for 30 minutes. Pierce orange in several places with a 2-pronged fork. In large saucepan, combine apple juice, lemon juice, cinnamon sticks and baked orange. Simmer, covered, over low heat for 30 minutes or longer. When ready to serve, remove cinnamon sticks and orange. Pour into heat-proof punch bowl. Float clove-studded orange in punch bowl. Serve hot.

Yield: 16 ($1/2$ cup) servings

Lisa Rodysill

HOT SPICED FRUIT PUNCH

1 ½ cups apple juice
3 cups orange juice
1 quart cranberry juice
   cocktail
3 cups pineapple juice
2 apples, cored, peeled and
   thinly sliced
¼ cup brown sugar
3 cinnamon sticks
½ teaspoon ginger
½ teaspoon nutmeg
½ teaspoon cloves
2 oranges, sliced

Combine all ingredients in a crockpot or large heavy kettle. Heat on low in crockpot or warm on stove for 2 to 3 hours, covered. Once mixture is thoroughly heated, serve immediately or keep warm. Can be made ahead and refrigerated. Rewarm before serving. Refrigerate any leftovers.

Yield: 3 quarts

Margo Stich

ORANGE SLUSH

1 (6-ounce) can frozen
   orange juice concentrate
1 cup cold water
1 cup 1% or 2% milk
1 teaspoon vanilla
6 to 8 ice cubes

Blend all ingredients in a blender on high speed. Pour into glasses and serve.

Serves: 4

Lisa Rodysill

PADDLER'S PASSION

3 cups crushed ice
6 tablespoons orange juice
6 tablespoons guava nectar
   or passion fruit juice
6 tablespoons vodka
6 tablespoons dark rum
3 tablespoons canned
   coconut cream (such as
   Coco Lopez)
2 teaspoons grenadine
Pineapple wedges for
   garnish

Combine first seven ingredients in a blender and blend until smooth. Pour into tall glasses. Garnish with pineapple wedges.

Serves: 4

Julie Roenigk

VIVALDI COCKTAILS

2 cups Quady Vinery
   Essensia
8 teaspoons grenadine
4 (750-ml) bottles
   champagne or white
   sparkling wine, chilled
8 to 10 pieces orange peel
   for garnish

Place 2 tablespoons Essensia and ½ teaspoon grenadine in each champagne goblet. Fill with champagne. Garnish with orange peel.

Serves: 8 to 10

Kay Love-Caskey

"Quady Vinery Essensia is an orange muscat wine which can be found at most liquor stores."

ROSÉ SPARKLE PUNCH

2 (10-ounce) packages
  frozen sliced
  strawberries, thawed
½ cup sugar
2 (750 ml.) bottles rosé
  wine or 2 (750 ml.) bottles
  sparkling pink grape
  juice
1 (12-ounce) can frozen pink
  lemonade concentrate,
  thawed
1 (1-liter) bottle club soda

1 ice ring made with fresh
  whole strawberries or
  other decorative fruit

In large non-metal bowl, mix
berries, sugar and one bottle of
wine. Let stand for one hour at
room temperature. Strain and mash
through strainer into punch bowl.
Just before serving, add lemonade
concentrate, second bottle of wine
and club soda. Serve over ice ring.

Yield: 24 (4-ounce) servings

*"Whoever makes the punch gets to savor the
strawberry pulp left in the strainer!"*

SOUPS

Beer Cheese and Bacon Soup

½ pound bacon
½ cup butter or margarine
½ cup minced onion
⅔ cup flour
1 teaspoon dry mustard
1 teaspoon paprika
⅛ teaspoon cayenne pepper
1 teaspoon salt
1 (10 ¾-ounce) can chicken
   broth
4 cups milk
1 (12-ounce) can beer
3 cups (12-ounces) sharp
   Cheddar cheese,
   shredded

Popcorn for garnish

Fry bacon, drain and crumble; set aside. In large kettle, sauté onion in butter until soft. Blend in flour and seasonings. Gradually stir in broth, milk and beer. Cook over medium heat, stirring constantly, until mixture comes to a boil. Boil and stir for 1 minute. Reduce heat and stir in cheese, until smooth. Add bacon. Serve garnished with popcorn.

Yield: 8 cups

Lisa Rodysill

Vegetable Cheese Soup

4 chicken flavored bouillon
   cubes
4 cups water
1 cup diced celery
1 cup diced onion
2 ½ cups cubed raw
   potatoes
1 (20-ounce) bag frozen
   mixed vegetables
2 (10 ¾-ounce) cans cream
   of chicken soup
1 pound processed cheese,
   cubed

Combine bouillon cubes, water, celery, and onions in a large kettle. Bring to a boil and simmer for 20 minutes. Add potatoes and mixed vegetables. Continue to simmer for another 30 minutes. Add chicken soup and cheese. Heat until cheese has melted, stirring constantly.

Yield: 4 quarts

Karen Petitt

"This soup freezes well."

Chicken Noodle Soup

2 tablespoons olive oil
2 chicken breast halves,
   skinned, boned and cut
   into ½-inch pieces
¼ to ½ cup chopped onion
2 celery stalks, diced
1 clove garlic, minced
1 large carrot, shredded
5 ½ cups water
5 ½ teaspoons chicken-
   flavored bouillon
⅛ cup dried parsley
¾ teaspoon dried basil
½ teaspoon oregano
1 bay leaf
2 ounces spaghetti, broken
   into 2-inch lengths

Heat oil in a large saucepan or Dutch oven over medium-high heat. Add chicken; cook, stirring frequently until chicken is cooked through. With slotted spoon, remove chicken; set aside. Add onion, celery and garlic to pan. (Add more oil if necessary to keep vegetables from sticking.) Sauté until tender. Add chicken, carrots, water, bouillon and seasonings, stirring well. Heat to boiling. Stir in pasta. Cover, reduce heat and boil gently 12 to 17 minutes or until pasta is tender. Remove bay leaf and serve.

Yield: 4 to 6 servings

Georgia Hurley

"This delicious soup is a wonderful way to warm yourself up from the winter chill. Serve with Beer Bread♪ for a hearty accompaniment."

HOT AND SOUR CHICKEN EGG DROP SOUP

3 tablespoons finely
   chopped green onion
2 tablespoons sesame oil
1 teaspoon white pepper
2 tablespoons vinegar
3 tablespoons cornstarch,
   divided
1 tablespoon cream sherry
3 tablespoons soy sauce,
   divided
1 teaspoon ginger, finely
   chopped
4 (8-ounce) chicken breasts,
   cut in strips
4 chicken bouillon cubes
5 cups water, divided
4 ounces fresh mushrooms
   or 2 to 3 black
   mushrooms soaked well
   in water and cut in strips
Small handful of tiger lilies,
   soaked for 10 minutes in
   water; pinch off the knot
   end
¼ head small cabbage, cut
   in strips
2 to 3 eggs, well beaten

Finely chopped green onion
   for garnish

Combine chopped green onion, sesame oil, white pepper and vinegar in a large bowl; set aside. Combine 1 tablespoon cornstarch, sherry, 1 tablespoon soy sauce, ginger and chicken, mixing well; set aside. Combine bouillon cubes and 4½ cups water in a saucepan. Bring to a boil. Add mushrooms, tiger lilies and cabbage; boil for approximately 45 minutes. Add chicken mixture and continue boiling for 10 minutes. In a small bowl, mix 2 tablespoons cornstarch, 2 tablespoons soy sauce and ½ cup water until smooth; pour into boiling soup. As soon as soup thickens and starts boiling again, add well-beaten eggs, stirring constantly. Remove from heat. Pour soup into bowl containing green onions. Mix well and serve hot.

Serves: 4 to 6

Lily Weinshilboum

LITE CHICKEN SOUP

1 (2 to 2 ½-pound) stewing
    hen
Water
1 medium onion, diced
1 ½ cups sliced celery
1 ½ cups sliced carrots
1 teaspoon pepper
1 teaspoon salt
Cooked noodles or rice, as
    desired

Wash chicken; cut into quarters. Place chicken in a large pot. Cover with cold water. Cook at low temperature for 2 ½ to 3 hours, until tender. Remove chicken, reserving broth, and let cool. Discard skin and dice meat. Place meat in a container and cover tightly. Strain broth. Place broth and chicken in refrigerator overnight. Remove chicken fat from top of broth. Pour broth into a large pot. Add vegetables and seasonings. Simmer over low heat until vegetables are almost tender. Add diced chicken. Simmer until chicken is heated and soup is hot. Add cooked noodles or rice, as desired.

Serves: 8

Lois Kennel

"Reduce the fat by making the chicken the day before. Enjoy!"

GIUSEPPI'S CLAM CHOWDER

¼ cup fresh oregano
¼ cup fresh basil
¼ cup chopped garlic
1 cup butter
2 cups white wine
1 tablespoon clam base
(chicken base can also be
used)
Flour
6 cups heavy cream
1 (25-ounce) can chopped
clams, drained with juice
reserved
¼ cup diced tomatoes
¼ cup chopped green onion

In a Dutch oven, combine spices
and butter; sauté briefly. Add white
wine and clam base; simmer 5
minutes. Stir in flour to make a
thick paste. Slowly stir in cream
and juice from the clams. Allow to
cook, stirring occasionally, until
heated to serving temperature. Add
tomatoes, green onions and clams.
Heat through; stir and serve.

Serves: 6 to 8

Mr. Loren Walters
Holiday Inn Downtown
Giuseppi's Olive Grove

*"Chicken and clam base is usually found in the
soup section at the grocery store."*

CREAMY CORN CHOWDER

⅓ cup chopped onion
2 tablespoons butter
2 (3-ounce) packages cream
cheese
4 cups skim milk
¼ teaspoon salt
¾ teaspoon thyme
¼ cup instant potato flakes
2 cups whole kernel corn,
cooked

In large saucepan, sauté onion in
butter, over medium heat, until soft
but not browned. Add cream
cheese. Stir until softened and
begins to melt. Stir in milk
gradually, stirring until smooth and
creamy. Add remaining ingredients.
Simmer, but do not boil, 5 to 8
minutes, stirring frequently. Serve
hot.

Serves: 4 to 6

Margo Stich

*"Cream cheese adds a rich flavor to this savory
soup thickened with instant potato flakes."*

QUICK LEEK SOUP

2 large potatoes, peeled and
   cut in one-inch cubes
Water
2 (10 ¾ -ounce) cans cream
   of potato soup
3 ¾ cups milk
1 large slice of ham, cut into
   bite-size pieces
1 medium size leek, rinsed
   well and sliced,
   including some green
1 tablespoon butter
⅛ teaspoon garlic salt
1 teaspoon chopped parsley
½ teaspoon dill weed
Salt and pepper to taste
1 (11-ounce) can whole
   kernel corn, with juice

In a large kettle, boil potatoes just covered with water for 10 minutes. Drain and return to kettle. Add potato soup, milk, ham, sliced leek, butter and seasonings. Stir well to combine over medium low heat. In a small pan, heat corn with its juice. Add to the soup kettle. Bring the soup slowly to a simmer and simmer 10 minutes.

Serves: 6 to 8

Sally Hanson

"This is great with crusty French bread."

CREAM OF LENTIL SOUP WITH GRILLED SHRIMP

12 cups water, divided
2 cups lentils, rinsed
2 large onions, chopped
2 large carrots, chopped
½ cup (1 stick) unsalted
   butter
10 fresh parsley sprigs
1 tablespoon fresh thyme
   leaves or 1 teaspoon
   dried crumbled thyme
½ teaspoon pepper
1 ½ pounds large uncooked
   shrimp, shells removed
   and reserved, deveined
2 tablespoons tomato paste
Salt to taste
Olive oil
Chopped fresh thyme for
   garnish

Combine 8 cups water, lentils, onion, carrot, butter, parsley sprigs, thyme and pepper in a heavy pan. Bring to boil, reduce heat and simmer until lentils are tender, about 50 minutes. Puree lentil mixture in batches in a blender. Transfer to a clean pan. Meanwhile, combine shrimp shells, 4 cups water and tomato paste in a heavy saucepan. Simmer until liquid is reduced to 1 cup, stirring occasionally, about 30 to 40 minutes. Strain shrimp mixture, discarding contents of strainer. Add shrimp stock to lentil puree. Season with salt and pepper. (Can be prepared 1 day ahead.) Cover and refrigerate. Preheat broiler. Brush shrimp with olive oil. Broil just until tender, about 2 minutes per side. Reheat soup. Divide shrimp among heated bowls. Pour in soup. Garnish with thyme and serve.

Serves: 8 to 10

Julie Larson
Rebecca Torgerson

Israeli Thick Lentil Soup

1 cup dried lentils, unrinsed
1 cup chopped onion
2 cloves garlic, minced
2 ribs celery, shredded or
   minced
2 carrots, shredded or
   minced
2 tablespoons fresh parsley,
   chopped
3 cups canned double-
   strength chicken broth
3 cups water
2 bay leaves
½ teaspoon cumin
Pinch of dried thyme
Pinch of turmeric or curry
   powder (optional)
Salt and pepper to taste
2 tablespoons lemon juice
1 cup cooked chicken, cut
   into bite-size pieces

Combine all ingredients, except lemon juice and chicken, in a large pan. Cover and cook until lentils are tender, about 1 hour. Stir in lemon juice and chicken. Heat through and serve.

Serves: 4

Almyra Whitehead

LENTIL AND BROWN RICE SOUP

8 cups water lightly flavored with vegetable bouillon (or broth)

1 ½ cups lentils, picked over and rinsed

1 cup uncooked long-grain brown rice

2 (14-ounce) cans stewed tomatoes

3 carrots, halved lengthwise and cut crosswise into ¼-inch pieces

1 cup chopped onion

½ cup chopped celery

3 large cloves garlic, minced

½ teaspoon dried basil

½ teaspoon dried oregano

½ teaspoon dried thyme

1 bay leaf

½ cup minced fresh parsley

2 tablespoons cider vinegar, or to taste

Salt and freshly ground black pepper to taste

In a large, heavy saucepan or Dutch oven, combine water or broth, lentils, rice, tomatoes, carrots, onion, celery, garlic, basil, oregano, thyme and bay leaf. Bring to a boil. Reduce heat. Cover pan and simmer, stirring occasionally, for 45 to 55 minutes, or until lentils and rice are both tender. Remove and discard bay leaf. Stir in parsley, vinegar, salt and pepper.

Serves: 8 to 10

Lois Milner

"This is a very favorite soup at our house. I've never served it to anyone who didn't love it. Very nutritious, and completely fat free. Serve with a tossed salad and breadsticks for a complete meal."

MEATBALL SOUP WITH PASTA RINGS

1 cup sliced carrots
1 cup sliced celery
½ cup sliced green onions
¼ cup chopped fresh
    parsley
3 beef bouillon cubes
3 teaspoons salt, divided
½ teaspoon pepper, divided
8 cups water
1 egg, slightly beaten
2 tablespoons milk
1 cup soft bread crumbs
¼ cup grated Parmesan
    cheese
1 pound lean ground beef
1 cup pasta rings
1 cup fresh spinach,
    chopped

Combine carrots, celery, green onions, parsley, bouillon cubes, 2 teaspoons salt, ¼ teaspoon pepper and water. Cover and bring to a boil; simmer for 20 minutes. Combine 1 teaspoon salt, ¼ teaspoon pepper, egg, milk and bread crumbs in a large bowl. Let stand a few minutes. Add Parmesan cheese and ground meat. Mix well and shape into 36 balls. Add to soup; cover and simmer for 15 minutes. Bring to a boil and add pasta rings. Cover and simmer for 5 minutes. Remove from heat. Stir in spinach. Serve.

Yield: 2 ½ quarts

Janet Engels

WINTER MINESTRONE

3 tablespoons olive oil
1 large onion, finely
  chopped
1 large stalk of celery, finely
  chopped
2 cloves garlic, minced or
  pressed
1 teaspoon dried basil
½ teaspoon dried rosemary
½ teaspoon dried oregano
½ teaspoon thyme
¼ cup pearl barley
1 potato, peeled and diced
1 rutabaga, peeled and
  diced
2 carrots, diced
8 cups chicken stock or
  chicken broth
1 large turnip, peeled and
  diced
1 (16-ounce) can red or
  white kidney beans,
  undrained
⅔ cup small shell or elbow
  macaroni
¼ cup tomato paste
2 cups finely shredded kale
  leaves or green cabbage
Salt and pepper to taste

1 ½ cups shredded jack
  cheese

Heat oil in a large pot or Dutch
oven. Add onion, celery, garlic,
basil, rosemary, oregano and thyme.
Cook over medium heat, stirring
occasionally, until onion is soft,
about 10 minutes. Add barley,
potato, rutabaga, carrots, stock and
turnip. Bring to a boil; reduce heat,
cover and simmer for 20 minutes.
Mix in beans and their liquid,
macaroni and tomato paste. Bring
to a boil over high heat; reduce
heat, cover and boil gently until
macaroni is tender, about 15
minutes. Add kale and cook,
uncovered, until kale is tender-
crisp, about 5 minutes. Season with
salt and pepper to taste. Pass cheese
to sprinkle over individual
servings.

Serves: 8 to 10

Karen Porayko

*"This is a hearty Italian soup made with winter
vegetables. We love it on a cold winter night,
served with Rosemary Focaccia♪ and a glass of
Beaujolais."*

Mushroom and Dill Soup

8 cups white onions,
  chopped
1 cup butter, divided
6 cups mushrooms, sliced
2 tablespoons fresh green
  dill, chopped in ¼-inch
  pieces
8 cups beef stock, divided
¼ cup sweet Hungarian
  paprika
1 tablespoon salt
4 cups non-fat dairy milk
¾ cup flour
3 tablespoons lemon juice
Pepper to taste
2 cups plain yogurt or sour
  cream
1 cup parsley, chopped

Sauté onions in ½ cup butter. Add mushrooms, dill, 4 cups beef stock and paprika. Simmer for 15 minutes. Add salt. In a separate pan, heat milk to simmer. Melt ½ cup butter in a heavy saucepan, sprinkle with flour and stir steadily with wooden spoon, scraping bottom of pan until mixture turns caramel color. Remove from heat, add hot milk and stir until well blended. Add remaining stock, mushroom/onion mixture, and lemon juice and pepper. Simmer for 15 minutes, covered. Before serving, add yogurt or sour cream and stir well while adding parsley.

Yield: 8 to 10 servings

Nan Douglas

"Use as a first course, or it makes a marvelous supper with French bread and a green salad on a cold winter night."

MUSHROOM AND POTATO SOUP

1 ½ pounds firm fresh
   mushrooms
6 tablespoons butter,
   divided
1 cup finely chopped onions
6 cups chicken stock, fresh
   or canned
6 small boiling potatoes,
   peeled and cut into
   ¼ -inch slices
1 teaspoon salt
¼ cup finely chopped
   celery
¼ cup finely chopped
   scallions, with green tops
2 tablespoons finely
   chopped fresh parsley
1 cup sour cream
1 tablespoon finely cut fresh
   dill leaves for garnish
Freshly ground black
   pepper

Wipe mushrooms with a dampened towel. Trim and cut lengthwise, including stems, into ⅛-inch-thick slices. In a heavy 4- to 5-quart casserole dish or pan, melt 4 tablespoons of butter over moderate heat. When foam begins to subside, add mushrooms and onions; stir until they are evenly coated with butter. Reduce heat to low, partially cover, and simmer for 20 minutes. Stir in chicken stock, potato slices and salt. Bring mixture to a boil over high heat. Reduce heat to low, cover partially, and simmer for about 25 minutes, or until potato slices are tender. Melt 2 tablespoons butter in a heavy 8- to 10-inch skillet. When foam begins to subside, add celery, scallions and parsley, stirring frequently. Cook, uncovered, over low heat for 15 minutes, until celery is tender, but not brown. In a small bowl, combine sour cream with ½ cup of simmering mushroom soup stock, mixing well. Stirring constantly, gradually pour sour cream mixture into the skillet and bring mixture to a boil over high heat. Add contents of the skillet to mushroom soup. Stir together gently but thoroughly. Taste for seasoning. Pour soup into a heated tureen or individual soup plates. Sprinkle with dill and a few grindings of pepper. Serve at once.
Serves: 8 to 10

Becky Brey

"Everyone loves this soup. It is delicious!"

OLD COUNTRY BORSCH

6 cups water
1 pound beef brisket, cut
  into 6 pieces
2 onions, sliced
2 stalks celery, cut into
  1-inch lengths
4 medium beets, pared and
  sliced (about 2 cups)
4 carrots, pared and thinly
  sliced
1 small head cabbage, cut
  into wedges
1 bay leaf
1 tablespoon salt
2 beets, coarsely grated
  (about 1 cup)
1 (6-ounce) can tomato paste
2 tablespoons vinegar
1 tablespoon sugar
2 teaspoons salt

1 cup sour cream for garnish

Place water, beef, onions, celery, sliced beets, carrots, cabbage, bay leaf and 1 tablespoon salt in a large kettle. Simmer, covered, about 2 hours. Add remaining ingredients, except sour cream. Simmer, covered, for another 15 to 20 minutes. Cool and then refrigerate. To serve, skim any fat from soup. Bring to boil over medium heat. Reduce heat and simmer covered for 10 minutes. Serve topped with sour cream.

Yield: 4 to 6 servings

Mary Creel

"Serve with a hearty bread and your favorite beer. Leftovers may be frozen."

POTATO SOUP WITH HAM

3 medium-sized potatoes, peeled and diced
1 large onion, finely chopped
1 smoked ham hock (about 1 pound)
1 tablespoon dried dill weed
2 teaspoons grated lemon peel
⅛ to ¼ teaspoon ground white pepper
2 ½ cups chicken broth
1 tablespoon cornstarch
½ cup whipping cream

Dill sprigs for garnish (optional)

In a 3-quart or larger electric slow cooker, combine potatoes, onion, ham hock, dill weed, lemon peel, white pepper and broth. Cover and cook at low setting until ham hock and potatoes are very tender when pierced, about 7 ½ to 8 hours. Remove ham hock and let stand until cool enough to handle. Meanwhile, remove about 1 cup of the potatoes with a little of the broth; whirl in a blender or food processor until pureed. Return puree to cooker. In a small bowl, mix cornstarch and cream; blend into potato mixture. Increase heat to high. Remove and discard fat and bone from ham. Tear meat into bite-size pieces and stir into soup. Cover and cook, stirring occasionally, for 20 minutes. Garnish with dill sprigs, if desired.

Serves: 4 to 6

Karen Porayko

SALMON CHOWDER

1 (16-ounce) can salmon,
  drained with juice
  reserved
½ cup chopped onion
¼ cup chopped green
  pepper
½ cup chopped celery
3 tablespoons butter
1 cup raw potato, cubed or
  sliced
1 cup chopped carrots
2 cups chicken broth
½ teaspoon dried dill weed
1 (13-ounce) can evaporated
  milk
1 (14-ounce) can cream style
  corn

In a large kettle, sauté onion, pepper and celery in butter until limp. Add potatoes, carrots, chicken broth, dill weed and reserved salmon juice. Simmer 20 minutes. Add evaporated milk and corn; bring to a simmer. Stir in the flaked salmon. Heat through before serving.

Serves: 6 to 8

Janet Engels

SPRINGTIME SOUP

2 tablespoons butter
2 leeks, chopped
1 small onion, chopped
6 cups hot water
2 potatoes, pared, quartered
  and thinly sliced
2 medium carrots, pared and
  thinly sliced
2 teaspoons salt
¼ cup rice
8 stalks fresh or frozen
  asparagus, cut into
  ½-inch pieces
½ pound fresh spinach,
  washed and chopped
1 cup light cream

Melt butter in a large pot. Add leeks and onion. Cover and cook over low heat for 5 minutes. Add hot water, potatoes, carrots and salt. Bring to boil. Cover, reduce heat and simmer for 15 minutes. Add rice and asparagus; cover and simmer for 25 minutes. Add spinach and simmer for 10 minutes more. Stir in cream and heat through (do not allow to boil).

Serves: 6 to 8

Janet Engels

"Flavor is enhanced if soup is refrigerated, covered, overnight and reheated at serving time."

ITALIAN TOMATO SOUP

1 (14 ½ -ounce) can stewed
    tomatoes
3 cups tomato juice
1 ½ cups water
1 ½ teaspoons dried basil
1 teaspoon dried oregano
1 teaspoon beef broth
    granules (or 1 bouillon
    cube)
½ pound mild Italian
    sausage
1 small onion, diced
1 cup sliced mushrooms
¾ cup sliced celery
½ cup sliced ripe olives
2 tomatoes, diced
1 ½ cups freshly grated
    Parmesan cheese, divided

Combine stewed tomatoes, tomato juice, water, herbs and beef bouillon in a large saucepan over medium-low heat. Cover and bring to a simmer. Meanwhile, brown Italian sausage in a large skillet. Add onion, mushrooms and celery. Sauté until onion is tender, about 3 minutes. Drain on paper toweling to remove excess grease. Stir sausage mixture into saucepan. Add olives and diced tomatoes. Cover and simmer over medium-low heat for 45 minutes. Stir in 1 cup grated Parmesan cheese about 5 minutes before serving. Ladle into soup bowls and sprinkle with remaining Parmesan cheese.

Yield: 8 to 10 (1 cup) servings

Margo Stich

"Great served with a fresh slice of Italian bread."

VEGETABLE-BASIL SOUP

3 tablespoons butter or
  margarine
1 medium onion, chopped
½ cup chopped celery
1 to 2 carrots, grated
1 large potato, peeled and
  cut into ½ -inch cubes
2 cups peeled and diced
  tomatoes
6 cups chicken stock or
  canned chicken broth
½ teaspoon salt
⅛ teaspoon pepper
2 tablespoons dried basil
½ small head of
  cauliflower, broken into
  florets
¼ pound green beans, cut
  into 2-inch lengths
½ pound green peas,
  shelled
¼ to ½ cup barley

Grated Parmesan cheese

In a 6-quart pan, melt butter over medium heat. Add onion, celery and carrots. Cook, stirring occasionally, until vegetables are soft but not browned, about 10 minutes. Add potato, tomatoes, stock, salt, pepper and basil. Bring to a boil over high heat; reduce heat, cover and simmer for about 20 minutes. Add cauliflower and green beans; simmer for 10 more minutes. Add peas and barley; cover and simmer until tender. Pass the cheese to sprinkle over individual servings.

Serves: 4 to 6

Karen Porayko

"Vary the vegetables to suit the season. Substitute 2 small zucchini, sliced ¼-inch thick, or 1 cup shredded cabbage. We love to add rutabagas to this soup too!"

"CREAMLESS" CREAMY WILD RICE SOUP

⅔ cup uncooked wild rice
½ cup chopped onion
½ cup diced celery
½ cup diced carrots
2 tablespoons butter
4 ½ cups chicken stock
½ teaspoon thyme
1 teaspoon crushed
    rosemary
1 ½ cups non-fat dairy milk
½ cup dried skim milk
Beurre manie (1 tablespoon
    flour and 1 tablespoon
    butter kneaded together)
3 to 4 strips of bacon,
    cooked crisp and
    crumbled
Salt and pepper to taste

Sauté rice, onion, celery and carrots in butter for 3 to 4 minutes. Stir in chicken stock, thyme and rosemary. Bring to a boil, reduce heat and cover. Simmer until rice is tender and has "popped", about 40 minutes. Stir in milk. Whisk in beurre manie until soup thickens. (If too thick, add more stock.) Stir in cooked and crumbled bacon. Season with salt and pepper to taste.

Yield: 6 servings

Nan Douglas

"This often brings back memories of college on Sunday nights! If you have leftover vegetables, carrots, peas, broccoli, pea pods, etc., add them. If it is to be a main course soup, add a chopped, cooked chicken breast."

HAM AND WILD RICE CHOWDER

5 ½ cups water, divided
¾ cups uncooked wild rice, rinsed
½ cup chopped onion
3 cloves garlic, minced
¼ cup margarine or butter
½ cup flour
4 teaspoons chicken-flavored bouillon (or 4 cubes)
1 ½ cups cubed, peeled potatoes
½ cup chopped carrots
½ teaspoon thyme leaves
½ teaspoon nutmeg
⅛ teaspoon pepper
1 bay leaf
1 (17-ounce) can whole kernel corn, undrained
2 cups half and half
3 cups cubed, cooked ham
2 tablespoons chopped fresh parsley for garnish

In a medium saucepan, combine 1 ½ cups water and wild rice. Bring to a boil. Reduce heat, cover and simmer for 35 to 40 minutes or until rice is tender. Do not drain. In a large saucepan or Dutch oven, sauté onion and garlic in margarine until crisp-tender. Stir in flour. Cook 1 minute, stirring constantly. Gradually stir in 4 cups water and bouillon. Add potatoes, carrots, thyme, nutmeg, pepper and bay leaf. Bring to a boil. Reduce heat, cover and simmer 15 to 30 minutes or until slightly thickened. Add corn. Cover; simmer an additional 15 to 20 minutes or until vegetables are tender. Stir in half and half, ham and rice. Cook until thoroughly heated. Do not boil. Remove bay leaf. Garnish with parsley.

Yield: 8 (1 ½ cup) servings

BLOODY MARY SOUP

1 medium onion, finely chopped
1 ½ cups chopped celery
2 tablespoons canola oil
1 tablespoon sugar
1 tablespoon lemon juice
4 cups tomato juice
2 ½ teaspoons Worcestershire sauce
¼ teaspoon black pepper
Dash of hot sauce
¾ cup vodka, chilled
8 celery sticks

In a medium saucepan, cook onion and celery in oil until tender. Add sugar, lemon juice, tomato juice, Worcestershire, black pepper and hot sauce. Cover pan and simmer for 15 minutes. Adjust seasoning to taste (you may want to add a little salt as well). Strain. Chill thoroughly. Just before serving stir in vodka. Serve in tall glasses, using celery sticks for stirrers.

Serves: 8

Margo Stich

SALADS
AND SALAD
DRESSINGS

BROCCOLI SLAW

1 (1-pound) package
   shredded broccoli mix
3 Roma tomatoes, sliced
1 (8-ounce) can pitted black
   olives, drained
1 (8-ounce) bottle Italian
   salad dressing
½ head iceberg lettuce, torn
   in bite-size pieces

Combine broccoli mix, tomatoes, and olives in a large bowl one hour before serving. Add ½ bottle of salad dressing. Toss to combine. Chill. Just before serving, add lettuce and remaining dressing. Toss again and serve.

Serves: 8 to 10

Sally Hanson

SUPER SLAW

3 cups finely shredded
   cabbage
½ cup orange juice
1 cup chopped fresh
   cranberries
¼ cup sugar
2 tablespoons chopped
   celery
2 tablespoons chopped
   green bell pepper
1 cup seedless green grapes,
   halved
2 tablespoons light
   mayonnaise
2 tablespoons yogurt

In a large bowl, stir cabbage and orange juice together to moisten. In a separate bowl, combine cranberries and sugar. Add the cranberry mixture to the cabbage along with the rest of the ingredients. Chill at least 30 minutes before serving.

Serves: 8

Janet Engels

Bibb Lettuce, Kiwi and Cucumber Salad with French Dressing

1 head Bibb lettuce, torn
   into bite-size pieces
3 kiwi fruits, peeled and
   thinly sliced
1 seedless cucumber, thinly
   sliced
4 scallions, sliced
Salt and freshly ground
   pepper to taste

French dressing:
1 teaspoon salt
1 teaspoon dry mustard
1 teaspoon paprika
1 teaspoon celery seed
1 tablespoon grated onion
¼ cup and 2 tablespoons
   sugar
¼ cup vinegar
1 cup oil

Place lettuce, fruit, cucumbers and scallions in a salad bowl. Cover and refrigerate until ready to serve. *For dressing,* combine all ingredients in the top of a double boiler; stir well. Heat over hot water until ingredients are lukewarm. Remove from heat and beat until slightly thickened. Cool completely. Cover and store in the refrigerator. Just before serving, toss salad with dressing and add salt and pepper to taste.

Variation: Substitute pears or mandarin oranges for kiwi fruit.

Yield: 4 servings
    1 pint dressing

Renda Meloy

Caesar Salad

2 cloves garlic
¾ cup olive oil
2 cups stale bread, cubed
2 large heads romaine
   lettuce
½ teaspoon salt
⅛ teaspoon freshly ground
   black pepper
Eggbeaters, equivalent to 2
   eggs
Juice of 1 large lemon
½ cup freshly grated
   Parmesan cheese

Crush garlic in a small bowl. Pour in oil. Let stand for 3 to 4 hours. In a skillet, brown bread cubes in ¼ of the garlic-oil mixture. Remove from skillet; let drain and cool. Tear lettuce into a large bowl. Season with salt and pepper. Pour remaining garlic-oil mixture over greens and toss. Combine Eggbeaters and lemon juice in a small bowl. Pour over greens and toss. Refrigerate. Just before serving, toss greens with Parmesan cheese and seasoned bread cubes.

Serves: 8 to 10

Cherie Miles

CRISPY ORIENTAL GREEN SALAD

½ cup butter
2 tablespoons sugar
½ cup sesame seeds
2 (3-ounce) packages Ramen
    noodles, uncooked and
    broken up (do not use
    seasoning)
1 (3-ounce) package sliced
    almonds
1 large or 2 small heads bok
    choy (about 2 pounds)
4 green onions with tops,
    sliced

Dressing:
¾ cup vegetable oil
¼ cup red wine vinegar
½ cup sugar
2 tablespoons soy sauce

In a large skillet, melt butter over medium heat. Add sugar, sesame seeds, broken Ramen noodles and almonds. Cook and stir until lightly browned, about 5 minutes. Cool to room temperature. Set aside until ready to serve. Meanwhile, coarsely chop bok choy, using both stalks and leaves. Combine with green onion and chill. *For dressing,* combine all ingredients and shake well. Just before serving toss greens with noodle mixture and dressing.
Serves: 12

Mary Jo Kelly

TOSSED FRESH GREENS WITH CUMIN VINAIGRETTE

1 shallot, finely minced
½ teaspoon grated lemon
    zest
1 teaspoon stone-ground
    mustard
¾ teaspoon ground cumin
1 tablespoon balsamic
    vinegar
⅓ cup fresh lemon juice
1 cup olive oil

8 to 10 cups assorted salad
    greens (ruby lettuce,
    Boston, oakleaf, spinach,
    etc.), torn into bite-size
    pieces

In a small jar, combine all ingredients except the greens. Shake until well mixed. Refrigerate for several hours. In a large bowl, toss greens together. Just before serving, drizzle vinaigrette over the greens and toss lightly until well combined.
Serves: 8 to 10

Kay Love-Caskey

SALAD GREENS WITH POTAGERIE DRESSING

½ cup sugar
2 tablespoons Dijon
   mustard
½ cup white vinegar
1 cup oil

8 cups assorted salad greens
   (red leaf lettuce, iceberg,
   romaine, etc.), torn into
   bite-size pieces

Combine sugar and mustard in a
small jar with a lid; shake, mixing
well. Gradually add vinegar. Stir in
oil and mix well. Refrigerate until
ready to serve. Toss greens together
in a serving bowl. Just before
serving, toss gently with dressing.

Serves: 8

Mona Price

*"This salad goes well with Chevre Stuffed
Chicken ♪."*

MIXED GREEN SALAD WITH RASPBERRIES, DIJON DRESSING AND BRIE TOASTS

Assorted salad greens (such
   as romaine, red top,
   Boston, arrugula,
   radicchio, water cress,
   spinach), washed and
   torn

Dressing:
1 teaspoon Dijon mustard
½ teaspoon salt
Pinch white pepper
¼ teaspoon finely minced
   garlic
¼ cup balsamic vinegar
1 cup olive oil

Brie Toasts:
1 loaf French bread
8 ounces Brie cheese, room
   temperature

Fresh raspberries for
   garnish

Prepare fresh greens, allowing
about 1½ loosely packed cups per
person. *For dressing,* mix together
mustard, salt, pepper and garlic.
Add a small amount of vinegar and
blend. Add remaining vinegar.
Whisk in oil. Refrigerate until ready
to serve. *For Brie toasts,* slice bread
into 20 pieces (not too large).
Spread some Brie cheese on each
slice. Broil until cheese melts and
bread turns light brown. *To serve,*
toss mixed greens with enough
dressing to coat lightly. Divide
among 10 plates. Garnish with fresh
raspberries. Place two Brie toasts on
each plate and serve.

Serves: 10

Sally Duffy

Orange and Red Salad

1 (2 ¼ -ounce) package
   sliced almonds
1 tablespoon butter
2 tablespoons fresh lemon
   juice
1 teaspoon Dijon mustard
½ teaspoon sugar
½ teaspoon salt
¼ teaspoon white pepper
½ cup oil
1 head romaine lettuce, torn
   in pieces
1 (11-ounce) can mandarin
   oranges, drained
1 small red onion, thinly
   sliced

Sauté almonds in butter until golden; set aside. Combine lemon juice, mustard, sugar, salt and pepper. Beat in oil. Combine lettuce, oranges, onion slices and almonds. Toss with dressing just before serving.

Serves: 4

Nancy Brubaker

Seventh Heaven Layered Salad

½ head iceberg lettuce,
   shredded
2 large tomatoes, chopped
   or 2 red bell peppers,
   chopped (optional)
4 stalks celery, diced
4 large carrots, peeled and
   sliced
1 (10-ounce) package frozen
   sugar peas, thawed and
   cut in half, or baby peas
2 cups (8-ounces) Cheddar
   cheese, shredded
8 slices bacon, cooked crisp
   and crumbled (optional)

Dressing:
1 cup mayonnaise
1 cup sour cream (optional)
2 tablespoons sugar
1 ½ teaspoon onion powder
1 teaspoon dried ground
   basil leaves or parsley
   (optional)

Layer vegetables in desired order in a trifle bowl or large glass container. *For dressing,* combine mayonnaise, sour cream, sugar and onion powder. Mix until smooth. Spread evenly over top of layered vegetables. Sprinkle with cheese. Garnish with crumbled bacon. Cover tightly and refrigerate.

Serves: 8 to 10

Mim Kurland

"A clear glass trifle bowl gives your guests a taste-tempting view of this heavenly salad. If you don't plan to use all the salad at one time, omit tomatoes & bacon, so it will remain crisp."

SPINACH SALAD

1 large bunch or bag fresh
  spinach
3 to 4 hard-cooked eggs,
  chopped
½ pound bacon, cooked
  crisp and crumbled
½ medium red onion,
  sliced thin

Dressing:
1 cup oil
¾ cup sugar
⅓ cup catsup
½ teaspoon salt
¼ cup vinegar
1 tablespoon Worcestershire
  sauce

Wash spinach, remove stems and
tear into bite-size pieces. Put leaves
in a salad bowl, cover with slightly
damp paper towels and refrigerate
to crisp. Lightly toss eggs, bacon
and onions with spinach. *For dressing,* combine dressing ingredients
and blend well. Serve dressing with
salad.

Serves: 6 to 8

Sheila Kramer

SPINACH SALAD WITH HONEY AND MUSTARD DRESSING

1 large bunch or bag fresh
  spinach
4 green onions, greens only,
  thinly sliced
1 (11-ounce) can mandarin
  oranges or 1 large orange,
  peeled and sliced
4 slices bacon, cooked crisp
  and crumbled

Dressing:
6 tablespoons olive oil
2 tablespoons cider vinegar
2 tablespoons honey
2 tablespoons Dijon
  mustard
2 tablespoons toasted
  sesame seeds
1 clove garlic, minced
½ teaspoon freshly ground
  pepper

Wash spinach, remove stems, and
drain well. Combine spinach,
onions, orange slices, and bacon.
Toss well and refrigerate until ready
to serve. *For dressing,* combine
dressing ingredients in a small jar.
Shake well and let sit to blend
flavors. Toss spinach salad and
dressing together just before
serving.

Serves: 6 to 8

Julie Huettner
Peggy King

SPINACH SALAD SUPREME

1 clove garlic, cut
½ cup oil
½ teaspoon Worcestershire
  sauce
¼ teaspoon dry mustard
¼ teaspoon paprika
1 teaspoon sugar
½ teaspoon salt
Dash of pepper
1 ½ cups crisp croutons
6 to 8 cups crisp spinach or
  mixed salad greens
1 (11-ounce) can mandarin
  orange sections, drained
1 (14-ounce) can artichoke
  hearts, drained
1 avocado, peeled and diced
Juice of ½ lemon

Combine garlic, oil, Worcestershire sauce, mustard, paprika, sugar, salt and pepper. Let stand for several hours or overnight. Ten minutes before serving, discard garlic and pour dressing over croutons. When ready to serve, break salad greens into a large salad bowl. Pour oil-crouton mixture over greens. Arrange oranges, artichoke hearts and avocado on top of greens. Squeeze lemon juice over salad. Toss gently.

Serves: 6

Margo Stich

SLICED AVOCADO VINIAGRETTE

3 avocados
Juice from 1 lemon
¼ cup vinegar
½ oil
Salt and pepper to taste
Bibb lettuce
Artichokes (optional)

Slice avocados in 8 wedges each. Sprinkle juice of 1 lemon over wedges. Combine vinegar, oil, salt and pepper to taste. Pour over avocados. Arrange avocados on Bibb lettuce-lined salad plates. Artichokes may also be added.

Serves: 6

Eleni George

MARINATED TRICOLOR BELL PEPPER AND MUSHROOM SALAD

1 ½ cups olive oil
6 cloves garlic, minced
2 tablespoons minced,
    seeded jalapeno chilies
¾ cup red wine vinegar
2 teaspoons fennel seeds
2 bay leaves, crushed
1 ½ pounds mushrooms,
    quartered
2 green bell peppers, thinly
    sliced
2 yellow bell peppers,
    thinly sliced
1 red bell pepper, thinly
    sliced
Salt and pepper to taste
2 heads curly endive,
    trimmed
3 heads radicchio, leaves
    separated
½ cup chopped fresh
    parsley

Heat olive oil in heavy large skillet over medium heat. Add garlic and jalapeno chilies; sauté 3 minutes. Pour into a large bowl. Cool slightly. Mix in vinegar, fennel seeds and bay leaves. Add mushrooms and all bell peppers; toss well. Season to taste with salt and pepper. Cover and refrigerate at least 4 hours or overnight, tossing occasionally. Place endive and radicchio around edge of plates. Using slotted spoon, remove vegetables from bowl and arrange in center of plates. Sprinkle with parsley.

Serves: 10

Julie Roenigk

PEA SALAD SUPREME

3 (16-ounce) cans peas
2 eggs, hard-boiled and
    chopped
1 cup shredded Cheddar
    cheese
4 strips bacon, cooked crisp
    and crumbled
2 tablespoons green onion,
    minced
1 ½ teaspoons prepared
    mustard
½ cup mayonnaise
½ cup low-fat sour cream
3 tablespoons milk
Salt and pepper to taste

Combine peas, hard-boiled eggs, cheese, bacon and onion in a serving bowl. In a small bowl combine mustard, mayonnaise, sour cream, milk and seasoning to taste, mixing until smooth. Pour dressing over salad and toss to coat. Chill well before serving.

Serves: 12 to 14

Margo Stich

KARTOFFELSALAT (POTATO SALAD)

3 pounds waxy potatoes, such as red-skinned or Michigan
½ pound bacon, chopped and fried until crispy
1 large onion or one bunch green onions, finely chopped
⅓ cup oil
2 to 4 tablespoons cider or red wine vinegar
1 ¼ cups soup stock or water
½ teaspoon salt, or to taste
¼ teaspoon pepper, or to taste
Chives for garnish
Hard-cooked eggs for garnish (optional)

Wash potatoes and cook with skins on just until pierceable with fork. Drain and peel potatoes while still warm; slice ⅛-inch thick. Add bacon, onion, oil, vinegar, soup stock, salt and pepper. Let marinate at least one hour at room temperature. Mix again before serving. Garnish with green onion tops, bacon, chives or sliced hard-cooked eggs.

Serves: 6 to 8

Diane Nippoldt

PICNIC POTATO SALAD

4 large potatoes
A few celery leaves
1 bay leaf
1 teaspoon salt
Water
1 cup sliced celery
3 tablespoons onion, chopped
¼ cup sweet gerkin pickle, chopped
¾ cup mayonnaise
¾ teaspoons prepared mustard
½ teaspoon salt
Celery seed to taste (optional)
Black pepper to taste

Combine potatoes, celery leaves, bay leaf and salt in a large saucepan. Add water to cover. Cook, covered, until tender (about 30 to 40 minutes). Drain. Peel and cube potatoes when cool enough to handle. Combine with celery, onion and pickle in a serving bowl. Combine mayonnaise, mustard, salt and seasonings to taste, in a small bowl, stirring until well blended. Toss into cooled potato-vegetable mixture. Cover and chill thoroughly before serving.

Serves: 6 to 8

Margo Stich

Spring Salad

10 to 12 small red potatoes,
  unpeeled
1 pound fresh asparagus,
  cut into 1 to 2-inch
  lengths
5 to 6 carrots, peeled and
  thinly sliced
¾ cup canola oil
6 tablespoons red wine
  vinegar
1 tablespoon sugar
½ cup chopped parsley
1 tablespoon dried basil (or
  fresh basil if you have it)
2 cloves garlic, chopped fine
Salt and freshly ground
  pepper
4 tablespoons chopped
  green onion

Cook potatoes until tender in salted water; drain and set aside. Steam asparagus just until tender; drain and set aside. Cook carrots for 5 minutes, until tender; drain and set aside. Put all vegetables in a large bowl and chill. In a blender, combine oil, vinegar, sugar, parsley, basil and garlic. Whirl until smooth. Add salt and pepper to taste. (Check flavor and add more vinegar, sugar, salt or pepper if you wish.) Add onions; toss with vegetables. Cover and chill. Serve cold or at room temperature.

Yield: 4 to 6 servings

Nan Douglas

"Great with ham, roast beef, lamb or even barbecued chicken."

Sweet Potato Salad

4 ounces snow peas,
  trimmed
3 large sweet potatoes,
  about 2 pounds, peeled
1 (¼ x ½-inch) piece of
  fresh ginger, peeled
½ cup fresh orange juice
⅓ cup safflower oil
4 to 5 tablespoons fresh
  lemon juice, divided
3 to 4 tablespoons honey,
  divided
¼ teaspoon salt
Dash of hot pepper sauce
2 medium yellow bell
  peppers, cored and
  seeded
4 medium green onions,
  chopped

Lettuce

In a large saucepan, cook snow peas in boiling salted water for about 1 minute. Remove with a slotted spoon and rinse under cold water. Chill. Return water to a boil. Cube the sweet potatoes and add to boiling water. Cook just until tender, about 2 ½ minutes. Drain well and place in a large bowl. In a food processor, with machine running, drop piece of ginger through the feed tube to mince. Add orange juice, oil, 4 tablespoons lemon juice, 3 tablespoons honey, salt and pepper sauce. Mix for 5 seconds. Pour dressing over warm sweet potatoes; toss gently. Cover and refrigerate for 3 hours. Cut bell peppers into small pieces; add to sweet potatoes along with green onions. Toss well. (Can be made 1 to 2 days ahead and chilled.) Just before serving, mix snow peas in. Add remaining tablespoons of lemon juice and honey; mix gently. Spoon into a lettuce-lined bowl and serve.

Serves: 6

Nina Sudor

"This salad is a nice addition to a summer buffet."

RED BELL PEPPER TERRINE WITH ASPARAGUS VINAIGRETTE

3 pounds red bell peppers
2 large cloves garlic,
   unpeeled
¼ teaspoon salt
Pinch of cayenne pepper
¼ cup dry white wine
1 ½ envelopes unflavored
   gelatin
¾ cup chilled whipping
   cream

1 ½ pounds asparagus

Vinaigrette:
¼ cup balsamic vinegar
2 teaspoons Dijon mustard
½ teaspoon salt
½ cup olive oil
2 tablespoons fresh basil,
   sliced

Line a baking sheet with foil. Arrange peppers and garlic cloves on sheet. Broil until peppers are black on all sides, turning as needed. Remove from oven and cover with a kitchen towel; let stand 10 minutes. Peel peppers, cut in half and remove seeds and stems. Squeeze pulp from garlic cloves. In a food processor or blender, puree garlic, peppers, salt and cayenne pepper until smooth. Transfer puree to a heavy saucepan. Cook over medium-low heat until puree is reduced to a scant 2 cups, stirring occasionally, about 10 minutes. Set puree aside. Pour wine into a small saucepan. Sprinkle gelatin over wine; let stand 10 minutes to soften. Place over low heat, stirring constantly until gelatin dissolves. Stir gelatin into puree. Let stand at room temperature just until cool, stirring occasionally, about 30 minutes. While puree is cooling, line a 4 or 5 cup loaf pan with plastic wrap, allowing a 3-inch overhang. In a large bowl, beat cream to stiff peaks. Fold in cooled puree. Pour into prepared loaf pan, bringing plastic carefully over the top. Chill until set, at least 4 hours. (Can be prepared up to this point two days ahead.) Cook asparagus in boiling salted water just until tender (do not overcook). Rinse immediately under cold water to stop cooking. Drain well, cover, and refrigerate until ready to serve. (Asparagus can be prepared one day ahead or early in the day.)

For vinaigrette, combine vinegar, mustard and salt. Whisk in olive oil. Add basil. Toss asparagus gently with vinaigrette. Remove plastic from top of terrine and turn out onto a large plate. Carefully remove remaining plastic. Cut terrine into 10 slices. Place one slice on each plate. Arrange asparagus around terrine slice. Serve.

Serves: 10

Sally Duffy

"Although the directions are long, this is easy to make."

TRIO OF SALADS

Vinaigrette:
¾ cup olive oil
¼ cup red wine vinegar
3 tablespoons Dijon mustard
2 shallots, quartered
1 clove garlic, halved
Pinch of sugar
Salt and pepper to taste

Vegetables:
1 ½ pounds celery root, peeled and grated
4 ½ cups coarsely grated carrots
4 (8 ¼ -ounce) cans julienne beets, drained
Salt and pepper to taste
Fresh parsley, minced
Fresh chives, minced

Blend all vinaigrette ingredients in a blender until smooth. Season to taste with salt and pepper. (Can be prepared 3 days ahead). Cover and refrigerate. In a large bowl, toss celery root with enough vinaigrette to season to taste. Refrigerate for 1 hour. Toss carrots and beets in two separate bowls with enough vinaigrette to season; salt and pepper to taste. Arrange salads on a platter. Sprinkle with fresh minced parsley and chives. Serve.

Serves: 10

Julie Larson
Rebecca Torgerson

VEGETABLES IN CELERY SEED MARINADE

Marinade:
1 tablespoon celery seeds
  (just covered with water)
4 teaspoons grated onion
¾ cup sugar
1 ½ teaspoons salt
1 teaspoon paprika
1 cup oil
½ cup red wine vinegar

Vegetables:
2 pounds small red
  potatoes, unpeeled
½ pound fresh green beans,
  trimmed
4 large carrots, pared and
  sliced
1 small head of broccoli,
  broken into pieces
1 (10-ounce) package frozen
  green peas
½ pound asparagus, cut
  into 2-inch pieces

Lettuce

Soak celery seeds in water for 24 hours. Drain, if necessary, and combine with the rest of the marinade ingredients in a jar with a tight cover. Shake well. *For vegetables,* cook potatoes in salted water, just until tender. Drain and rinse with cold water; drain again. Let cool. Meanwhile, cook green beans and carrots, separately, until crisp tender. Cook broccoli for about 3 minutes. Thaw peas in hot water. Cook asparagus for 3 to 5 minutes, until crisp tender. Drain all vegetables after cooking and rinse with cold water; drain again. Peel and slice potatoes. Combine vegetables in a large bowl. Pour marinade over; stir gently. Chill for several hours or overnight. Spoon into a lettuce lined bowl to serve.

Serves: 12

Nina Sudor

"This salad was served at the fall kick-off meeting of the Guild Board in 1992."

TABBULI

1 cup bulgar wheat
1 cup water
⅓ cup olive oil
¼ cup lemon juice
1 teaspoon salt
1 teaspoon ground allspice
1 bunch green onions,
   chopped
⅓ cup lightly packed fresh
   mint leaves, finely cut
1 ½ cups packed parsley
   sprigs, finely cut
2 tomatoes, cut into ¼ -inch
   cubes

Romaine lettuce

Combine wheat and water in a saucepan. Bring to a boil. Reduce heat and simmer until water is absorbed and wheat is puffed. Remove from heat. Combine oil, lemon juice, salt and allspice together; add to wheat, mixing well. Allow mixture to cool. Add onions, mint and parsley; mix well. Cover and chill. Add tomatoes just before serving. Stir gently to mix. Serve on a bed of lettuce leaves.

Variation: Omit tomatoes. Add ½ cup finely grated carrots and ½ cup raisins or currants.

Serves: 4 to 6

Ann Groover
Margo Stich

TORTELLINI SALAD

Dressing:
½ cup olive oil
3 tablespoons white wine
   vinegar
1 teaspoon white
   Worcestershire sauce
1 teaspoon dry mustard
½ teaspoon black pepper
1 tablespoon sugar
1 ¼ teaspoons salt
3 drops red pepper sauce
1 small clove garlic, minced

Salad:
1 (7 to 9-ounce) package
   tortellini egg pasta with
   cheese filling
1 teaspoon basil
⅓ cup sliced black olives
½ cup sliced green onions
½ cup diagonally sliced
   celery
¼ cup snipped parsley
1 (4-ounce) package
   shredded Cheddar cheese

Combine all dressing ingredients together; set aside. Cook tortellini following package directions until al dente, about 15 minutes. Drain. Spoon tortellini into a large bowl. Toss pasta with dressing; cool to lukewarm. Fold in remaining ingredients. Refrigerate, covered, for several hours or overnight. Remove from refrigerator ½ to 1 hour before serving. Toss lightly and serve.

Yield: 12 (½ cup) servings

Margo Stich

COLD TORTELLINI WITH TOMATO SALAD

2 (9-ounce) packages
   refrigerated cheese
   tortellini
¼ cup olive oil

Dressing:
¼ cup olive oil
½ cup fresh basil leaves,
   packed
½ cup fresh parsley leaves,
   packed
1 clove garlic, finely
   chopped
2 tablespoons balsamic
   vinegar
¼ teaspoon salt
Freshly ground pepper to
   taste

4 plum tomatoes, seeded
   and diced
1 small onion, finely
   chopped
½ cup sliced, pitted black
   olives

Prepare tortellini according to package directions. Drain well and place in a large bowl. Toss with ¼ cup olive oil. Cool to room temperature. *For dressing,* combine ingredients in a food processor with a chopping blade. Process until well blended. Add diced tomatoes, onion and sliced olives to cooled tortellini. Pour dressing over all; stir gently to mix. May be served at room temperature or chilled.

Serves: 6 hearty servings

Nina Sudor

"This was served at the fall kick-off meeting of the Guild Board in 1992. Serve with another salad and rolls for a satisfying lunch."

CRANBERRY ORANGE GELATIN

2 (3-ounce) packages cherry
   gelatin
2 ½ cups boiling water
1 (8-ounce) can crushed
   pineapple
1 (10-ounce) package frozen
   cranberry orange sauce,
   thawed

Lettuce

Dissolve gelatin in boiling water. Stir in undrained pineapple and cranberry orange sauce. Pour into mold. When set, unmold onto a bed of lettuce.

Serves: 6

Lois Swanson

"A tasty accompaniment to poultry or beef."

FESTIVE MOLDED STRAWBERRY SALAD

¾ cup (1 ½ sticks) butter or margarine, melted
2 cups pretzels, crushed
3 tablespoons brown sugar
2 (3-ounce) packages strawberry gelatin
2 cups boiling water
2 (10-ounce) packages frozen strawberries, undrained
1 (8-ounce) package cream cheese, softened
⅓ cup sugar
1 (9-ounce) container whipped topping, thawed

Lettuce leaves

In a medium saucepan, over medium heat, melt butter. Remove from heat. Stir in crushed pretzels and brown sugar. Press into a 9 x 13-inch pan. Bake at 350° for 15 minutes. Remove from oven and cool. Dissolve gelatin in boiling water. Add frozen strawberries. Stir until strawberries are thawed and gelatin is slightly thickened. Pour over pretzel crust. Chill until gelatin is set, about 2 hours. In a large bowl, beat together cream cheese and sugar until smooth. Fold in whipped topping. Spread over the chilled gelatin. Return salad to the refrigerator; chill another 2 hours. *To serve,* cut into squares and place on lettuce leaves.

Serves: 12

Mary Jo Kelly

"The pretzels give this salad a nice nutty flavor."

WALDORF SALAD EXTRAORDINAIRE

4 apples, chopped
1 tablespoon lemon juice
1 (3-ounce) package cream cheese, softened
2 tablespoons honey
Milk (for desired consistency)
⅛ teaspoon apple pie spice
¼ cup chopped dates
¼ cup chopped walnuts

Place chopped apples in a medium size bowl. Sprinkle lemon juice over; toss lightly. In a small bowl, blend cream cheese, honey, milk and apple pie spice. Pour over apples. Add dates and walnuts. Toss lightly to coat ingredients with dressing.

Serves: 4 to 6

Margo Stich

"Leave red peel on apples for a colorful salad."

CHINESE CHICKEN SALAD

2 whole chicken breasts,
   cooked, cooled and diced
½ head lettuce, shredded
4 green onions, chopped
2 tablespoons sesame seeds
2 tablespoons slivered
   almonds

Dressing:
2 tablespoons sugar
2 teaspoons salt
3 tablespoons vinegar
1 tablespoon sesame oil
¼ cup salad oil
1 tablespoon monosodium
   glutamate (optional)

Toss diced chicken, lettuce, green onions, sesame seeds and almonds together in a serving dish; cover tightly with plastic wrap. Refrigerate until ready to serve. *For dressing,* combine all ingredients, mixing well. Toss salad and dressing together just before serving.

Serves: 4 to 6

Chuck Canfield

Chicken Mandarin Orange Salad

Marinade:
2 cloves garlic, crushed
1/2 cup soy sauce
6 green onions, sliced
Juice from a fresh orange

4 skinless chicken breasts

Dressing:
1/3 cup white distilled
    vinegar
1 cup oil
1 teaspoon dry mustard
1 1/2 tablespoons sesame
    seeds, toasted
1 teaspoon soy sauce
1 1/2 tablespoons onion
    juice
3/4 cup sugar
1 teaspoon salt

Lettuce leaves
1 (11-ounce) can mandarin
    oranges
Slivered almonds, toasted
Additional sliced green
    onions
Slivered mushrooms
Chow mein, or other
    crunchy noodles

Combine marinade ingredients together. Pour over chicken breasts. Cover and marinate in the refrigerator for at least 3 hours. *For dressing,* combine ingredients in a container with a tight lid. Shake well to mix. Refrigerate. Cook chicken under broiler until done, turning once. Remove from oven to cool slightly. Cut chicken into bite-size pieces. *To serve,* make a bed of lettuce on individual plates. Top with mandarin orange slices, slivered almonds, freshly sliced green onions and sliced mushrooms. Add cut up chicken. Sprinkle with dressing. Top with crunchy noodles.

Serves: 4

Julie Larson

CHICKEN SALAD

2 whole chicken breasts
1 cup chicken broth
¼ pound bacon, cooked,
   drained, and crumbled
½ cup mayonnaise
1 tablespoon lemon juice
1 tablespoon horseradish
½ tablespoon capers
1 (8-ounce) can water
   chestnuts, sliced
Lettuce

In a skillet, simmer chicken breasts in broth for 20 minutes or until done. Cool. Cut chicken into bite-size pieces and mix with bacon. Combine mayonnaise and lemon juice in a small bowl. Add horseradish, capers, and water chestnuts. Mix with chicken and bacon. Serve over shredded lettuce.

Serves: 4

Betsy Ogle Weitz

"Horseradish is the secret ingredient in this delicious salad!"

CHICKEN-VEGETABLE SALAD

3 cups chicken, cooked and
   diced
1 cup broccoli flowerets,
   steamed tender crisp
1 cup frozen peas, thawed
   and drained
1 cup carrots, thinly sliced
1 small zucchini, sliced
¼ cup red bell pepper,
   diced
1 cup mayonnaise
¼ cup green onions, sliced
¼ cup fresh parsley,
   chopped
½ teaspoon salt
Pepper to taste
Fresh basil to taste

Prepare chicken and vegetables. Combine mayonnaise, green onion, parsley and seasonings; mix well. Toss together with chicken and vegetables. Chill until ready to serve.

Serves: 4 to 6

Margo Stich

"Low calorie mayonnaise may be substituted as desired."

TUNA SALAD

⅓ cup minced red onion
2 ribs of celery, sliced thin
2 tablespoons minced fresh
　parsley leaves
1 ½ teaspoons dried dill,
　crumbled
2 (6 ½-ounce) cans solid
　white tuna packed in
　water, drained
½ cup small-curd cream-
　style cottage cheese
½ cup mayonnaise
1 tablespoon Dijon mustard
Salt and pepper to taste

In a bowl, toss together onion, celery, parsley and dill. Add tuna, and toss until coated well. Add cottage cheese, mayonnaise and mustard. Toss to combine well. Season with salt and pepper to taste.

Serves: 4 to 6

CRUNCHY TUNA SALAD

1 (10-ounce) package petite
　frozen peas, thawed
1 cup celery, diced
1 (6-ounce) jar cocktail
　onions, drained
2 (6 ½-ounce) cans tuna
1 cup mayonnaise
1 tablespoon lemon juice
1 teaspoon soy sauce
⅛ teaspoon garlic salt

1 cup chow mein noodles
½ cup chopped almonds,
　toasted, for garnish
6 to 8 lettuce cups

In a large bowl, combine peas, celery, onions and tuna. In a small bowl, stir mayonnaise, lemon juice, soy sauce and garlic salt together. Combine tuna and mayonnaise mixtures, mixing thoroughly; chill for 1 hour or more. *To serve*, stir in chow mein noodles. Spoon salad into lettuce cups. Garnish with almonds.

Serves: 6 to 8

Janet Engels

MEDITERRANEAN SALAD DRESSING

1 clove garlic, peeled
3 teaspoons salt
3 teaspoons pepper
1 teaspoon dry mustard
1 teaspoon prepared
  horseradish
1 teaspoon Worcestershire
  sauce
½ cup red wine vinegar
1 ½ cups olive oil

Mix all the ingredients together in a large mayonnaise jar or quart canning jar with a tight-fitting lid. Shake well to blend. Let garlic clove sit in jar. Store in refrigerator.

Yield: 2 cups

Ann Jost

"This recipe is from Cindy Keating Pelone, who grew up in Rochester and now lives in Rome with her husband and two daughters. Our daughters came back from their European semesters with wonderful memories of Cindy's hospitality toward homesick American college students!"

ROSY SALAD DRESSING

1 teaspoon Worcestershire
  sauce
1 cup olive oil
1 (8-ounce) can tomato sauce
¼ cup red wine vinegar
1 teaspoon dry mustard
1 teaspoon paprika
1 teaspoon salt
1 tablespoon sugar
⅛ teaspoon garlic powder
  or 3 cloves garlic, peeled

Combine all ingredients, except garlic cloves, in a blender or food processor and blend well. Will keep several weeks, refrigerated. (Remove garlic cloves after 3 days.)

Yield: about 2 cups

Janet Engels

Honey Rum Dressing for Fruit

¼ cup honey
2 tablespoons dark rum
1 tablespoon fresh lemon or
   lime juice
⅛ teaspoon ground ginger

Canned or fresh fruit

Blend all ingredients well. Drizzle over canned or fresh fruits. Refrigerate, covered, at least one hour before serving, to blend flavors.

Note: Add fruits which tend to brown, bananas and apples particularly, just before serving, or treat with an anti-browning agent first.

Variation: Add sour cream and brown sugar to taste, to give a richer, differently flavored and textured dressing.

Yield: ½ cup

Margo Stich

Lime Honey Dressing

⅓ cup fresh lime juice
   (about 2 large limes)
1 cup oil
1 tablespoon lime zest
1 teaspoon ground ginger
½ cup honey, or more to
   taste

Blend all ingredients in a blender or process in a food processor.

Yield: About 2 cups

Nina Sudor

"This dressing is delicious on fresh fruit and melon."

ENTREES

MARINATED TENDERLOINS

1 ½ pound beef tenderloin
  roast
3 cloves garlic, crushed
Salt and pepper to taste
¾ cup catsup
¼ cup Worcestershire sauce
1 pound fresh mushrooms,
  sliced
½ cup (1 stick) cold butter,
  sliced

Rub meat with garlic, salt and pepper. Combine catsup and Worcestershire sauce. Pour over meat and marinate for 8 to 10 hours. Before baking, top with mushrooms and butter slices. Bake at 350° for about 40 minutes or use meat thermometer for desired doneness.

Serves: 4

Julie Larson

TERIYAKI ROAST TENDERLOIN

½ cup dry sherry
¼ cup soy sauce
2 tablespoons dry onion
  soup mix
2 tablespoons brown sugar
2 pounds beef tenderloin
2 tablespoons water

Combine sherry, soy sauce, onion soup mix and brown sugar. Place beef tenderloin in a large plastic bag or glass baking dish; pour marinade over. Seal bag or cover dish and let meat marinate overnight in refrigerator. *To bake,* place tenderloin and marinade in a 9 x 13-inch glass baking dish. Roast, uncovered, at 425° for 30 minutes, basting meat occasionally with marinade. In a saucepan, heat half of the marinade and water until mixture bubbles. Slice meat in ¼-inch slices. Spoon marinade over meat. Serve hot or cold.

Serves: 6

Pam Smoldt

ITALIAN STUFFED BEEF TENDERLOIN WITH ROASTED RED PEPPER AND GARLIC SAUCE

Sauce:
2 large whole heads of
  garlic, unpeeled
5 tablespoons olive oil,
  divided
4 large red bell peppers
½ teaspoon salt
½ teaspoon freshly ground
  black pepper
1 teaspoon finely minced
  fresh rosemary
⅓ cup dry vermouth or
  white wine

Filling:
½ cup olive oil
2 shallots, minced
1 green bell pepper,
  julienned
½ pound fresh mushrooms,
  finely minced
2 teaspoons minced fresh
  rosemary
½ cup finely chopped fresh
  parsley

Meat:
1 (4-pound) beef fillet,
  butterflied
Salt
Freshly ground black
  pepper
6 fresh rosemary sprigs
2 tablespoons olive oil

Fresh rosemary for garnish

Cut off tops of garlic heads to expose cloves. Place them in a small, foil-lined pan, and drizzle 1 ½ teaspoons olive oil over each garlic head. Cover with foil and bake at 350° for 1 hour. Remove from oven, uncover, and allow the garlic to cool about 15 minutes. With your fingers, squeeze garlic pulp onto a small plate and divide in half; set aside. Preheat broiler, with rack approximately 6 inches from heat. Core red peppers and cut in half. Flatten peppers out on a foil-lined baking pan. Rub surfaces liberally with 2 tablespoons olive oil. Broil for 10 to 12 minutes, turning occasionally, or until the skin is black and charred. Remove from oven, and with a spatula, transfer peppers to a small brown paper sack and allow them to steam for 15 minutes. With a sharp knife, peel away the charred skin and discard. Place red peppers and half of the garlic pulp in a food processor bowl with the remaining 2 tablespoons olive oil. Add salt and pepper. Process until smooth; set aside. *For filling,* heat olive oil in a deep skillet over medium heat. Add shallots and sauté until golden, about 3 minutes. Add green bell pepper, remaining garlic pulp, mushrooms and rosemary. Sauté until green pepper begins to soften, about 5 minutes. Remove from heat and let the filling cool, then stir in parsley. *For meat,* line a shallow baking pan with foil and coat with vegetable spray. Place opened fillet in the pan and sprinkle with salt and pepper to taste. Place three-fourths of the filling lengthwise down one side of the fillet and flip the other side over it to cover. Tie fillet at 1-inch intervals with kitchen string. Place rosemary sprigs on top of the fillet, tucking them under the string. Rub meat and rosemary with olive oil. Insert a meat thermometer and bake at 425° for 10 minutes. Reduce heat to 350° and bake 15 to 20 minutes longer for rare or 25 to 30 minutes for medium rare. *To finish sauce,* place remaining filling in a small saucepan. Add red pepper-garlic puree, rosemary and vermouth. Cook over medium heat, stirring often, until heated through. Let fillet rest for 10 minutes, then slice it ³/₄ inch thick, discarding string. Arrange on a bed of rosemary and serve with warmed sauce.

Serves: 8

Kay Love-Caskey

Marinated Brisket of Beef

6 pounds beef brisket
1 ½ teaspoons nutmeg
1 tablespoon salt
Freshly ground pepper to
taste
⅓ cup red wine vinegar
1 cup red wine
2 medium yellow onions,
quartered
2 large carrots, chopped
2 lemons, thinly sliced
8 cloves garlic, peeled
8 peppercorns
2 bay leaves

1 ½ cups sour cream
2 tablespoons dill weed

Rinse brisket under cold water and dry with paper towels. Rub nutmeg, salt and pepper all over brisket. In a non-corrosive bowl or kettle large enough to hold brisket, combine vinegar, wine, onions, carrots, lemons, garlic, peppercorns and bay leaves. Place brisket in marinade, turning it once. Cover tightly. Refrigerate for 48 hours, turning brisket several times. *To bake*, place brisket in a large baking pan. Pour marinade, including vegetables and spices, over brisket. Cover tightly and bake at 300° for 6 to 8 hours. (Add more red wine if roast cooks dry.) Remove from pan to cool. Refrigerate overnight. In a small bowl, stir together sour cream and dill weed. Spread over brisket (as you would frost a cake). Refrigerate until ready to serve. *To serve*, cut in thin slices against the grain.

Serves: 12 to 15

Nina Sudor

"This is a delicious and unusual meat dish that is wonderful at a cold buffet as well as at an informal picnic."

SMOKED BRISKET

3 to 4 pound beef brisket
1 (3 ½ -ounce) bottle liquid
   smoke, to taste
Salt
Garlic powder
Celery salt/flakes
1 large onion, chopped
¼ to ⅓ cup Worcestershire
   sauce
¾ cup barbeque sauce

Pour liquid smoke over meat and liberally season with salt, garlic powder, and celery salt. Place chopped onions over top. Cover meat and refrigerate overnight. Before baking, drain off excess juice and douse meat with Worcestershire sauce. Cover meat, sealing pan, with foil. Bake at 275° for 5 hours. Uncover and pour barbeque sauce over meat. Cover and bake for an additional hour.

Serves: 6 to 8

Sheila Kramer

FILET OF BEEF IN PHYLLO PASTRY WITH MADEIRA SAUCE

3 pound filet mignon,
  trimmed
Salt
½ cup (1 stick) plus 4
  tablespoons sweet butter,
  divided
½ pound mushrooms,
  rinsed and thoroughly
  dried
2 shallots, minced
1 (1-pound) package phyllo
  pastry

Madeira Sauce:
3 tablespoons butter
1 ½ tablespoons flour
¾ cup beef stock
1 teaspoon browning sauce
  (such as Kitchen Bouquet
  or Maggi)
¼ cup Madeira wine

Rub filet mignon with salt. In a large heavy skillet, melt 2 tablespoons butter. Sear meat over high heat, until brown on all sides, to seal in juices. Remove from heat; set aside. In a small saucepan, sauté mushrooms and shallots in 2 tablespoons butter for 2 to 3 minutes or until soft. Remove from heat; set aside. Melt ½ cup butter. Layer 12 pieces of phyllo pastry together, brushing each layer with melted butter. Spread half of the mushroom mixture on pastry and place seared beef on top. Spread remaining mushroom mixture on top of filet and fold phyllo dough around filet. Prepare an additional 5 to 6 layers of phyllo pastry, each brushed with butter. Seal all edges of filet by overlapping them with the additional pastry. Brush with butter. Place beef on a greased pan. Bake at 400° for 40 to 45 minutes or until pastry is brown and flaky. Remove from oven and serve with Madeira sauce. *For sauce,* melt butter in a small saucepan. Stir in flour. Cook 5 minutes. Add beef stock, browning sauce and wine. Cook until thickened. Serve over beef.

Serves: 6 to 8
        1 ½ cups Madeira Sauce

Julie Huettner
Peggy King

BUL KO KEE

1 pound flank steak
¼ cup soy sauce
¼ cup sugar
2 cloves garlic, crushed
7 green onions, thinly sliced
2 tablespoons sesame oil
2 tablespoons sesame seeds,
   toasted

Slice flank steak, very thin, on the diagonal. Combine remaining ingredients to make a marinade. Pour marinade over meat slices and refrigerate overnight or for 4 hours outside refrigerator. Line a baking sheet or jelly roll pan with aluminum foil. Place meat slices side by side in one layer on foil. Broil meat about 3 to 4 minutes, six inches from heat source. Watch closely as meat should be rare. Serve in marinade. (Can be made one day ahead and refrigerated. To reheat, pile steak slices in a pan and bake, uncovered, at 350° for 20 minutes.) Serve hot or at room temperature.

Serves: 4

Marion Kleinberg
Cindy Ullman

"Your guests will rave over this very flavorful meat! Great for a crowd too, as this recipe can be doubled or tripled and made ahead."

PELICAN LAKE FLANK STEAK

¼ cup salad oil
¼ cup soy sauce
1 tablespoon vinegar
2 tablespoons catsup
¼ teaspoon pepper
1 clove garlic, crushed
1 pound flank steak

Combine first six ingredients, mixing thoroughly. Pour over flank steak and marinate for 3 to 4 hours or overnight in the refrigerator. *To grill,* place flank steak over heat source, grilling about 10 minutes on a side. Do not overcook. Meat should be pink in the middle. Slice thinly on the diagonal. If desired, heat marinade and pour over sliced meat. *To broil,* thinly slice raw flank steak on the diagonal. Marinate slices for 3 to 4 hours or overnight in the refrigerator. Place meat slices in one layer on an 11 x 7-inch baking pan lined with aluminum foil. Broil meat six inches from heat source for 3 to 4 minutes. Watch closely; meat should be rare. Serve immediately.

Serves: 4

Nancy Brubaker

"Everyone who eats this for the first time asks for the recipe! The meat is also good served cold."

FAVORITE COMPANY CASSEROLE

1 pound lean ground beef
1 medium onion, chopped
1 (30-ounce) can tomatoes
1 (8-ounce) can tomato sauce
1 teaspoon celery salt
1 teaspoon paprika
Freshly ground pepper to taste
1 cup converted rice, cooked
2 cups grated American cheese
½ to 1 cup shredded Cheddar cheese

In a large skillet, brown beef with chopped onion. Add tomatoes with their juices, tomato sauce and spices. Stir to mix thoroughly, breaking up tomatoes. Simmer for 15 to 20 minutes. Combine rice and beef mixture together in a 3-quart casserole dish. Stir in cheese, mixing well. Bake, uncovered, at 350° for 1 hour.

Serves: 8

Maren Stocke

WILD RICE CASSEROLE

⅔ cup wild rice
2 cups boiling water
1 pound ground beef
3 tablespoons chopped
  onion
1 (10 ¾ -ounce) can cream of
  chicken soup
1 (4-ounce) can sliced
  mushrooms, undrained
⅛ teaspoon celery salt
⅛ teaspoon onion salt
⅛ teaspoon garlic salt
⅛ teaspoon paprika
⅛ teaspoon pepper
1 bay leaf, crumbled
Parmesan cheese

Combine wild rice and boiling water; let stand for 15 minutes or longer. Drain. Brown ground beef and onion; set aside. In a large bowl combine chicken soup, mushrooms and their liquid, and remaining ingredients except Parmesan cheese. Add drained rice and beef mixture; mix well. Place in a 1 ½ -quart casserole dish. Sprinkle with Parmesan cheese. Bake, covered, at 350° for 1 hour.

Serves: 6

Betsy Ogle Weitz

"My family loves this recipe!"

KNEADERY CHILI

2 pounds ground beef
1 large onion, chopped
1 green bell pepper,
  chopped
3 (16-ounce) cans kidney
  beans, drained and
  rinsed
1 (24-ounce) can whole
  tomatoes
1 (16-ounce) can tomato
  sauce
2 teaspoons parsley flakes
  or ½ cup chopped fresh
  parsley
½ teaspoon chopped garlic
2 tablespoons ground cumin
4 teaspoons chili powder
1 (4-ounce) can chopped
  mild green chili peppers
1 (16-ounce) bottle green
  salsa ("salsa verde")

Grated Cheddar cheese
Tortilla chips

Brown ground beef in a 6-quart Dutch oven. Add onions and green pepper to sauté slightly. Add remaining ingredients, except cheese and chips, mixing well. Adjust seasoning to taste. Simmer for 30 minutes. Serve in individual bowls topped with grated cheese and tortilla chips.

Yield: 8 to 10 servings

Nan Douglas

LA LASAGNE SANS SOUCI

1 pound ground beef or
  Italian sausage, browned
1 (30-ounce) jar spaghetti
  sauce
1 ½ cups water
1 (16-ounce) box lasagna
  noodles
1 (15-ounce) carton ricotta
  cheese, divided
8 ounces shredded
  mozzarella cheese,
  divided
¾ cup grated Parmesan
  cheese, divided

Brown meat; set aside. Grease a 9 x 13-inch baking dish. Combine spaghetti sauce and water in a large bowl. Cover bottom of baking dish with 1 ½ cups of sauce. Arrange a layer of uncooked noodles, slightly overlapping, on top of sauce. Spread half of the ricotta cheese and half of the mozzarella cheese over noodles. Sprinkle with 2 tablespoons Parmesan cheese. Spread half of the browned meat over the cheeses. Add another layer, 1 ½ cups, of sauce. Repeat with another layer of noodles, remaining ricotta and mozzarella cheeses, and 2 tablespoons Parmesan cheese. Add remaining meat. Top with a layer of noodles. Pour remaining sauce over top, spreading evenly to cover edges of noodles. Sprinkle with ½ cup Parmesan. Cover tightly with foil. Bake for one hour or until knife cuts easily through noodles.

Serves: 8 to 10

Jeanette Howe

"Lasagna without trouble!"

LORI'S HAMBURGER STROGANOFF

1 pound ground beef
½ cup chopped onion
¼ cup butter or margarine
2 tablespoons flour
1 teaspoon salt
1 clove garlic, minced
¼ teaspoon pepper
1 (4-ounce can) sliced
  mushrooms, drained
1 (10 ¾-ounce) can cream of
  chicken soup
1 cup sour cream

Cooked noodles, rice, or
  baked potatoes

In a large skillet, cook meat and onions until meat is browned and onions are tender. Stir in butter, flour, salt, garlic, pepper and mushrooms. Cook for 5 minutes, stirring constantly. Stir in soup and heat to boiling, stirring constantly. Reduce heat; simmer uncovered for 10 minutes. Stir in sour cream and heat through; do not boil. Serve over noodles, rice or baked potatoes.

Serves: 4

Georgia Hurley

Spring Rolls

1 stalk celery
3 to 4 ounces dried black
  mushrooms
1 (8-ounce) can water
  chestnuts, drained
1 (8-ounce) can bamboo
  shoots, drained
6 to 8 scallions
1 tablespoon ginger root,
  finely chopped (optional)
1 pound shrimp, shelled
  and deveined
1 pound extra lean ground
  beef
5 to 6 tablespoons soy sauce
5 tablespoons cornstarch
2 tablespoons sherry
1/3 cup oil, divided
1 (16-ounce) can bean
  sprouts
1 teaspoon salt

1 (1-pound) package spring
  roll wrappers
Oil for deep frying

Soy sauce
Mustard sauce

Cut celery into 1 1/2-inch long
strips; set aside. Soak mushrooms
in warm water until soft, then cut
into thin strips; set aside. Cut water
chestnuts into thin strips; set aside.
Cut bamboo shoots into 1 x 1/2-inch
thin strips; set aside. Cut scallions
into very small pieces, approximately 1/8-inch long; set aside. Chop
ginger root into fine pieces; set
aside. Cut shrimp into approximately 1/4-inch pieces. In a large
bowl, combine shrimp, ground
beef, soy sauce, cornstarch, scallions, ginger root and sherry. Add
1 1/2 tablespoons oil to the mixture to
prevent sticking; set aside. In a
large skillet or wok, sauté mushrooms in 2 tablespoons oil for 5
minutes. Add celery. Cook, stirring
constantly, until celery is soft. Add
bean sprouts, water chestnuts,
bamboo shoots and salt. Continue
cooking, stirring constantly, for 10
minutes or longer, until vegetables
become soft. Remove vegetables
with a slotted spoon; set aside. Add
remaining 2 tablespoons oil to
skillet; increase heat to high. When
oil begins to smoke, add shrimp
and beef mixture. Stir constantly
until the meat is cooked. Add
cooked vegetables; mix well.
Remove from heat. *To assemble
spring rolls,* have a cup of water and
a fork ready. Cut the square
wrappers into 2 triangles; keep
wrappers in a plastic bag to prevent
them from drying out. Take 15 to 20
wrappers out at a time. Put
triangular wrappers in a stack, with
the base facing you (the point away

from you). Put 1 to 1½ heaping teaspoons of filling in the middle third, at the base near the edge. Fold sides to center, one over the other. Press the wrapper in front of the filling area and wet the edges of the remaining triangle with water and roll forward until it is completely wrapped and sealed. *To cook,* deep fry spring rolls in hot oil at 375° until golden brown. Serve hot or warm with soy sauce or mustard sauce.

Yield: 60 to 70

Lily Weinshilboum

"Uncooked spring rolls can be kept in the freezer for weeks, so one can make them in large quantity ahead of time. Spring rolls can be served as a main dish or as an appetizer."

BEEF FRIED RICE NOODLE
(MEI FUN)

1 pound flank steak or extra
  lean ground beef
4 to 5 green onions, chopped
2 to 3 slices ginger root,
  finely chopped
1 to 2 ounces black
  mushrooms
1 tablespoon cooking sherry
2 to 3 tablespoons
  cornstarch
3 tablespoons soy sauce
¾ to 1 pound rice noodles
6 to 7 tablespoons oil,
  divided
1 to 2 (8-ounce) packages
  frozen snow peas
1 (16-ounce) can bean
  sprouts, drained
1 teaspoon salt, or to taste

Cut flank steak into thin slices. Chop green onions and ginger root into fine pieces; set aside. Soak black mushrooms in hot water and then cut into strips; set aside. Mix green onion, sherry, cornstarch, ginger root and soy sauce with sliced beef (or ground beef); set aside. In a large bowl, soak dried rice noodles in water until softened. In a large skillet or wok, sauté black mushroom strips in 2 tablespoons oil for 5 to 10 minutes. Add snow peas and bean sprouts; cook, stirring constantly, for 10 minutes or until they are soft. Remove vegetables with a slotted spoon; set aside. Add 2 to 3 tablespoons oil to skillet, and increase heat to high. When oil begins to smoke, add beef and cook, stirring occasionally, until browned. Add cooked vegetables to meat, stirring gently to mix well. Remove with a slotted spoon; set aside. Add 2 more tablespoons oil to the skillet. Reduce heat to medium-high. Add noodles to hot oil and cook, stirring constantly, for 5 to 10 minutes. Add meat and vegetables; mix well. Season with salt. Serve hot.

Serves: 6 to 8

Lily Weinshilboum

WONTONS

Filling:
½ pound lean ground beef
  or pork
1 teaspoon salt
¼ teaspoon monosodium
  glutamate (optional)
3 tablespoons soy sauce
1 ½ tablespoons cornstarch
2 teaspoons pale dry sherry
1 tablespoon sesame oil
  (optional)
5 to 6 teaspoons minced
  scallions
4 to 5 tablespoons minced
  black mushrooms
  (optional)
4 to 5 tablespoons minced
  bamboo shoots (optional)
½ pound shelled shrimp,
  minced

1 pound wonton wrappers
Oil for deep frying

Soup:
Chicken bouillon
1 tablespoon minced
  scallions
1 small bunch watercress

Duck sauce
Mustard sauce

In a large bowl, mix all filling ingredients together; set aside. Have a cup of cold water ready. Put 1 to 1 ½ teaspoons filling in the center of the wonton skin. Using a finger dipped in water, wet the front edge and side edges of wonton skin. Fold the back edge even with the front edge by using your thumbs and two index fingers. Using both thumbs, press the wonton skin firmly around the filling. The fold you have just made will form two wings on either side of the filling. Now fold these two wings together backwards. Wet the corners of these two wings with water overlap, and press them firmly together between your right thumb and index finger. *To deep fry,* cook wontons in hot oil at 375° until golden brown. Serve hot with duck sauce and mustard sauce. *For soup,* gently place wontons in a large saucepan with desired quantity of boiling chicken bouillon. Do not crowd wontons as they may stick together. Allow wontons to boil approximately 20 minutes. Add scallions and watercress 5 minutes before serving. Soup must be served hot.

Yield: 15 to 20

Lily Weinshilboum

"Wontons can be kept in freezer for weeks, so one can make them in large quantity ahead of time. Five to six wontons would be a good quantity per person for soup."

EASY ROAST BEEF

1 (3 to 4-pound) beef roast
(rump, arm, etc.)
1 (10 ¾-ounce) can double
strength beef broth
1 soup can of water
1 (0.8-ounce) package au jus
mix
1 (0.6-ounce) envelope
Italian salad dressing mix

Place beef roast in a crock pot. Mix broth, water and dry mixes together. Pour over beef roast. Cook on low heat for 4 hours. (Or bake at 300° for 3 to 4 hours, or until desired doneness.)

Serves: 6 to 8

Diane Hurley

MARINATED RIB-EYE ROAST

1 (6-pound) boneless beef
rib-eye roast
½ cup cracked black
pepper
1 cup soy sauce
¾ cup red wine vinegar
1 tablespoon tomato paste
1 teaspoon paprika
½ teaspoon garlic powder

Apricot halves (optional)
Hot pepper jelly (optional)
Parsley sprigs (optional)

Trim excess fat from roast. Pat pepper onto roast and place in a shallow dish. Combine next five ingredients and pour over roast. Cover; marinate overnight in refrigerator, turning occasionally. Remove roast from marinade; discard marinade. Wrap roast in foil and place in a shallow baking pan. Insert meat thermometer, making an opening so that thermometer does not touch foil. Bake at 325° for 2 hours or until thermometer registers 140° (rare) or 160° (medium). Place roast on a serving platter and carve. Fill centers of apricot halves with jelly and arrange around roast along with parsley sprigs to garnish, if desired.

Serves: 12 to 14

Carolyn Rorie

ROULADEN (FILLED BEEF ROLLS)

2 pounds beef sirloin or
   round steak, sliced thin
   (about ³⁄₁₆-inch thick)
Salt and pepper to taste
German mustard (optional)
12 ounces bacon, finely
   diced
1 large onion, finely minced
Whole dill pickles
Toothpicks or string
Lard or fat
2 cups beef stock or
   bouillon
¼ cup flour
¼ cup water

Rinse steak slices and pat dry with paper towel. Cut overly thick ones in half. Lightly salt and pepper one side of each slice. Spread some mustard evenly on one side of each slice, if desired. Fry bacon and onion together until bacon starts to crisp and onions are limp and golden but not browned. Drain mixture on paper toweling. Cut pickles lengthwise into quarters or eighths, depending on size. Place a pickle spear on each slice of meat with a spoonful of bacon-onion mixture. Roll up, tucking in the sides. Secure with toothpicks or string. Heat fat in a large Dutch oven. Brown beef rolls well on all sides, adding fat as needed. Do not overcrowd the pan while browning. After all the beef rolls are browned, remove meat with a slotted spoon and pour off any excess fat. Add beef stock or bouillon and scrape up any browned bits on the bottom of the pan. Return rolls to the pan. Cover and simmer for about 1 hour. Remove rolls from pan. Take out toothpicks or cut off string. Blend flour with water to form a smooth paste. Add to the liquid in the pan, stirring constantly. (Add only as much as needed to thicken to a smooth gravy.) Season gravy as needed. Return rouladen to the pan and heat through.

Serves: 6 to 8

Diane Nippoldt

Scrumptious Beef Burgundy

2 pounds top round beef or
  sirloin tip roast, cut into
  small pieces
2 tablespoons butter
2 tablespoons sherry,
  warmed
3 or 4 small onions
12 mushrooms
1 teaspoon tomato paste
3 tablespoons flour
1 cup beef stock
1 cup burgundy wine,
  divided
1 bay leaf
Salt and pepper to taste

Cooked rice or noodles
Parsley for garnish

In a large skillet, brown meat in butter. Sprinkle sherry over meat, and then remove meat. Brown onions, then mushrooms in the same pan. Combine tomato paste, flour and beef stock in a small bowl. Add to vegetables in skillet. Return meat to pan, bring to a boil and add ¼ cup burgundy wine and bay leaf. Cook slowly until meat is tender, about 1 hour 45 minutes. Add remaining wine. Remove from stove to cool. Refrigerate overnight. Reheat before serving. Season with salt and pepper to taste. Serve over rice, noodles or wild rice. Garnish with parsley.

Serves: 4 to 6

Janet Engels

CUMBERLAND SAUCE

4 tablespoons butter (do not
   substitute), divided
2 tablespoons shortening
1 beef bouillon cube
1 (10 ¾ -ounce) can beef
   consomme
1 ⅓ cups red wine, divided
3 tablespoons flour
3 tablespoons cornstarch
½ teaspoon salt (optional)
¼ teaspoon black pepper
1 cup water
2 teaspoons sugar
⅓ cup tomato juice
1 teaspoon wine vinegar
1 teaspoon browning sauce
   (such as Maggi or
   Kitchen Bouquet)

In a large heavy saucepan, ·melt 2 tablespoons butter and shortening together. In a small bowl, combine bouillon cube, consomme, 1 cup wine, flour, cornstarch, salt and pepper; stir until mixed. Pour mixture slowly into hot shortening, stirring constantly. When thick and bubbly, add water, sugar, tomato juice, ⅓ cup wine, vinegar and browning sauce, blending well. Rinse another saucepan with cold water and pour sauce into wet pan. Place over low heat, cover and simmer for 15 to 20 minutes. Whisk in 2 tablespoons butter and adjust seasonings to taste if necessary.

Variations: Can add finely minced parsley, sliced mushrooms sautéed in butter, capers, herbs or anchovy paste.

Yield: about 4 cups sauce

Ann Jost

"This is a recipe from my husband's mother, Peggy Jost, the best cook I've ever known! It is wonderful on roast beef."

LAMB SHISH KEBAB

**1 (2 ½ -pound) boneless
lamb shoulder or leg
roast**

Marinade:
Olive oil
**¼ cup red wine vinegar or
lemon juice**
2 cloves garlic, minced
1 ½ teaspoons salt
1 teaspoon oregano leaves
¼ teaspoon pepper

16 small white onions
1 large green bell pepper
3 firm medium tomatoes
½ pound large mushrooms

Cut strings and unroll lamb
shoulder, trimming excess fat. Cut
lamb into 1½-inch chunks. In a
large bowl, combine ½ cup olive
oil, vinegar, garlic, salt, oregano and
pepper, mixing well. Add lamb and
stir to coat with marinade. Cover
and refrigerate overnight, turning
occasionally. Preheat broiler or grill.
Cook onions in a 2-quart saucepan,
in 2 inches of boiling water for 10
minutes or just until tender-crisp.
Cut green pepper into 1½-inch
chunks and tomatoes into quarters.
Remove stems from mushrooms.
Skewer lamb chunks, alternating
with green pepper chunks and
onions, on five 12 or 14-inch all-
metal skewers; reserve marinade.
Place skewers on rack in broiling
pan. Stir 3 tablespoons olive oil into
reserved marinade. Brush vegetables with some of the marinade
mixture. Broil skewers of lamb (or
place skewers on rack over grill) for
10 to 12 minutes. Meanwhile, on
two or three more 12 to 14-inch all-
metal skewers, thread mushroom
caps and tomato quarters. Turn
lamb; place skewers containing
tomatoes and mushrooms on broil-
ing-pan rack. Brush meat and
vegetables with remaining marinade mixture and broil for 10 to 12
minutes more, until lamb is of
desired doneness.

Yield: 8 to 10 servings

Georgia Hurley

*"This is our favorite lamb kebab recipe. It is
excellent!"*

ROAST LAMB

2 lamb racks, leg of lamb, or
  rolled, boneless lamb
  roast
1 ½ teaspoons salt
½ teaspoon pepper
4 cloves garlic, crushed
1 teaspoon paprika
2 teaspoons rosemary,
  crushed
2 tablespoons lemon juice
2 tablespoons vegetable oil

Score the fat on the lamb in a diamond pattern. Combine salt, pepper and garlic in a small bowl; mash to a paste. Add remaining ingredients, mixing well. Spread mixture over meat. Place lamb in roasting pan, fat side up and roast at 350° for about 30 minutes a pound for medium. (Add 10 minutes per pound for rolled roast.) Baste occasionally with pan drippings.

Serves: 4

Betsy Ogle Weitz

"Very easy and delicious!"

HAM BALLS

2 pounds ground ham
½ pound ground beef
2 eggs
2 slices bread, crumbled
½ to ¾ cup milk

Sauce:
½ cup cider vinegar
1 ½ cups brown sugar
½ cup water
1 tablespoon butter
½ teaspoon dry mustard

Combine meats, eggs, bread and ½ cup milk in a large bowl, mixing well. If mixture seems too dry, add remaining milk by tablespoons. Using a heaping tablespoon, roll into balls. Place in a 9 x 13-inch pan. (Ham balls may be frozen at this point. Thaw in the refrigerator before continuing.) Combine sauce ingredients, mixing until well blended. Pour over ham balls. Bake at 325° for 1 hour.

Serves: 6

Ramona Kisrow

IRISH LOIN OF PORK WITH LEMON AND HERBS

1 (5 to 6-pound) boneless
   pork loin
½ cup chopped fresh
   parsley
¼ cup minced onion
¼ cup finely grated lemon
   peel
1 tablespoon chopped fresh
   basil
3 medium cloves garlic,
   crushed
½ cup plus 3 tablespoons
   olive oil
¾ cup dry sherry

Fresh parsley for garnish
Lemon slices for garnish

Rinse and pat pork dry; score well with a sharp knife. Combine parsley, onion, lemon peel, basil and garlic in a small bowl. Whisk in ½ cup olive oil. Rub mixture into pork. Wrap meat in foil and refrigerate overnight. Let pork stand at room temperature for 1 hour before roasting. Brush pork with remaining 3 tablespoons olive oil. Set on a rack in a shallow pan. Roast in oven at 350° until meat thermometer, inserted in the thickest part of meat, registers 170°, about 2 ½ hours. Remove from oven and set meat aside. Degrease pan juices. Blend sherry into pan juices. Cook over low heat for 2 minutes. Pour into sauceboat. Transfer pork to platter. Garnish with fresh parsley and lemon slices. Pass sauce separately.

Serves: 10

Renda Meloy

ROASTED LOIN OF PORK

3 to 4-pound boneless pork
   loin roast
1 (8-ounce) jar pineapple
   preserves
⅓ cup horseradish mustard

Place roast on a rack in baking pan. Roast at 350° for 2 to 2 ½ hours or to internal temperature of 185°. In a small saucepan, heat preserves and mustard together. Baste roast during last half hour of cooking. Pass remaining sauce with roast.

Serves: 6 to 8

Connie Gambini

BACON CHEVRE CHICKEN SAUTÉ

¼ cup flour
¼ teaspoon salt
¼ teaspoon pepper
1 whole chicken breast,
   skinned, boned, and split
1 tablespoon unsalted
   butter

Sauce:
½ cup heavy cream
1 shallot, minced
2 tablespoons mild goat
   cheese
1 tablespoon fresh lemon
   juice
¼ cup minced watercress
   leaves, divided
2 slices bacon, cooked crisp
   and crumbled

Mix flour, salt and pepper on a plate. Lightly coat chicken with seasoned flour. Heat butter in medium skillet over medium heat. Add chicken and sauté, turning once, until cooked through, about 8 to 10 minutes. Remove to serving plate and keep warm. *For sauce,* pour cream into skillet and increase heat to medium-high. Deglaze skillet by heating cream to boiling and scraping loose browned bits on bottom of pan. Add shallot and cook, stirring frequently, until cream is thickened, about 4 minutes. Add cheese, lemon juice, and half of the watercress. Stir until thoroughly blended. Adjust seasoning with salt and pepper to taste. Spoon sauce over chicken and sprinkle with remaining watercress and bacon.

Serves: 2

Diane Nippoldt

APRICOT STUFFED CHICKEN BREASTS WITH SAUCE SUPREME

½ pound dried apricots
1 ½ cups Marsala wine
¼ pound prosciutto ham
1 cup soft bread crumbs
1 stalk celery, thinly sliced
¼ cup chopped green onion
Pinch of rosemary
Pinch of thyme
½ teaspoon sage
¼ pound Gruyere cheese, cut into 12 paper thin slices
6 whole chicken breasts, skinned, boned, halved and pounded to thickness of ¼ inch
6 tablespoons dry white wine

Sauce:
1 cup half and half, room temperature
½ cup sour cream, room temperature
6 tablespoons butter
½ pound chanterelles or shiitaki mushrooms, thinly sliced
3 cups peeled, seeded and diced fresh tomatoes
Salt
Freshly ground pepper

Lemon slices for garnish
Parsley for garnish

Soak apricots in Marsala wine for 2 hours. Drain, reserving liquid for sauce. In a food processor, process apricots with prosciutto until chopped fine. Combine apricot-prosciutto mixture with bread crumbs, celery, green onion and herbs to make a fine stuffing. (The stuffing can be prepared a day ahead and refrigerated until ready to use. Bring to room temperature.) Arrange 1 slice Gruyere cheese (folded if necessary) on each chicken breast. (Chicken breasts can be readied for stuffing early in day and refrigerated until ready to stuff.) Spread about a heaping tablespoonful of stuffing mixture on top of cheese. Fold in the short ends, and beginning at long edge, roll chicken up jelly roll fashion. Pour white wine into a greased 9 x 13-inch pan. Arrange chicken breasts seam side down. Cover pan with foil and bake at 350° for 30 minutes, until tender. *For sauce*, whisk half and half and sour cream together in a bowl; set aside. Melt butter in a heavy skillet over medium heat. Add mushrooms and sauté until tender, about 5 minutes. Add tomatoes and cook until thickened, about 10 minutes. Add reserved Marsala wine and cook until liquid is reduced to ½ cup, stirring occasionally, about 10 minutes. Remove from heat. Blend in cream mixture. Return to medium heat and stir until thickened to sauce-like consistency. Season with salt and pepper to taste. Arrange 2 chicken rolls on each plate. Spoon sauce over chicken. Garnish with lemon slices and parsley. Serve immediately.

Serves: 6

Nina Sudor

"This is a recipe I have used for a long time and have added my own interpretations."

BAKED CHICKEN SUPREME

4 to 6 boneless chicken
   breasts
1 cup sour cream
1 (10 ¾-ounce) can cream of
   mushroom soup
½ cup dry sherry (optional)

Place chicken in a 7 x 11-inch baking dish. Combine remaining ingredients and pour over chicken. Bake, covered, at 350° for 45 minutes. Uncover; bake an additional 45 minutes.

Yield: 4 to 6 servings

Mary-Jean Martens

CHEVRE STUFFED CHICKEN

2 ounces dried tomatoes
1 cup dry white wine,
   divided
4 whole chicken breasts,
   skinned, boned, and cut
   in halves
1 (6-ounce) package chevre
   or similar goat cheese
½ cup chicken broth
Salt and pepper to taste

Marinate tomatoes in ½ cup wine for 2 hours or overnight. Pound chicken breasts to flatten. Cut up tomatoes and mix with cheese. Divide tomato-cheese mixture into eight portions and place on each piece of chicken. Roll up chicken. Place seam side down in a 9 x 13-inch baking dish. Combine broth, seasonings and remaining ½ cup wine in a small bowl. Pour over chicken. Bake at 350° for 1 hour.

Serves: 8

Mona Price

"I serve this with the Crisp Salad Greens with Potagerie Dressing,♪ Popovers ♪ and a glass of our favorite Chardonnay wine for a wonderful meal."

CHICKEN BREASTS SUPREME

¼ cup flour
2 ½ teaspoons salt
1 teaspoon paprika
6 whole chicken breasts,
    boned, skinned and cut
    in halves
¼ cup butter or margarine
¼ cup water
2 teaspoons cornstarch
1 ½ cups half and half,
    divided
¼ cup cooking sherry
1 teaspoon lemon peel
1 tablespoon lemon juice
1 cup grated Swiss cheese

½ cup chopped parsley for
    garnish
1 (16-ounce) jar spiced
    whole crab apples,
    drained (optional)

Up to 1 week before serving: Combine flour, salt and paprika in a plastic resealable bag; shake to mix thoroughly. Place halved chicken breasts, one at a time, in bag and shake to coat with flour mixture. Heat butter in large skillet. Lightly brown chicken on both sides. Add water, cover and simmer for 30 minutes or until chicken is almost tender. Arrange chicken in a freezerproof and ovenproof 9 x 13-inch baking dish. Mix cornstarch with ¼ cup half and half; stir into drippings in skillet. Cook, stirring, over low heat. Gradually stir in remaining half and half, sherry, lemon peel and lemon juice. Continue cooking and stirring until sauce is thickened. Cool sauce slightly, then pour over chicken. Cover and refrigerate if serving the next day or wrap dish tightly and freeze. To thaw, remove dish from freezer and thaw on counter top about 4 to 5 hours until almost defrosted, yet still cold. If necessary, refrigerate until reheating time. Bake chicken, covered, at 350° for 35 minutes or until sauce is bubbly hot. Remove cover; sprinkle with cheese and bake a minute or two more to melt cheese. Garnish with chopped parsley and spiced apples, if desired.

Serves: 8

Nancy Brubaker

"If served buffet style, place the chicken breasts on a large platter interspersed with spiced whole crab apples. The red apples contrasted with the green parsley on the chicken makes a very attractive presentation."

IMPERIAL GRILLED CHICKEN

3 ½ to 4 pounds split
   chicken breasts

Marinade:
1 clove garlic, finely
   chopped
1 teaspoon black pepper
⅛ teaspoon cayenne pepper
½ cup white wine vinegar
1 cup dry white wine
¼ cup olive oil
2 teaspoons dried leaf
   thyme, crushed
½ teaspoon grated lemon
   peel
2 tablespoons fresh lemon
   juice
1 teaspoon honey

Rinse chicken and pat dry. Place in a 9 x 13-inch pan in a single layer. To prepare marinade, combine ingredients in a jar with a tight lid. Shake well to thoroughly mix ingredients (marinade will take on a cloudy appearance). Pour over chicken, then turn pieces to coat with marinade. Cover and refrigerate for at least 6 hours or overnight. Lift chicken from marinade and drain briefly, reserving marinade. Place chicken, skin side up, on a lightly greased or sprayed grill, 4 to 6 inches above medium hot coals. Cook, turning and basting frequently with marinade, for 20 to 30 minutes, until meat near bone is no longer pink; cut to test.

Serves: 6 to 8

Margo Stich

LEMON HERB CHICKEN SAUTÉ

¼ cup flour
¼ teaspoon salt
¼ teaspoon pepper
1 whole chicken breast,
    skinned, boned, and split
1 tablespoon unsalted
    butter

Sauce:
½ cup heavy cream
1 shallot, minced
2 teaspoons grated lemon
    zest
1 teaspoon minced fresh
    tarragon or ½ teaspoon
    dried tarragon
2 teaspoons fresh thyme
    leaves or ¼ teaspoon
    dried thyme
2 tablespoons fresh lemon
    juice

Mix flour, salt and pepper on a plate. Lightly coat chicken with seasoned flour. Heat butter in a medium skillet over medium heat. Add chicken and sauté, turning once, until cooked through, about 8 to 10 minutes. Remove chicken to a serving plate and keep warm. *For sauce*, pour cream into skillet; increase heat to medium-high. Deglaze skillet by heating cream to boiling and scraping loose browned bits on bottom of pan. Add shallot, lemon zest, tarragon and thyme. Cook, stirring frequently, over medium-high heat until cream is thickened, about 3 minutes. Remove from heat and stir in lemon juice. Adjust sauce seasonings with additional salt and pepper to taste. Spoon sauce over chicken and serve.

Serves: 2

Diane Nippoldt

CHICKEN PARMESAN

6 to 8 skinless chicken
    breasts
¼ cup Zesty Italian salad
    dressing
½ cup Parmesan cheese
½ cup Italian style bread
    crumbs
2 tablespoons parsley
½ teaspoon salt
½ teaspoon paprika
¼ teaspoon pepper
1 egg
1 tablespoon water

Rinse chicken and pat dry. Place chicken in a 9 x 13-inch baking dish and pour dressing over chicken. Cover and refrigerate for 4 hours. In a large plastic bag, combine cheese, bread crumbs, parsley, salt, paprika and pepper. Shake to mix well. In a small bowl, beat egg and water together. Drain dressing off chicken and save. Dip chicken in egg and then in crumbs. Return chicken to baking dish. Spoon dressing over top. Bake at 350° for 40 to 45 minutes.

Serves: 6 to 8

Sheila Kramer

Chicken Marbella

16 (6 to 8-ounce) boneless,
   skinless chicken breasts
1 head garlic, peeled and
   finely pureed
¼ cup dried oregano
Coarse salt and freshly
   ground black pepper to
   taste
½ cup red wine vinegar
½ cup olive oil
1 cup pitted prunes
½ cup pitted Spanish green
   olives
½ cup capers with a bit of
   juice
6 bay leaves
1 cup brown sugar
1 cup white wine

¼ cup Italian parsley or
   fresh coriander (cilantro),
   finely chopped

Combine chicken, garlic, oregano, salt and pepper to taste, vinegar, olive oil, prunes, olives, capers and juice, and bay leaves in a large bowl. Cover and let marinate, refrigerated, overnight. Arrange chicken in a single layer in one or two large, shallow baking pans, and spoon marinade over it evenly. Sprinkle chicken pieces with brown sugar. Pour white wine around them. Bake at 350° for 50 to 60 minutes, basting frequently with pan juices. Chicken is done when pricking with a fork in its thickest area yields clear yellow juice. With a slotted spoon, transfer chicken, prunes, olives and capers to a serving platter. Moisten with a few spoonfuls of pan juices and sprinkle generously with parsley or cilantro. Remove bay leaves and discard. Pass remaining juices in a sauceboat. This dish may be served hot or cold. *To serve cold,* cool to room temperature in cooking juices before transferring to a serving platter. You may cover and refrigerate at this time. Allow chicken to return to room temperature before serving. Spoon juices over chicken before serving.

Yield: 16 servings

Cherie Miles

"Your guests will love this dish, which first appeared in The Silver Palate Cookbook."

NORMANDY CHICKEN SAUTÉ

¼ cup flour
¼ teaspoon salt
¼ teaspoon pepper
1 whole chicken breast,
   skinned, boned, split
3 tablespoons butter,
   divided
5 tablespoons applejack or
   Calvados, divided
½ Granny Smith or red
   delicious apple, cored
   and cut into thin wedges
2 shallots, minced
Pinch of dried thyme
⅓ cup creme fraiche

Mix flour, salt and pepper on a plate. Lightly coat chicken with seasoned flour. Heat 1 tablespoon butter in a medium skillet over medium heat. Add chicken and sauté, turning once, until cooked through, about 8 to 10 minutes. Remove to serving plate and keep warm. Pour 4 tablespoons applejack into skillet; increase heat to medium-high. Deglaze skillet by heating liqueur to boiling and scraping loose browned bits on bottom of pan. Add 2 tablespoons butter, apple wedges, shallots and thyme. Cook, stirring frequently, until apple is softened, about 3 minutes. Stir in creme fraiche and remaining applejack. Cook, stirring occasionally, until thickened, about 3 minutes longer. Adjust sauce seasonings with additional salt and pepper to taste. Spoon sauce over chicken and serve.

Serves: 2

Diane Nippoldt

OPULENT CHICKEN

6 whole chicken breasts,
  boned, skinned, and cut
  in halves
Paprika
Salt
Pepper
1 cup (2 sticks) butter,
  divided
2 (15-ounce) cans artichokes,
  drained
1 pound fresh mushrooms,
  sliced
¼ teaspoon tarragon
6 tablespoons flour
1 cup sherry, dry or sweet
3 cups chicken bouillon

Coat chicken breasts with paprika, salt, and pepper. Sauté in 1 stick of butter until brown. Place in a large casserole dish. Add artichokes. In a large skillet, sauté mushrooms in 1 stick of butter for 5 minutes or until done. Season with tarragon. Sprinkle in flour. Add sherry and bouillon, stirring to mix well. Simmer for 5 minutes. Pour sauce over chicken. Cover and bake at 350° for 45 minutes.

Variation: Sauté chicken in 3 tablespoons of butter. Arrange in casserole dish. In a medium bowl, combine 1 ½ teaspoons salt, ½ teaspoon paprika, 2 tablespoons flour, 1 (10 ¾-ounce) can cream of mushroom soup, 3 tablespoons sherry and 3 tablespoons melted butter. Pour over chicken. Add artichokes. Cover and bake at 375° for 40 minutes.

Serves: 8

Ann Groover
Jim and LouAnn Eppard

"This is wonderful as it makes its own gravy."

PROVENCAL CHICKEN SAUTÉ

¼ cup flour
¼ teaspoon salt
¼ teaspoon pepper
1 whole chicken breast,
    skinned, boned, and split
1 tablespoon butter

Sauce:
½ cup dry white wine
1 (14-ounce) can Italian
    plum tomatoes, drained
    and chopped
½ cup julienned red bell
    pepper
1 clove garlic, minced
1 tablespoon minced fresh
    parsley
⅛ teaspoon dried thyme

¼ cup pitted Nicoise olives
1 tablespoon capers, drained

Mix flour, salt and pepper on a plate. Lightly coat chicken with seasoned flour. Heat butter in medium skillet over medium heat. Add chicken and sauté, turning once, until cooked through, about 8 to 10 minutes. Remove to serving plate and keep warm. Pour wine into skillet and increase heat to medium-high. Deglaze skillet by heating wine to boiling and scraping loose browned bits on bottom of pan. Add tomatoes, bell pepper, garlic, parsley and thyme. Cook, stirring frequently, until thickened, about 4 to 6 minutes. Adjust seasoning with additional salt and pepper to taste. Spoon sauce over chicken and sprinkle with olives and capers. Serve hot.

Serves: 2

Diane Nippoldt

CHICKEN SPAGHETTI

1 large onion, thinly sliced
2 tablespoons olive oil
4 ounces mushrooms, sliced
1 green bell pepper,
    chopped
1 (16-ounce) can tomatoes,
    cut up
1 (8-ounce) can tomato sauce
2 teaspoons salt
3 cups cooked chicken
    breast, cut into bite-size
    pieces
8 ounces spaghetti, cooked
½ cup Parmesan cheese

In a large skillet, sauté onion in olive oil until soft. Add mushrooms, green pepper, tomatoes, tomato sauce and salt. Bring to a boil; simmer for 5 minutes. Add cooked chicken to the skillet; simmer for about 10 minutes. Butter a 2-quart casserole dish. Layer spaghetti, chicken mixture and cheese. Bake, covered, at 350° for 30 minutes or until thoroughly heated through.

Yield: 5 to 6 servings

Lois Swanson

CHICKEN TETRAZZINI

2 pounds whole chicken
  breasts, split
3 pounds chicken legs and
  thighs
3 cups water
3 celery tops
3 parsley sprigs
2 medium carrots, pared and
  sliced
1 onion, quartered
2 teaspoons salt
10 whole black peppercorns
1 bay leaf

Sauce:
¾ cup butter or margarine
¾ cup flour
3 teaspoons salt
⅛ teaspoon nutmeg
Dash of cayenne pepper
4 cups milk
4 egg yolks
1 cup heavy cream
½ cup dry sherry

1 (1 pound) package thin
  spaghetti
2 (6-ounce) cans whole
  mushrooms, drained
2 (8-ounce) packages sharp
  Cheddar cheese, grated

Wash chicken. Place in a 6-quart kettle. Add water, celery, parsley, carrots, onion, salt, peppercorns and bay leaf. Bring to a boil; reduce heat and simmer, covered, for 1 hour, or until chicken is tender. Remove chicken; set aside. Strain stock and return liquid to kettle. Bring to a boil; boil gently, uncovered, until reduced to 2 cups, about 30 minutes. Remove chicken meat from bones in large pieces (about 6 cups); set aside. *For sauce,* melt butter in a large saucepan. Remove from heat. Stir in flour, salt, nutmeg, and cayenne until smooth. Gradually stir in milk and 2 cups stock. Bring to a boil, stirring constantly. Boil gently, stirring constantly, for 2 minutes, or until slightly thickened. In a small bowl, beat egg yolks with cream. Gently beat in a little of the hot mixture. Pour into saucepan; cook over low heat, stirring constantly, until sauce is hot (do not let it boil). Remove from heat. Add sherry. Cook spaghetti as package label directs; drain. Return spaghetti to kettle. Add 2 cups sauce, and toss until well blended. Remove another 2 cups sauce, cover and refrigerate. To remaining sauce, add cut-up chicken and mushrooms. Divide spaghetti into two 8 x 12-inch baking dishes, arranging it around edges. Spoon half of chicken mixture into center of each. Sprinkle 2 cups cheese over spaghetti in each dish. Cover with foil; refrigerate until ready to bake. Bake at 350° for 30 to 45 minutes, or until piping hot. Just before serving, reheat reserved sauce, and spoon over spaghetti in baking dishes.

Serves: 12

Renda Meloy

Viva la Chicken Tortilla Casserole

1 (10 ¾-ounce) can cream of chicken soup
1 (10 ¾-ounce) can cream of mushroom soup
2 cups milk
1 small onion, minced
1 (16-ounce) can green chili salsa
2 tablespoons chicken stock
1 dozen corn tortillas, cut in 1-inch strips
4 whole chicken breasts, cooked and boned, cut in bite-size pieces
1 pound Cheddar cheese, shredded

In a large bowl, mix together soups, milk, onion and salsa. Grease a 9 x 13-inch baking dish. Place chicken stock on bottom of dish. Layer half of the tortillas, chicken pieces, soup mixture and cheese. Repeat layers, ending with cheese. Refrigerate for 24 hours. Bake at 300° for 1 to 1 ½ hours until hot and bubbly.

Serves: 8

Janet Engels

"Wonderful with just a tossed salad."

CURRIED CHICKEN DIVAN

1 (20-ounce) package frozen
   cut broccoli
2 cups cooked chicken,
   cubed
2 (10 ¾-ounce) cans cream
   of chicken soup
1 cup mayonnaise
1 tablespoon lemon juice
1 teaspoon curry powder
2 to 3 cups cooked rice or
   cooked orzo (pasta)
2 cups shredded Gouda
   cheese, divided

Put broccoli in colander and run hot water over it. Drain thoroughly. Spread broccoli on the bottom of a 9 x 13-inch pan. Combine remaining ingredients, reserving 1 cup cheese. Pour over the broccoli. Bake at 350° for 35 minutes. Top with the remaining shredded Gouda for the last 5 minutes.

Yield: 6 servings

Vicki Valente

"Serve with a crisp green salad and hard rolls."

CORNISH GAME HEN WITH SAUSAGE AND WILD RICE STUFFING

1 large box (6.25 ounces)
    long grain and wild rice
1 pound hot sausage,
    browned and drained
1 (8-ounce) can whole water
    chestnuts, drained and
    quartered
½ cup (1 stick) butter
1 onion, sliced
6 Cornish hens
Salt and pepper to taste

Cook rice according to package directions. Mix cooked rice with sausage and chestnuts; set aside. Place butter and onion in a 10 x 15-inch baking dish (you may want to use 2 pans). Preheat oven to 350°. Melt butter in the oven. Rinse hens. Dry, then salt cavity. Stuff hens with rice mixture. (Use remaining rice for side dish.) Place hens on top of onions. Season with salt and pepper. Baste with butter-onion mixture. Bake at 350° for 1 hour, basting twice.

Serves: 6

Eleni George

GAME HENS WITH HONEY-SAUTERNES SAUCE, SPINACH AND PEARL ONIONS

Sauce:
½ cup plus 4 tablespoons honey
3 cups sauternes or other sweet white dessert wine
2 cups chicken stock or canned low-salt chicken broth
4 tablespoons soy sauce

Caramelized Onions:
2 (10-ounce) baskets pearl onions
4 tablespoons butter
½ cup water
2 tablespoons honey

Game Hens:
5 or 6 (1 ¼ pounds each) Cornish game hens, cut in half
Salt and pepper to taste
1 cup plus 6 tablespoons butter, cut into pieces, room temperature
2 bunches spinach, trimmed

Heat honey in a small heavy skillet over medium-high heat for about 3 minutes, until honey darkens and becomes fragrant, swirling pan occasionally. Carefully add sauternes and chicken stock. Boil mixture until reduced to 2 cups, about 20 to 30 minutes. Add soy sauce and boil 4 minutes longer. (Can be prepared 1 day ahead.) Cover and refrigerate. *For caramelized onions,* bring a medium saucepan of water to boil. Add onions and blanch for 2 minutes. Drain. Rinse onions under cold water to cool. Drain. Using a small sharp knife, trim off root end of onions and peel off skin. Melt butter in a heavy medium skillet over medium heat. Add onions and sauté until golden brown and almost tender, about ten minutes. Add water and honey. Cover and simmer until onions are tender, about 5 to 6 minutes. Uncover and continue cooking until onions are caramelized, stirring occasionally, for about 2 minutes. Remove from heat. (Can be prepared 8 hours ahead). Cover and let stand at room temperature. *For game hens,* season halves with salt and pepper. Arrange hens, skin side up, on baking sheet. Bake at 425° for about 25 minutes, until juices run clear when thighs are pierced. Keep warm. Melt 2 tablespoons butter in a large heavy skillet over medium-high heat. Add spinach. Cover and cook until spinach is just wilted, about 2 minutes. Drain. Season with salt and pepper. Keep warm. Reheat onions over medium heat, stirring constantly. Bring sauce to boil; remove from heat and gradually whisk in remaining 1 cup plus 4 tablespoons butter. *To serve,* divide spinach among plates. Place 1 hen half on each plate. Spoon sauce over hens. Garnish with caramelized onions and serve.

Yield: 10 to 12 servings

Julie Larson

BEST-EVER ROAST TURKEY

1 turkey
Cooking bags for poultry
1 recipe of your favorite
     poultry stuffing
1 cup mayonnaise, plus
     more if needed

Buy the cheapest turkey you can find. The size depends on the size of the cooking bag and the number of people you wish to serve. Follow the directions for the cooking bag, except use one for turkey and one for stuffing. Prepare your favorite poultry stuffing as your recipe directs. Place in a cooking bag. Close bag with accompanying tie and cut 15 1-inch slits all over plastic bag (this is so flavorful meat juices can get in). Place bag in cavity of turkey; let extra hang out. Place turkey in second cooking bag, following directions, except just before closing spread mayonnaise in a thin coating over entire turkey. Use more mayonnaise if necessary. Seal bag and bake according to cooking bag instructions.

Sally Hanson

"When finished, you'll have a golden brown turkey, good juices, and stuffing that can easily be cut from bag. The marvelous thing about this method is the juicy, moist, wonderful turkey meat and best of all, no crusty pans to scrape and wash."

Roast Turkey "Herb Rub"

3 tablespoons butter
2 tablespoons
  Worcestershire sauce
1 clove garlic, minced
1 ½ teaspoons dried basil
1 ½ teaspoons dried thyme
¾ teaspoon dried ground
  sage
1 ½ teaspoons salt
1 teaspoon black pepper

1 (10 to 12-pound) turkey

Combine all ingredients, except turkey, mixing well. Rinse turkey and pat dry. Rub herb mixture over turkey. Roast per your favorite method and directions.

Margo Stich

Spirited Turkey Chili

1 tablespoon oil
2 medium onions, chopped
2 cloves garlic, minced
3 pounds skinless turkey
  breast, coarsely ground
2 tablespoons chili powder
½ teaspoon dried oregano
1 teaspoon salt
½ cup dark rum
1 (6-ounce) can tomato paste
1 (28-ounce) can tomatoes,
  undrained
3 (16-ounce) cans kidney
  beans, drained

Heat oil in an 8 to 10-quart pot. Lightly sauté onions and garlic. Add meat, breaking it up and stirring with a wooden spoon until just brown. Add remaining ingredients. Stir. Cover and simmer for 2 hours. Check seasoning and adjust to taste.

Serves: 10

Cherie Miles

TURKEY SUPREME

2 cups cubed cooked turkey
2 cups cooked wild rice
1 cup chopped celery
1 cup sliced almonds
¼ cup chopped green bell
  pepper
2 tablespoons lemon juice
1 (10 ¾-ounce) can cream of
  chicken soup
½ to 1 teaspoon curry
  powder, or to taste
Salt and pepper to taste
1 cup crushed wheat flakes
  (cereal)
2 tablespoons margarine or
  butter, melted

Combine turkey, wild rice, celery, almonds, green pepper, lemon juice, soup, curry powder, salt and pepper. Pour into a 9 x 9-inch baking dish. Combine wheat flakes and melted margarine or butter. Spread over top of turkey mixture. Bake, uncovered, at 350° for 30 minutes until heated through.

Yield: 6 to 8 servings

Amy Waugh

CRUSTLESS CRABMEAT QUICHE

½ pound fresh mushrooms,
  sliced, sauteed in
  2 tablespoons butter or
  2 (4-ounce) cans
  mushrooms, drained
4 large eggs
1 cup sour cream
1 cup small-curd cottage
  cheese
½ cup grated Parmesan
  cheese
¼ cup flour
½ to 1 teaspoon dill weed
½ to 1 teaspoon basil, or
  your favorite herb
1 teaspoon onion powder
4 drops hot pepper sauce
  (such as Tabasco)
½ cup sliced green onions
2 cups (8 ounces) shredded
  Monterey Jack or mixed
  colby and jack cheeses
8 ounces fresh or frozen
  crabmeat, thawed and
  well-drained, or
  1 (8-ounce) package
  frozen mock crabmeat,
  cut into chunks

Grease and flour a 10-inch quiche dish or a 10-inch deep-dish glass pie plate. If using fresh mushrooms, sauté them in butter or margarine and drain on paper towels. In blender or food processor, blend eggs, sour cream, cottage cheese, Parmesan, flour, herbs, onion powder and hot pepper sauce. Place mushrooms, green onions, shredded cheese and crabmeat in a large bowl. Pour in egg mixture, stirring gently to mix well. Pour into prepared dish. (At this point, quiche can be refrigerated, covered with plastic wrap. Bring to room temperature before baking.) Bake at 350° for 45 minutes or until quiche is puffed, golden brown and knife inserted near center comes out clean. Remove from oven and let stand for 5 to 10 minutes before cutting into wedges.

Variation: Substitute ½ pound cooked, cubed ham for crabmeat.

Serves: 8 as a main course
        10 to 12 as an appetizer

Ann Jost

Baked Salmon Fillets

Sauce:
1 teaspoon Dijon mustard
Juice of ½ lemon
Pinch of cayenne pepper
**1 tablespoon chopped
    parsley**

Fish:
1 ½ pounds fillet of salmon
Olive oil
Salt and pepper to taste

Combine all sauce ingredients in a small bowl; set aside. Arrange salmon in a single layer, skin side down, in a greased baking dish. Brush with olive oil. Season with salt and pepper. Cover and bake at 350° for 15 minutes. Uncover and top with sauce. Bake, uncovered, for another 10 minutes or until done.

Serves: 4

Lois Swanson

Grilled Salmon Fillets With Citrus-Avocado Sauce

2 oranges
2 small onions, diced
**2 cups chopped fresh
    pineapple**
**2 large tomatoes, peeled,
    seeded, and chopped**
¼ cup vegetable oil
**½ cup chopped fresh
    cilantro**
**6 small serrano chilies,
    minced**
**10 (6-ounce) center-cut
    salmon fillets, about
    1 ½ inch thick**
3 cups pink grapefruit juice
**1 avocado, halved, pitted,
    and diced**

Peel oranges and remove white pith. Separate into segments and remove membrane. Chop coarsely. Combine chopped oranges, onions, pineapple, tomatoes, oil, cilantro and chilies in a large bowl; set aside. Place salmon fillets into a shallow dish. Pour grapefruit juice over fillets and marinate for 1 hour at room temperature, turning occasionally. Prepare barbecue grill (medium high heat). Place salmon skin side down on grill. Cook until opaque, turning once. Transfer salmon to plates. Just before serving, add avocado to citrus-chile sauce. Spoon over salmon and serve.

Serves: 10

Sally Duffy

"Just a few notes: If fresh serrano chilies are not available, use jalapeno. Wear gloves when seeding and chopping chilies or be prepared not to get your hands near your mouth or eyes for 24 hours. Do not let salmon marinate longer than 1 hour. Sauce (without avocado) may be made 8 hours ahead."

Barbecued Garlic Shrimp

1 ¼ cups (2 ½ sticks)
  unsalted butter
12 green onions, chopped
15 cloves garlic, minced
2 cups dry white wine
6 tablespoons fresh lemon
  juice
Pepper to taste
1 ½ pounds large unpeeled
  shrimp
1 cup plus 3 tablespoons
  minced fresh parsley,
  divided

Bamboo skewers
Hot pepper sauce (such as
  Tabasco)
3 tablespoons minced green
  onion tops
Salt to taste

Lemon wedges

Melt butter in a large heavy skillet over medium-low heat. Add chopped green onions and garlic; sauté for 3 minutes. Add white wine; simmer for 15 minutes, stirring occasionally. Mix in fresh lemon juice. Season to taste with pepper. Transfer to a large bowl and let cool. Cut shrimp down the back, through shell; do not peel. Remove veins. Add shrimp and 1 cup parsley to garlic mixture; toss well. Cover and chill for 6 hours, turning occasionally. Soak bamboo skewers in water for 30 minutes before grilling. Prepare barbecue grill (medium-high heat). Remove shrimp, reserving marinade. Thread 2 shrimp on each bamboo skewer. Transfer marinade to a medium heavy saucepan. Simmer over medium heat until thick, stirring occasionally, about 12 minutes. Strain through sieve set over bowl, pressing on solids. Season with pepper sauce and salt. Spoon into 8 small bowls. Sprinkle with onion tops and remaining 3 tablespoons of parsley. Place bowls on individual plates. Cook shrimp on grill until pink and cooked through, turning once, about 3 minutes. Divide shrimp among plates, garnish with lemon wedges and serve immediately.

Serves: 8

Julie Roenigk

Scallops and Linguine

½ cup chicken broth
2 tablespoons lemon juice
1 pound scallops (slice sea scallops in thirds)
12 ounces linguine
1 tablespoon olive oil
2 cloves garlic, minced
3 red bell peppers, seeded, deveined and julienned
Dash of red pepper sauce
½ cup chopped parsley

Combine chicken broth and lemon juice in a large skillet; bring to a boil. Add scallops; reduce heat and simmer for 3 minutes. Drain scallops, reserving ½ cup of liquid. Prepare linguine as directed on package. In a small pan, heat olive oil. Sauté garlic and red pepper strips about 2 to 3 minutes. Combine all ingredients together in a large serving dish. Toss and serve.

Serves: 4

Bev Olander

Scampi N' Pasta

1 ½ pounds fresh shrimp, shelled and deveined
3 tablespoons butter or margarine
3 large cloves garlic, minced
½ cup minced onion
¼ cup dry white wine
½ cup tomato sauce
1 ¼ cups whipping cream, divided
½ teaspoon dried basil, crumbled
½ teaspoon dried oregano, crumbled
1 teaspoon salt
⅛ teaspoon white pepper
3 egg yolks
12 ounces dry vermicelli
2 tablespoons minced fresh parsley

Rinse shrimp; pat dry with paper towels. Melt butter in a large skillet. Sauté garlic over medium heat, stirring constantly, for 1 minute. Add shrimp and onion; sauté over medium-high heat until shrimp are bright pink on both sides, about 5 minutes. Add wine, tomato sauce, 1 cup cream, basil, oregano, salt and pepper. Heat through. Beat egg yolk with remaining ¼ cup cream; add to sauce. Cook over medium heat, stirring constantly, until sauce thickens; do not boil. Cook vermicelli following package directions until al dente, about 8 to 10 minutes; drain. Arrange vermicelli on a heated platter. Pour sauce over pasta. Sprinkle with parsley and serve immediately.

Serves: 6

Diane Nippoldt

SEAFOOD SUPREME

2 (7 ½ -ounce) cans crab,
    drained
1 (4 ½ -ounce) can large
    shrimp, drained
4 eggs, well beaten
1 cup grated sharp Cheddar
    cheese
1 cup finely chopped celery
½ cup finely sliced green
    onion tops
1 ¼ cups mayonnaise
¼ cup sour cream
1 tablespoon prepared
    mustard
Salt and pepper to taste
4 ounces fresh mushrooms,
    sliced
¼ cup chopped green bell
    pepper
½ cup seasoned crouton
    crumbs

Remove cartilage from crab.
Combine remaining ingredients,
except crouton crumbs, in a large
bowl; mix well. Place in a buttered
9 x 13-inch casserole dish. Top with
crouton crumbs. Bake at 350° for 30
to 35 minutes until firm.

Serves: 4 to 6

Janet Engels

"Rice makes a nice accompaniment for this dish."

SHRIMP CHINESE

3 cups sliced celery
1 cup chopped onion
½ cup water
2 tablespoons butter
8 ounces fresh mushrooms
¾ cup chopped green bell
    pepper
1 (4-ounce) jar pimentos,
    drained and chopped
1 (5-ounce) can water
    chestnuts, drained and
    sliced
1 (6-ounce) can cashew nuts
1 pound shrimp, cooked
    and cleaned
2 to 3 (10 ¾ -ounce) cans
    cream of mushroom
    and/or cream of celery
    soup
2 (5-ounce) cans chow mein
    noodles

Combine celery, onion and water in
a large pan; simmer until onion is
soft. Drain. Heat butter in a small
pan. Sauté mushrooms until
browned. Combine all ingredients
except noodles. Season to taste.
Sprinkle one can of noodles over
bottom of a greased 4-quart shallow
casserole dish. Spread vegetable
mixture over noodles and top with
remaining can of noodles. Bake at
350° for 30 minutes.

Serves: 8

Bev Olander

GRILLED MARINATED SWORDFISH STEAKS

2 tablespoons lemon juice
1 clove garlic, chopped
1 teaspoon dry mustard
2 tablespoons olive oil
4 swordfish steaks

Prepare grill. Combine first four ingredients, mixing well. Brush mixture evenly over steaks. Place on a well-greased cooking grill. Cook about 4 to 5 inches from heat for 10 minutes per 1-inch of thickness. Turn fish over halfway through the estimated cooking time. Steaks may be broiled in the same manner.

Serves: 4

Janet Engels

GRILLED SWORDFISH WITH GINGER BUTTER

2 tablespoons shallots
¼ cup lemon juice
¼ cup white wine
2 tablespoons finely
  chopped fresh ginger
  root
1 cup (2 sticks) unsalted
  butter
Salt and freshly ground
  pepper to taste
⅛ teaspoon cayenne pepper
  (optional)
2 ½ pounds swordfish, in
  two steaks, 1-inch thick
Corn oil

Chopped parsley or basil
  for garnish

In a small saucepan, combine shallots, juice, wine and ginger root. Cook until liquid is reduced to ¼ cup. Reduce heat to low. Add butter, a little at a time, stirring constantly; do not let mixture boil. Season with salt, pepper and cayenne. Sprinkle both sides of fish with salt and pepper. Brush with oil. Broil over a medium-hot grill for 8 to 12 minutes. Turn carefully to cook other side. Transfer to serving plate and cover with sauce. Garnish with chopped parsley or basil.

Serves: 6 to 8

Julie Roenigk

CHEDDAR RAMEKIN

12 ounces sharp Cheddar
   cheese, grated
1 (10-inch) pie shell, baked
½ cup diced green chilies
4 eggs
2 egg yolks
2 tablespoons freshly grated
   Parmesan cheese
1 ½ tablespoons flour
¼ teaspoon salt
1 ½ cups whipping cream

Sprinkle half of the Cheddar cheese over the bottom of the pie crust. Top with chilies. Cover with remaining Cheddar cheese. Beat together eggs, egg yolks, Parmesan cheese, flour and salt. Add cream, stirring until just blended. Gently pour over cheese. Bake at 350° for 50 to 60 minutes. Serve warm.

Serves: 6

Bev Olander

"Makes a nice brunch dish, served with muffins and fresh fruit. This dish is also good when baked, frozen, thawed and reheated."

THREE-CHEESE SPINACH FRITTATA

¼ cup olive oil
1 (10-ounce) package frozen
   chopped spinach, thawed
   and well drained
8 ounces fresh mushrooms,
   sliced
1 medium onion, chopped
6 eggs, lightly beaten
¾ cup shredded provolone
   cheese
2 cloves garlic, minced
¾ teaspoon dried Italian
   seasoning
Salt and pepper to taste
4 ounces shredded
   mozzarella cheese
¼ cup grated Parmesan
   cheese

In a large skillet, heat olive oil until light haze forms. Add spinach, mushrooms and onion. Cook and stir until onion is transparent. Remove from heat. Add eggs, provolone cheese, garlic and seasonings; mix well. Spoon into a greased 9-inch pie plate. Sprinkle with mozzarella cheese and Parmesan cheese. Bake at 350° for 25 minutes or until set.

Yield: 6 servings

Margo Stich

EGGS AND POTATOES

4 tablespoons butter,
   divided
6 eggs, lightly beaten
½ cup plus 1 tablespoon
   half and half
¼ teaspoon salt
Pinch of pepper
1 tablespoon dried onion
1 tablespoon chives (or
   green onion)
1 cup shredded Cheddar
   cheese
1 ½ cups diced ham
1 (12-ounce) package frozen
   hash brown potatoes

Blend together 2 tablespoons melted butter, eggs, cream, salt and pepper; set aside. In a large bowl, stir together remaining ingredients. Add egg mixture, stirring to mix thoroughly. Melt 2 tablespoons butter in a 9 x 9-inch pan. Gently pour in potato-egg mixture. Bake at 375° for 30 to 40 minutes, until top is lightly browned.

Serves: 6

Jennie Wilson

SAVORY EGGS AND HAM

8 hard-cooked eggs
¼ cup melted butter or
   margarine
½ teaspoon Worcestershire
   sauce
½ teaspoon dry mustard
Chopped parsley to taste,
   and for garnish
1 tablespoon grated onion
⅓ cup chopped ham
Ham strips (optional)
Mushrooms (optional)
1 cup grated American
   cheese

Bechamel Sauce:
3 tablespoons melted butter
¼ cup flour
1 chicken-flavored bouillon
   cube
1 cup boiling water
Salt and pepper to taste
Paprika
¾ cup milk

Halve hard-cooked eggs length-wise. Remove yolks, reserving whites, and mash yolks in a small bowl. Add butter, Worcestershire sauce, mustard, parsley, onion and ham. Stuff whites of eggs with this mixture. Arrange eggs in a buttered chafing dish or 9 x 13-inch baking dish. Sprinkle strips of ham and mushrooms over eggs. (Can be prepared ahead to this point, covered and refrigerated.) *For Bechamel Sauce,* blend butter or margarine with flour. Dissolve bouillon cube in boiling water and gradually add to flour mixture. Season with salt, pepper and paprika to taste. Add milk. Cook over low heat, stirring constantly, until thick. When ready to serve, pour Bechamel Sauce over eggs. Sprinkle with cheese and parsley. Cover and bake at 325° for 20 minutes or until hot.

Yield: 6 servings

Suzanne Dinusson

"Wonderful for brunch."

SPINACH ARTICHOKE CASSEROLE

2 (10-ounce) packages
  frozen spinach
½ pound fresh mushrooms
½ large onion, chopped
5 tablespoons butter,
  divided
1 tablespoon flour
½ cup milk
½ teaspoon salt
⅛ teaspoon garlic powder
1 cup sour cream
¼ cup mayonnaise
⅛ cup lemon juice
2 (14-ounce) cans artichoke
  hearts
Paprika

Grease a 2-quart casserole dish. Cook and drain spinach according to package directions. Remove stems from 10 mushrooms. Chop stems and set aside. Melt 2 tablespoons butter in a small skillet. Sauté mushroom caps. Remove mushroom caps from skillet with a slotted spoon; set aside. Add 1 tablespoon butter to skillet. Sauté mushroom stems and chopped onions. Melt 2 tablespoons butter in a saucepan; add flour and cook until bubbly. Add milk; stir until smooth and thickened. Remove from heat. Stir in salt, garlic powder, spinach and mushroom-onion mixture; set aside. In a separate bowl, combine sour cream, mayonnaise and lemon juice, mixing well; set aside. Place drained artichoke hearts on the bottom of prepared casserole dish. Cover with spinach mixture. Pour sour cream mixture over spinach. Top with mushroom caps. Bake at 350° for 25 minutes. Garnish with paprika.

Serves: 6 to 8

"This is a wonderful vegetarian dish."

SPINACH AND HAM FRITTATA

½ pound fresh mushrooms,
    sliced
½ cup minced onion
1 clove garlic, minced
    (optional)
2 tablespoons olive oil
1 (10-ounce) package frozen
    chopped spinach, thawed
    and drained
6 eggs, slightly beaten
1 cup (4 ounces) grated
    Romano cheese, divided
1 cup (4 ounces) shredded
    provolone cheese,
    divided
1 teaspoon dried basil
½ teaspoon dried marjoram
¼ teaspoon pepper
1 cup cooked ham, cubed

Sauté mushrooms, onion and garlic in olive oil until lightly browned. Stir in spinach and cook for 3 minutes; set aside. In a large bowl, combine eggs, ⅔ cup Romano cheese, ⅓ cup provolone cheese, basil, marjoram and pepper. Add onion mixture, stirring until mixed well. Stir in ham. Pour into a greased 10-inch pie plate or a 7 x 11-inch baking dish. Sprinkle with remaining ⅓ cup Romano cheese and ⅔ cup provolone cheese. Bake at 350° for 30 to 40 minutes or until set.

Serves: 6 to 8

Margo Stich

SPINACH PIE

1 (10-ounce) package frozen
    chopped spinach,
    thawed, with all moisture
    squeezed out
½ pound grated Cheddar
    cheese
1 (16-ounce) container
    cottage cheese
1 tablespoon onion powder
    or fresh minced onion
4 eggs, beaten
½ teaspoon pepper
2 tablespoons margarine,
    melted

Grease a 9-inch glass pie plate. Mix all ingredients together in a bowl, adding spinach last. Spoon into greased pie plate. Bake at 350° for 1 hour. (Pie can be frozen before baking; add 15 minutes to baking time.)

Serves: 4

Marilyn McKeehen

"Add muffins and fresh fruit such as strawberries, bananas, kiwi, or apple slices for a colorful and light lunch."

ZIPPY EGGS

12 eggs, beaten
2 (17-ounce) cans cream-
 style corn
4 cups (16 ounces) grated
 sharp Cheddar cheese
2 (4-ounce) cans chopped
 green chilies, drained
1 tablespoon Worcestershire
 sauce
1 tablespoon salt
½ teaspoon pepper

Grease a 9 x 13-inch ovenproof serving dish. Combine all ingredients in a large bowl and beat until well mixed. Pour into greased dish. (At this point, casserole may be covered with plastic wrap and refrigerated up to 24 hours.) Bake at 325° for 1 hour 15 minutes, or until firm to the touch.

Serves: 10 to 12

Ann Jost

FETTUCCINE ALFREDO

8 ounces fettuccine
1 tablespoon olive oil
¾ cup evaporated skim
 milk
⅓ cup freshly grated
 Parmesan cheese
¼ cup chopped green onion
2 tablespoons fresh snipped
 basil, or ½ tablespoon
 dried basil
¼ teaspoon finely shredded
 lemon peel
⅛ teaspoon pepper
¼ teaspoon garlic powder
Cooked peas (optional)

Lemon slices for garnish

In a medium saucepan, cook fettuccine according to package directions. Drain and return to pan. Add oil; toss to coat. Add milk, cheese, onion, basil, lemon peel, pepper and garlic powder. Cook, stirring constantly, over medium heat until bubbly. Add cooked peas if desired. Garnish with lemon slices, fresh basil or Parmesan cheese.

Serves: 2

Janet Engels

"A low cholesterol version of an old favorite."

MANICOTTI EXTRAORDINAIRE

12 manicotti shells
1 (32-ounce) jar meatless
  spaghetti sauce
3 tablespoons butter
⅓ cup chopped white
  onion
1 clove garlic, finely
  chopped
1 pound Italian sausage
½ pound fresh mushrooms,
  sliced
1 (10-ounce) package frozen
  chopped spinach, thawed
  and well drained
⅓ cup grated fresh
  Parmesan cheese
½ teaspoon dried Italian
  seasonings
¾ teaspoon salt
Pepper to taste
2 eggs, beaten
2 tablespoons milk

Cheese Sauce:
¼ cup margarine
¼ cup flour
2 cups milk
½ cup shredded mozzarella

Cook manicotti shells according to package directions. Rinse in cold water. Drain well; set aside. In a large skillet, melt butter. Sauté onion, garlic, sausage and mushrooms until meat is brown. Remove from heat and drain well. Stir in drained spinach, Parmesan cheese, seasonings, salt and pepper. Stir in beaten eggs and milk. *For cheese sauce*, melt margarine in a medium saucepan. Stir in flour. Add milk all at once. Cook and stir over medium heat until thickened. Remove from heat. Stir in cheese until melted. With a small spoon, fill each manicotti shell with ⅓ cup sausage filling. Spread half of the cheese sauce in the bottom of a 9 x 13-inch baking dish. Spoon or pour half of the spaghetti sauce over the cheese sauce. Top with the filled shells and pour remaining spaghetti sauce over. Top with remaining cheese sauce. Bake, covered, at 375° for 40 minutes.

Serves: 6

Margo Stich

"This colorful dish incorporates both a red tomato-based sauce and a creamy white cheese sauce to make a memorable main dish. Store-bought spaghetti sauce facilitates easy preparation or substitute 4 cups of your favorite homemade sauce."

Straw and Hay

2 tablespoons chopped
  onion
1 clove garlic, minced
½ cup (1 stick) butter or
  margarine, divided
8 ounces fresh mushrooms,
  sliced
8 ounces cooked ham, cubed
1 tablespoon basil
¼ teaspoon nutmeg
¼ teaspoon sage
¼ teaspoon thyme
½ teaspoon salt
Pepper to taste
1 cup whipping cream,
  divided
6 ounces plain fettuccine
6 ounces spinach-flavored
  fettuccine
½ cup grated Parmesan
  cheese

In a medium skillet, sauté onion and garlic in ¼ cup butter until lightly browned. Add mushrooms, ham and seasonings; sauté for 3 more minutes. Stir in ½ cup cream. Cook over medium heat until slightly thickened. Meanwhile, cook fettuccine in boiling salted water for 5 minutes. Drain. In a deep skillet, melt ¼ cup butter. Stir in remaining ½ cup cream. Add cooked fettuccine and toss. Stir in half of the vegetable-ham sauce and Parmesan cheese; toss again. Stir in remaining sauce and serve.

Note: Fresh pasta does not 'grow' when cooked as much as dry pasta.
½ pound dry pasta=¾ pound fresh
  pasta
1 pound dry pasta=1 ½ pounds
  fresh pasta

Serves: 4 to 6

Joan Hinds

"All you need is a tossed salad and crunchy rolls for a delicious lunch or supper."

CHICAGO-STYLE DOUBLE-CRUST PIZZA

Crust:
1 ½ cups very warm water
1 ½ packages active dry
    yeast
¼ cup butter, melted and
    cooled
3 to 3 ½ cups flour, divided
¾ cup yellow cornmeal
1 tablespoon sugar
2 teaspoons salt

Sauce:
3 tablespoons olive oil
1 large onion, chopped
3 cloves garlic, minced
1 (28-ounce) can tomatoes
    and juice, chopped
1 (6-ounce) can tomato paste
1 tablespoon oregano
1 tablespoon basil
1 bay leaf
¼ teaspoon ground red
    pepper
1 tablespoon parsley
4 tablespoons honey
¼ teaspoon black pepper

Topping:
1 pound shredded
    Mozzarella cheese
1 ½ pounds hot Italian
    sausage

In a large bowl, sprinkle yeast over water; let stand until bubbly. Stir in butter. Add 2 ½ cups flour, cornmeal, sugar and salt, stirring until smooth. Knead on lightly floured surface until smooth and elastic, adding remaining flour as needed. Place in a greased bowl, cover and let rise in a warm place for 1 hour or until doubled. *For sauce,* heat oil in a large skillet. Sauté onion until soft. Stir in garlic; sauté for 1 minute. Add remaining sauce ingredients. Bring sauce to a boil, reduce heat and simmer uncovered for 1 hour, stirring occasionally. Remove from heat and take out bay leaf. In another skillet, sauté sausage until brown and cooked thoroughly. Pour off grease. Set aside. To make pizza, punch down dough. Lightly oil bottom and sides of 14-inch deep round pizza pan. Dust with cornmeal. Divide dough into two balls. Roll one ball flat and thin to lay out on pan, covering bottom and sides of pan. Bake at 425° for 5 to 10 minutes. Remove from oven; cool slightly. Spread cheese evenly over crust. Spread sausage evenly over cheese. Roll out second ball of dough, flat and thin; place on top of sausage. Pinch together the edges of the two dough layers, along edge of pan. Return to oven and bake for 5 to 10 minutes. Remove from oven. Ladle sauce, smooth and flat, over top of pizza. Return to oven and bake for 20 to 30 minutes. Let stand 5 minutes before serving.

Serves: 6 to 8

Renee and Bob Jacobson

TORTELLINI BARONESSA

3 cups whipping cream, room temperature
1 egg yolk, room temperature
1 pound grated fresh Parmesan cheese
Salt and pepper to taste
Dash of nutmeg
2 pounds cheese tortellini
4 ounces fresh mushrooms, sautéed in butter
1 cup frozen peas
4 ounces prosciutto ham, cut in strips

Pour cream into saucepan; heat to boiling. In a small bowl, add a small amount of hot cream to egg yolk; whisk to blend. Return egg mixture to saucepan. Reduce heat to simmer. Add Parmesan cheese, a little at a time, whisking constantly until sauce is thick enough to coat a spoon. Season to taste with salt, pepper and nutmeg. Remove from heat. Cook tortellini as directed; drain. Stir into cream sauce. Add sautéed mushrooms, peas and ham. Heat through and serve.

Serves: 6 to 8

Lisa Rodysill

LASAGNA PRIMAVERA

1 (8-ounce) package lasagna
  noodles
3 carrots, cut into ¼-inch
  slices
1 cup broccoli florets
1 cup sliced zucchini,
  ¼-inch thick
1 cup sliced crookneck or
  yellow squash, ¼-inch
  thick
1 (10-ounce) package frozen
  chopped spinach, thawed
1 (15-ounce) carton ricotta
  cheese
1 (26-ounce) jar marinara
  style spaghetti sauce with
  mushrooms
12 ounces mozzarella
  cheese, shredded
½ cup grated Parmesan
  cheese

In a large kettle, boil lasagna
noodles for 5 minutes. Add carrots;
boil for 2 minutes. Add broccoli,
zucchini and squash, boiling for 2
more minutes. Remove from heat
and drain well. Squeeze all the
liquid out of the spinach. In a large
bowl, combine spinach with ricotta
cheese; set aside. In a greased 9 x
13-inch pan, pour one-third of the
marinara sauce, spreading to coat
the bottom evenly. Arrange half of
the noodles over sauce. Layer half
of the vegetables, half of the
spinach mixture and half of the
mozzarella cheese over noodles.
Repeat with one-third of the
marinara sauce and remaining
layers of noodles, vegetables,
spinach mixture and mozzarella
cheese. Pour remaining third of the
marinara sauce on top. Sprinkle
with Parmesan cheese. Bake at 400°
for 30 minutes.

Serves: 8 to 10

Marion Williams

VEGETABLES AND SIDE DISHES

COLLEEN'S BAKED BEANS

4 (1-pound) cans pork 'n
  beans
1 cup brown sugar
½ cup cider vinegar
1 (10-ounce) can diced
  tomatoes and green
  chilies
1 (6-ounce) can tomato paste
1 large bell pepper, seeded
  and diced
3 celery sticks, diced
1 large onion, diced
Salt and pepper to taste
Garlic salt to taste
1 teaspoon dry mustard
6 strips bacon, uncooked

Combine all ingredients, except
bacon strips, in a large crockpot or
casserole dish. Layer bacon strips
on top. Bake uncovered at 275° for 4
hours.

Serves: 12

Colleen Hodges

HARLEQUIN BAKED BEANS

½ pound bacon, chopped
3 cloves garlic, chopped (or
  to taste)
3 large onions, cut in rings
½ cup brown sugar
¼ cup cider vinegar
1 teaspoon dry mustard
1 (28-ounce) can baked
  beans
1 (16-ounce) can dark red
  kidney beans, drained
  and rinsed
1 (16-ounce) can lima beans,
  drained

Brown bacon in a large skillet. Add
garlic and onions; sauté until
tender. Just before bacon becomes
crisp, drain off most of bacon grease
and add brown sugar, vinegar and
mustard. Simmer for 10 minutes,
stirring to prevent sticking. Place
the three types of beans in a large
oven-proof casserole and pour
sauce over beans. Mix gently. Bake,
uncovered, at 325° for one hour or
more, or until ready to serve.

Serves: 8 to 10

Ann Jost

*"I usually double the recipe, cook the bacon
mixture in a dutch oven and add the beans, which
saves washing another pan! Adding 2 pounds of
ground beef, browned and drained, turns this
into a main dish."*

DILLED BEAN AND CARROT STICKS

2 cups cider vinegar
¾ cup water
¾ cup sugar
1 tablespoon salt
1 ½ teaspoons dried dill
    weed or 1 ½ tablespoons
    chopped fresh dill
1 teaspoon onion powder
2 cups carrots, cut in 3-inch
    sticks
2 cups trimmed whole fresh
    green beans

In a large non-corrosive saucepan, combine vinegar, water, sugar, salt, dill and onion powder. Bring to a boil, reduce heat and simmer for 15 minutes. Add carrots and beans, cover and simmer until crisp-tender, about 3 to 5 minutes. Place mixture in a jar with a tight-fitting lid. Cover and refrigerate for at least 12 hours. Drain and serve cold.

Yield: 4 cups

Nina Sudor

"Nice accompaniment to a salad buffet and good with burgers. Will keep several days, refrigerated."

HERBED GREEN BEANS

1 pound fresh green beans
4 tablespoons butter
½ cup chopped onion or 2
    tablespoons dry minced
    onion
½ clove garlic, minced
¼ cup minced celery
½ cup minced fresh parsley
1 teaspoon rosemary
1 teaspoon basil
¾ teaspoon salt

Cook beans in boiling water while preparing sauce. In saucepan, melt butter. Add onion, garlic and celery; cook for 5 minutes. Add parsley, rosemary, basil and salt. Cover and simmer for 10 minutes. Drain beans; toss with herb sauce just before serving.

Serves: 6

Judy Mellinger

ITALIAN BEANS WITH WATER CHESTNUTS AND ALMONDS

3 (9-ounce) packages frozen
  Italian cut green beans
1 (8-ounce) can water
  chestnuts, sliced, drained
Butter to taste
1 (2 ½ ounce) package
  slivered almonds, toasted

Cook beans according to package directions; drain. Add sliced water chestnuts to beans. Add butter to taste and sprinkle with toasted almonds.

Serves: 8 to 10

Nancy Brubaker

"Easy! Enjoy the contrasting texture of water chestnuts and slivered almonds."

BROCCOLI FOR GARLIC LOVERS

1 ½ pounds broccoli
4 tablespoons olive oil
8 medium cloves garlic,
  peeled
¼ teaspoon turmeric
½ teaspoon salt

Cut broccoli into flowerets. Cut stems diagonally into ½-inch slices. Rinse with water and drain for 5 minutes. Heat oil in large saucepan over medium heat. Add garlic and sauté for 2 minutes. Add turmeric. Stir to mix well. Add broccoli to pan and let sizzle for 1 minute. Add salt, stirring to mix well. Cook, covered, for 8 to 10 minutes. Uncover and cook until moisture evaporates.

Yield: 4 servings

Zola Vantaggi

"Cauliflower may be substituted for broccoli."

SESAME BROCCOLI

1 ½ pounds broccoli,
   trimmed
¼ cup butter or margarine
Toasted sesame seeds

Cut stems of broccoli into 1-inch pieces. Cut flowerets into 1 to 1 ½ - inch pieces. Fill Dutch oven half full of water; bring to boiling. Drop broccoli stems into water; boil 3 to 4 minutes. Add flowerets; boil 2 minutes longer. Drain. Drop broccoli into ice water until cold. Drain and refrigerate, covered. To serve, melt butter in a large skillet. Add broccoli. Cook over medium heat, stirring often, just until heated through, about 5 minutes. Garnish with sesame seeds.

Serves: 4 to 5

Diane Nippoldt

BROCCOLI SUPREME

2 (10-ounce) packages
   frozen chopped broccoli
1 (10 ¾-ounce) can cream of
   mushroom soup
1 cup cubed Velveeta cheese
2 eggs, beaten
1 cup salad dressing (such
   as Miracle Whip)
2 tablespoons chopped
   onion
Salt and pepper to taste
1 cup cheese cracker crumbs

Steam broccoli for 5 minutes and drain. Combine all ingredients, except cracker crumbs, with broccoli. Pour into a greased 9 x 13-inch casserole dish, sprinkle crumbs on top and bake at 400° for 30 minutes.

Serves: 6 to 8

Ellen Hurley

"Excellent for brunch, evening meals, or late suppers."

BRUSSEL SPROUTS ALMONDINE

1 ½ pounds fresh brussel
 sprouts
½ teaspoon sugar
1 inch of boiling water in
 saucepan
3 tablespoons butter, melted
1 tablespoon lemon juice
3 tablespoons slivered,
 toasted almonds

Wash brussel sprouts. Remove imperfect outer leaves and stems. Soak for 20 minutes in cold salted water, using 1 teaspoon salt to one quart of water. Place sprouts in saucepan. Add sugar and boiling water. Cover. Cook 10 to 15 minutes until just tender. Lift lid occasionally to retain green color. Drain off water. Combine butter, lemon juice and almonds. Add to sprouts and stir gently to blend.

Serves: 6 to 8

Almyra Whitehead

BLAUKRAUT (RED CABBAGE)

1 large head red cabbage
 (about 2 pounds)
1 ½ tablespoons lard or
 shortening
1 medium onion, finely
 chopped
2 bay leaves
10 whole cloves
2 tablespoons cider or red
 wine vinegar
½ teaspoon sugar
Water
1 or 2 large apples
Salt
1 teaspoon cornstarch

Cut cabbage in quarters and remove stem. Cut finely. Melt shortening in a large pot. Add onions and cook, stirring occasionally, until lightly browned. Add cabbage; stir until fat is absorbed. Add bay leaves, cloves, vinegar, sugar and a little water to steam. Steam, covered, for 30 minutes. Peel, core and slice apples about ¼-inch thick. Add apples and salt to taste; steam an additional 30 minutes. Mix cornstarch with a little cold water. If there is about a cup of liquid left in the pot, add cornstarch mixture and stir in. If not, add water and then the cornstarch mixture. Remove bay leaves and cloves before serving.

Serves: 6

Diane Nippoldt

CARROT DELIGHT

4 tablespoons butter
1 pound carrots, peeled and
  sliced
¼ cup whipping cream
Salt and white pepper to
  taste
Freshly grated nutmeg

In a medium sized saucepan, melt butter. Add carrots and cook slowly over medium-low heat until they are soft. Carefully pour them into a blender or food processor and puree until smooth. Add whipping cream. Return carrots to the pan. Season with the salt, pepper, and grated nutmeg (about ½ to 1 teaspoon). Stir well and reheat, if necessary, over very low heat. Serve hot.

Serves: 4

Janet Engels

GLAZED BABY CARROTS

1 pound fresh baby carrots
2 tablespoons brown sugar
3 tablespoons butter
1 teaspoon real maple syrup

Cook carrots until tender. Combine carrots, brown sugar, butter and syrup. Stir to mix well. Serve.

Serves: 4

Julie Huettner

CARROT AND PARSNIP MEDLEY

6 to 8 medium carrots, peeled and cut into 3-inch julienne strips
¾ cup water
½ teaspoon salt
3 medium parsnips, cut into 3-inch julienne strips
2 ½ tablespoons butter
1 ½ tablespoons brown sugar

Place carrots in a medium saucepan and cover with water. Add salt and bring to a boil. Reduce heat and simmer, covered, until crisp-tender, 5 to 7 minutes. Remove carrots from the pan with a slotted spoon and transfer to a bowl. Cover to keep warm. Add parsnips to the simmering water (add more water if necessary to cover). Return to boil, lower heat and simmer about 5 minutes or until crisp-tender. Drain. Meanwhile, melt the butter in a large deep skillet. Add brown sugar and stir until sugar dissolves. Add the drained parsnips to the carrots. Carefully add the carrot-parsnip mixture to the butter mixture in skillet. Toss gently to coat vegetables with the butter mixture. Heat through and serve.

Serves: 6 to 8

Nina Sudor

ORANGE CARROTS

6 to 8 fresh carrots
½ cup water
1 teaspoon sugar
¼ teaspoon salt
3 to 4 tablespoons butter or margarine
½ cup orange marmalade

Peel carrots and cut into sticks or diagonal slices. Combine water, sugar and salt in a saucepan and bring to a boil. Add carrots; cover and reduce heat to simmer. Cook carrots until tender-crisp, about 10 minutes. Add butter and marmalade. Increase heat to bring to a boil. Cook, uncovered, until syrupy.

Serves: 6 to 8

Sheila Kramer

GOURMET CARROTS

1 ½ pounds carrots, peeled
and cut into 4-inch
lengths
3 tablespoons unsalted
butter
3 tablespoons almond
liqueur (Amaretto
preferred)
¼ teaspoon ground ginger,
or to taste
⅓ cup sliced unblanched
almonds, lightly toasted
Salt and pepper to taste

Steam carrots over boiling water,
covered, for 10 minutes. Quarter the
carrots lengthwise. In a skillet, cook
carrots in butter over moderate
heat, stirring occasionally, for 3
minutes. Stir in liqueur and ginger.
Cook the mixture, covered, over
low heat for 3 minutes. Stir in
almonds. Add salt and pepper to
taste. Simmer the mixture, covered,
for 1 minute. Serve immediately.
Serves: 6 to 8

Renda Meloy

STEAMED CARROT AND ZUCCHINI JULIENNE

1 pound carrots, cut into
2-inch julienne strips
1 ½ pounds zucchini, cut
into 2-inch julienne
strips, with core
discarded
2 tablespoons butter or
margarine
Fresh lemon juice
Salt and pepper to taste

Steam carrots over boiling water for
3 minutes or until they are crisp-
tender. Rinse under cold water to
stop cooking process. Drain
thoroughly, saving water, and
transfer to a large bowl. Using the
same water, steam the zucchini for
1 or 2 minutes. Rinse and drain as
for carrots. At this point, vegetables
may be covered and refrigerated. To
serve, melt butter or margarine in a
large skillet over low heat. Toss the
vegetables in the butter until they
are heated through. Season with
lemon juice, salt and pepper.
Serves: 10

Sally Duffy

BAKED CORN PUDDING

1 (16-ounce) can cream style
   corn
1 (16-ounce) can whole
   kernel corn, drained
½ cup butter, melted
2 eggs, beaten
¼ cup sugar (or less to
   taste)
1 cup sour cream
1 (9-ounce) package corn
   bread mix

Combine all ingredients, mixing well. Pour into a greased 9 x 13-inch pan. Bake at 350° for 50 to 60 minutes. Serve hot.

Serves: 10

Maren Stocke

CORN PUDDING

2 cups whole-kernel corn (if
   using canned corn, drain)
1 cup milk
2 eggs, beaten
¼ teaspoon salt
¼ teaspoon pepper
¼ cup sugar
3 tablespoons margarine

Combine corn, milk, eggs, salt, pepper and sugar. Mix well. Melt margarine in a 1-quart casserole dish. Add pudding mixture. Bake at 350° for 1 hour.

Serves: 4

Dorothy Hartman

ONION KUCHEN

1 pound sweet onions,
   chopped (about
   3 ½ cups)
6 tablespoons butter,
   divided
4 eggs, divided
1 ½ cups sour cream
½ teaspoon salt
1 teaspoon caraway seed
½ cup milk
1 ¾ cups buttermilk biscuit
   mix

In a 10-inch skillet, sauté onions in 4 tablespoons butter for 20 to 30 minutes. In a medium bowl, beat 3 eggs thoroughly. Gradually stir in onions, sour cream, salt and caraway seed; set aside. Melt remaining 2 tablespoons butter; set aside. In medium bowl beat 1 egg with milk to combine. Add melted butter and biscuit mix. Stir until barely moistened. Pour batter into a well-greased 7 x 12-inch glass loaf pan and spread evenly. Spread onion mixture over dough. Bake at 375° for 30 minutes or until browned. Cut into squares and serve warm.

Serves: 4 to 6

Almyra Whitehead

QUICK MINTED PEAS

4 teaspoons butter or
   margarine, divided
1 to 4 sprigs fresh mint
1 (10-ounce) package frozen
   petite peas
¼ teaspoon salt

Place 2 teaspoons butter, mint and frozen peas in a 1-quart saucepan. Cook, covered, over low heat, shaking pan occasionally until heated through, 12 to 15 minutes. Remove lid to let any extra moisture escape. Remove mint. Stir in salt and remaining butter.

Serves: 4

Diane Nippoldt

COLCANNON (IRISH POTATOES)

6 large potatoes, peeled and
  diced
2 pounds cabbage, cut fine
½ cup (1 stick) butter, cut in
  1-inch cubes
2 tablespoons onion or
  chives, chopped
½ cup milk
Salt and pepper to taste
1 ½ cups grated Cheddar
  cheese

Boil potatoes in salted water until soft; drain. Boil cabbage in salted water for about 10 minutes; drain. Mash potatoes. Stir in butter, chives or onions, milk, cabbage, salt and pepper. Place in greased 2-quart baking dish. Sprinkle cheese on top. Bake at 350° for 30 minutes.

Yield: 6 to 8 servings

Zola Vantaggi

DELICIOUS POTATO CASSEROLE

8 medium potatoes,
  unpeeled
1 bay leaf
1 (10 ¾-ounce) can cream of
  chicken soup
1 ½ cups sour cream
½ teaspoon salt
¼ teaspoon pepper
3 green onions, sliced,
  including tops
1 ½ cups grated Cheddar
  cheese
¼ cup butter, melted

Topping:
½ cup shredded Cheddar
  cheese
½ cup crushed cornflakes

In a large kettle, boil potatoes in salted water with bay leaf for 15 minutes. Drain. Discard bay leaf. Peel and slice potatoes into a greased 3-quart casserole. In a large bowl, mix together soup, sour cream, salt, pepper, onions, 1½ cups grated cheese and butter. Pour over the potatoes. Bake, uncovered, at 350° for 30 minutes. Combine the topping ingredients and sprinkle over top of casserole. Bake 10 to 15 minutes longer.

Serves: 8 to 10

Janet Engels

HASH BROWN BAKE

½ cup (1 stick) butter
½ cup processed American
cheese
3 cups half and half
1 teaspoon salt
1 (24-ounce) package frozen
hash brown potato
squares
½ cup grated Parmesan
cheese

Heat butter, American cheese and half and half until cheese is melted. Add salt. Place potato squares in a 9 x 13-inch pan. Pour cheese mixture over top. Cover with aluminum foil. Bake at 325° for 30 minutes. Sprinkle Parmesan cheese on top. Bake, uncovered, 10 to 15 minutes, until lightly browned on top.

Serves: 8

Julie Larson

HASH BROWN POTATOES

1 (10 ¾ -ounce) can cream of
chicken soup
1 cup grated Cheddar cheese
½ cup chopped onion
1 teaspoon salt
½ teaspoon pepper
1 (16-ounce) carton sour
cream
1 (2-pound) bag frozen hash
browns, thawed
½ cup (1 stick) margarine,
melted
1 ½ cups corn flake crumbs

Combine soup, cheese, onion, salt, pepper and sour cream in a large bowl. Mix thoroughly. Add potatoes, mixing well. Pour into a lightly buttered 9 x 13-inch baking dish. Combine melted margarine and corn flake crumbs, mixing well. Spread over potatoes. Bake at 350° for 1 hour.

Serves: 8

Sheila Kramer

OVEN-FRIED POTATOES

3 medium potatoes, peeled
   or unpeeled
2 tablespoons margarine,
   melted
1 ½ teaspoons olive oil
Paprika

Halve potatoes lengthwise and slice into ½-inch thick strips. Combine margarine and olive oil. Add potatoes to coat well. Arrange potato strips in single layer on a non-stick baking sheet. Sprinkle with paprika. Bake at 450° for 30 to 40 minutes.

Serves: 6

Zola Vantaggi

OVEN ROASTED POTATO WEDGES

4 medium-sized baking
   potatoes, peeled
¼ cup butter, melted
¾ teaspoon dried thyme
Salt

Cut potatoes in half lengthwise. Slice each half in thirds, making 3 wedge-shaped pieces. Blanch wedges in rapidly boiling water to cover for 3 minutes. Drain and pat dry. Place potatoes side by side in single layer in a greased 9 x 13-inch baking dish. Drizzle melted butter over potatoes and sprinkle with thyme and salt. Bake at 450° for 15 minutes. Turn potatoes and bake another 15 minutes.

Serves: 4 to 6

Carolyn Rorie

"Rosemary may be substituted for thyme."

POTATO GRATIN WITH BOURSIN CHEESE

2 cups heavy cream
1 (5-ounce) package garlic-
  herb Boursin cheese
3 pounds new potatoes,
  sliced
Salt and pepper to taste
1 ½ tablespoons chopped
  fresh parsley

Heat cream and cheese over medium heat, stirring constantly, until smooth. Lightly grease a 9 x 13-inch pan. Arrange half the potatoes on bottom in overlapping rows. Season with salt and pepper. Pour half of cheese mixture over potatoes. Repeat layers. Bake, covered, at 400° for 1 hour until potatoes are fork tender. Sprinkle with fresh parsley before serving.

Serves: 8 to 10

Julie Larson

ROSEMARY POTATOES

20 medium red potatoes
½ cup olive oil
10 garlic cloves, minced
2 tablespoons chopped
  fresh rosemary
Salt and pepper to taste

Cook potatoes in a large pot of boiling water just until tender, about 20 minutes. Drain and cool. Peel potatoes and cut in half. Place potatoes in a large roasting pan. Add oil, garlic, rosemary, salt and pepper. Toss to coat potatoes. Bake at 375° for 1 hour, or until potatoes are crisp and brown. Turn occasionally during baking.

Serves: 10

Sally Duffy

Savory Roast Potatoes

½ cup (1 stick) butter or
  margarine
8 large baking potatoes
1 tablespoon seasoned salt
½ cup chicken broth

Melt butter in a 9 x 13-inch baking pan. Pare potatoes. Roll in melted butter to coat well. Sprinkle with seasoned salt. Bake, uncovered, at 350° for 1 hour. Remove pan from oven; turn potatoes. Add chicken broth. Bake 1 hour longer, turning several times.

Serves: 8

Renda Meloy

Scalloped Potatoes

4 to 5 large potatoes, peeled,
  sliced and boiled
Salt and pepper to taste
¼ cup butter or margarine
1 (10 ¾-ounce) can cream of
  celery soup
½ soup can milk
6 strips of bacon, cooked
  and crumbled
1 cup grated Cheddar cheese

Place potatoes in a greased 9 x 9-inch baking dish. Season with salt and pepper. Dot with butter. Combine cream of celery soup and milk, mixing until smooth. Pour over potatoes. Sprinkle with bacon and Cheddar cheese. Bake at 350° for 30 minutes.

Serves: 6

Sheila Kramer

SKILLET NEW POTATOES WITH GARLIC

2 pounds small new
  potatoes
2 tablespoons margarine
2 tablespoons cooking oil
2 large peeled, whole garlic
  cloves
½ teaspoon salt
Ground pepper to taste

Wash potatoes. Peel narrow band
around the center of each potato, if
desired. Combine all ingredients in
a large heavy skillet. Cover and
cook over low heat for 40 to 60
minutes, or until potatoes are
brown and tender. Shake pan occasionally during cooking. Remove
garlic and serve.

Serves: 4

Lois Swanson

SWEDISH GREEN POTATOES

6 large potatoes
¼ pound soft butter
¾ cup sour cream
1 teaspoon sugar
2 teaspoons salt
¼ teaspoon white pepper
2 tablespoons chopped
  chives
1 ½ teaspoons dried dill
1 (10-ounce) package frozen
  chopped spinach,
  partially cooked and well
  drained

Boil potatoes until tender. Drain
and mash. Combine potatoes,
butter, sour cream, sugar, salt and
pepper. Whip until light and fluffy.
Add chives, dill and spinach. Place
in a shallow greased 2-quart casserole dish. Bake at 350° for 30
minutes or until piping hot.

Serves: 6 to 8

Faye Waldo

SAUERKRAUT

1 or 2 pork hocks
1 or 2 medium yellow
  onions, chopped
3 quarts sauerkraut (in glass
  jars, plastic bags, or
  fresh), drained and
  lightly rinsed
1 tablespoon lard or
  shortening
1 bay leaf
12 whole dried juniper
  berries (in spice section)
1 apple, peeled and
  chopped
1 cup dry white wine,
  optional
1 medium potato, peeled
  and finely grated
Freshly ground black
  pepper to taste

Place all of the ingredients in a heavy kettle. Cover and simmer gently for 3 hours. (Or use pressure cooker for 1 ½ to 2 hours, or until meat is tender.) Remove pork hock, bay leaf and juniper berries. After pork hock has cooled, remove fatty outer layer and discard. Remove any lean pork and mix into sauerkraut. Discard bone. (Can be made ahead to this point and refrigerated.) Heat through before serving.

Serves: 6

Diane Nippoldt

SPINACH PROVENCALE

2 (10-ounce) packages
  frozen chopped spinach
1 tablespoon olive oil
1 large onion, chopped
1 clove garlic, minced
Butter or margarine
2 eggs, beaten
1 cup freshly grated
  Parmesan cheese, divided
Salt and pepper, to taste

Cook spinach according to package directions, or thaw before cooking. Squeeze out as much liquid from spinach as possible. Heat olive oil in large skillet. Sauté onion and garlic for about 2 to 3 minutes, until onion is transparent. Add spinach; mix thoroughly. Remove from heat and cool slightly. Stir in eggs and ½ cup grated Parmesan cheese. Add salt and pepper to taste. Pour into a buttered medium-sized baking dish. Sprinkle remaining Parmesan cheese over the top and dot with butter. Bake at 375° for 10 to 15 minutes. Serve steaming hot.

Serves: 4 to 6

Diane Nippoldt

TENNESSEE SUMMER SQUASH

12 yellow summer squash (6
   to 7 inches each)
Water
6 tablespoons butter, melted
2 medium onions, chopped
2 teaspoons sugar
Salt and black pepper, to
   taste
1 teaspoon ground nutmeg
1 cup cracker crumbs

Cook squash covered with water for 15 minutes or until just tender. Cut in half. Carefully scrape out the pulp. Place shells in a shallow greased pan. Mash pulp in a large bowl. Stir in remaining ingredients, mixing well. Fill shells. Bake at 300° for 15 to 20 minutes. Serve hot.

Serves: 8 to 10

Almyra Whitehead

SUPREME CANDIED SWEET POTATOES

8 medium sweet potatoes or
   yams
½ cup (1 stick) butter
2 cups granulated sugar
1 cup light brown sugar,
   packed
¼ cup maple syrup
1 tablespoon flour
1 tablespoon vinegar
1 ½ tablespoons boiling
   water

Wash potatoes. In a large saucepan, cover potatoes with water and boil until just tender, 20 to 30 minutes. Drain and place potatoes on a rack until cool enough to handle. Meanwhile, melt butter in a heavy medium saucepan. Add remaining ingredients. Boil gently for 5 minutes. Keep warm so syrup stays liquid. Reheat if syrup starts to harden. Peel and cut potatoes into ¾-inch lengthwise pieces. Layer in a 3-quart baking dish. Pour the warm syrup over potatoes. Bake at 350° for 1 hour, basting generously every 15 minutes. (Can be made the day before. Reheat to serve.) Serve hot.

Serves: 6 to 8

Maren Stocke

"These are rich and delicious! They will make you famous as they did my mother."

TOMATOES BAKED WITH SPINACH AND FETA

6 medium tomatoes,
  hollowed out and
  drained
½ cup finely chopped
  onions
¼ cup butter or margarine
2 (10-ounce) packages
  frozen chopped spinach,
  thawed and drained
2 eggs
½ pound feta cheese,
  crumbled
¼ cup chopped fresh
  parsley
½ teaspoon dill
½ teaspoon salt
⅛ teaspoon pepper
Bread crumbs

Prepare tomatoes. In a large saucepan, sauté onions in butter for 5 minutes, until golden. Add spinach; stir to mix well. Remove from heat. Beat eggs in a large bowl. Stir in cheese, parsley, dill, salt, pepper and spinach-onion mixture. Fill tomatoes with mixture. Sprinkle with bread crumbs. Bake at 350° for 20 to 30 minutes.

Serves: 6

Eleni George

LEMON RICE

¼ cup butter or margarine
1 medium onion, minced
1 cup thinly sliced celery
2 cups sliced mushrooms
½ teaspoon thyme
½ teaspoon salt
Pepper to taste
2 cups water
Rind of 1 lemon, finely
  grated
½ cup lemon juice
1 ½ cups uncooked long
  grain white rice

Sauté onion in butter until transparent. Add celery and mushrooms; sauté 2 minutes longer. Add thyme, salt and pepper to taste. Stir to blend. Remove from heat; set aside. In a 2-quart saucepan, combine water, lemon rind and lemon juice. Bring mixture to a boil. Add rice and onion mixture. Return to boil. Stir, reducing heat to low. Cover and simmer 20 minutes longer.

Serves: 6

Diane Nippoldt

PILAF OF BARLEY, MUSHROOMS, PEAS AND RADICCHIO

2 tablespoons olive oil
1 medium onion, chopped
1 sprig fresh rosemary or
    ½ teaspoon dried
    rosemary, crumbled
⅔ pound mushrooms,
    sliced
⅔ cup pearl barley or
    quick-cooking barley
1 cup chicken stock
Salt and pepper to taste
1 cup tiny frozen peas
2 cups radicchio or escarole,
    cut into strips

Heat oil in heavy medium saucepan over medium-low heat. Add onion and rosemary and cook until onion is translucent, stirring occasionally, about 8 minutes. Add mushrooms and cook until they begin to soften, stirring frequently, about 5 minutes. Add barley and stir 2 minutes. Add chicken stock, salt and pepper; bring to a boil. Reduce heat to low, cover and cook until barley is almost tender, 50 minutes for pearl barley or 12 minutes for quick-cooking barley. Stir peas and radicchio into pilaf. Cover and cook until peas are tender, about 3 minutes. Serve immediately.

Serves: 2 to 4

Diane Nippoldt

MUSHROOM HERB RICE

1 ½ cups uncooked rice
3 chicken bouillon cubes
¾ teaspoon salt
¾ teaspoon rosemary
¾ teaspoon marjoram
¾ teaspoon thyme
1 ½ teaspoons chopped
    chives
3 cups cold water
1 ½ tablespoons butter
1 (4 ½-ounce) jar sliced
    mushrooms

Combine all ingredients except mushrooms in a large saucepan. Heat until mixture comes to a boil; reduce heat. Stir once with a fork. Cover tightly and simmer for 15 to 20 minutes or until all liquid is absorbed. Stir in sliced mushrooms.

Serves: 8

Nancy Brubaker

Rice and Pecan Casserole

1 pound mushrooms, sliced
4 green onions, sliced
1 clove garlic, minced
1 cup (2 sticks) unsalted
  sweet butter
2 cups uncooked brown rice
½ teaspoon dried thyme
  leaves
¼ teaspoon turmeric
1 teaspoon salt
¼ teaspoon freshly ground
  pepper
1 ½ cups chopped pecans
6 cups beef stock or broth (3
  cans (10 ¾-ounce)
  condensed beef broth
  mixed with 2 ¼ cups
  water can be substituted)
Whole pecans
Green onions, tops only,
  sliced

Sauté mushrooms, onions and garlic in butter in a large Dutch oven until onions are golden, 5 to 7 minutes. Stir in rice. Cook, stirring with fork, until rice is hot, about 3 minutes. Add thyme, turmeric, salt and pepper. Stir in chopped pecans. Pour in beef stock. (May be prepared ahead to this point and refrigerated.) Heat to boiling. Bake at 400° for 1 hour and 20 minutes, until liquid is absorbed and rice is tender. Adjust seasoning to taste. Garnish with pecans and onion slices.

Serves: 10 to 12

Renda Meloy

Spiced Rice

2 cups water
1 cup uncooked regular rice
1-inch piece fresh unpeeled
  ginger
1 teaspoon salt
¼ cup seedless raisins
¼ cup currants
2 ounces dried apricots,
  chopped
½ teaspoon ground nutmeg
2 teaspoons minced shallots
2 tablespoons lemon juice
½ teaspoon coriander
1 tablespoon olive oil
Freshly ground pepper to
  taste
½ cup pine nuts, toasted

In a medium saucepan, bring water to a boil. Add rice, ginger and salt. Cook, covered, for 20 minutes until rice is tender. Remove ginger. In another pan, cover the dried fruit with hot water and soak until plump, about 30 minutes. Drain. Place the cooked rice in a warm, buttered 2-quart casserole. Stir in nutmeg, shallots, lemon juice, coriander, olive oil and pepper. Fold in fruit and pine nuts. Heat in a 325° oven just until hot, about 20 minutes.

Serves: 4 to 6

Bunny Young

POLENTA NOTES

2 cups water
1 cup half and half
1 cup yellow cornmeal
¼ cup olive oil
1 medium onion, finely
    chopped
½ cup chopped oil-packed
    sun-dried tomatoes
Fresh basil, minced
¼ teaspoon cayenne pepper
1 teaspoon salt
2 cups grated sharp Italian
    cheese

In a deep saucepan, bring water and half and half to a boil. Slowly add cornmeal, whisking constantly until thoroughly blended. Reduce heat to low and cook, uncovered, for 30 minutes, continuing to whisk until the polenta is smooth and creamy. (You may need to add a little more half and half if it seems too thick.) In a small skillet, heat olive oil over medium heat. Add onion and sauté until soft. Add tomatoes, basil, pepper and salt. Sauté until basil is wilted. Stir onion mixture into polenta; mix well. Lightly oil a platter or baking sheet. Pour mixture onto it. Shape into a rectangle about 9 x 7 inches and about ¼-inch thick. Refrigerate, uncovered, until firm. Cut the polenta into large music notes and place on a greased, foil-lined baking sheet. Sprinkle the notes with cheese and bake at 350° for 5 minutes. Turn heat to broil. Place under broiler to brown the cheese, about 2 minutes.

Serves: 8

Kay Love-Caskey

SPATZLE

3 cups flour
1 cup water
4 eggs
1 teaspoon salt
2 tablespoons butter

Combine flour, water, eggs and salt. Beat well. Bring a large pot of salted water to a boil. On a cutting board, cut dough into small pieces. (You can also use a spatzle press to form the noodles.) Drop into the boiling water. Boil until noodles float to the surface, indicating they are done. Remove with a slotted spoon, allowing water to drain off. Mix with butter. Serve warm.

Serves: 4 to 6

Diane Nippoldt

CRANBERRY-APPLE RELISH

1 pound cranberries, rinsed
1 ½ cups water
4 large unpeeled cooking
    apples, cored and sliced
2 cups sugar
1 teaspoon ground
    cinnamon
Dash of ground cloves

Combine all ingredients in a heavy pan. Bring to a boil. Simmer 15 minutes or until cranberries have all popped. Cool, then refrigerate until ready to serve.

Yield: 8 cups

Zola Vantaggi

SCALLOPED PINEAPPLE

¾ cup butter
¾ cup sugar
3 eggs
¼ cup milk
2 tablespoons lemon juice
1 (20-ounce) can crushed
   pineapple, with juice
4 cups day-old bread, cubed
   (about 8 slices)

In a large bowl, cream butter and sugar together. Beat in eggs, milk and lemon juice. Stir in pineapple with juice and bread cubes. Mix well. Pour into a lightly buttered 9 x 13-inch baking dish and bake at 325° for about 1 hour or until top is golden.

Serves: 6 to 8

Joan Hinds

"This makes an unusual and delicious accompaniment to ham, chicken or turkey."

SHERRIED HOT FRUIT

1 (16-ounce) can pears
1 (16-ounce) can dark pitted
   cherries
1 (16-ounce) can pineapple
   chunks
4 bananas, sliced (more if
   desired)
1 (16-ounce) can peaches
½ cup (1 stick) butter,
   divided
½ cup brown sugar
1 (2 ½ -ounce) package
   slivered almonds
½ (16 ounce) package
   macaroons, crumbled
¼ cup sherry or juice from
   canned fruit

Drain fruit and cut into bite-sized pieces. In a 3-quart casserole dish, layer fruit, dotting each layer with butter, a sprinkle of brown sugar and almonds. Top with macaroons. Sprinkle with sherry or fruit juice. Bake at 350° for 20 minutes.

Serves: 10 to 12

Sheila Kramer

"ENJOY!!!!!"

BREADS

HEALTHY APPLESAUCE BREAD

¾ cup quick-cooking
    oatmeal
¼ cup flour
1 teaspoon baking powder
1 teaspoon baking soda
½ teaspoon salt
1 ½ teaspoons cinnamon
¾ cup sugar
3 egg whites
6 tablespoons canola oil
1 teaspoon vanilla
1 cup applesauce
¾ cup plain yogurt

Spray a 9 x 5-inch loaf pan with nonstick cooking spray; set aside. In a large mixing bowl, stir together oatmeal, flour, baking powder, baking soda, salt, cinnamon and sugar. Set aside. In a large bowl, using an electric mixer, beat together the egg whites, oil, vanilla, applesauce and yogurt. With mixer on medium speed, blend in dry ingredients, beating just until smooth. Pour into prepared pan. Bake at 350° for 50 to 55 minutes or until tester comes out clean. Let cool 10 minutes in pan, then turn out onto wire rack. Slice and serve warm or at room temperature.

Yield: 1 loaf

Margo Stich

BEER BREAD

3 cups self-rising flour
¼ cup sugar
1 (12-ounce) can beer
¼ cup melted butter
    (optional)

Grease and flour one 9 x 5-inch bread pan; set aside. Mix flour, sugar and beer together in a bowl. Pour into prepared pan. Bake at 375° for 40 minutes. Pour melted butter over top. Return pan to oven and bake an additional 20 minutes. (You can omit the melted butter and bake loaf for 60 minutes.)

Yield: 1 loaf

Kathy Johnstone

"This recipe works especially well using a popular light Mexican beer and is a wonderful accompaniment to Chicken Noodle Soup♪."

CHEESY CORN BREAD

1 large onion, chopped
3 tablespoons butter or
  margarine
2 eggs
6 tablespoons milk
1 (17-ounce) can cream-style
  corn
1 (16-ounce) package
  cornmeal muffin mix
2 cups shredded sharp
  Cheddar cheese

In a medium skillet, sauté onion in butter or margarine until golden; set aside. In a medium bowl, mix eggs and milk until blended. Add corn and muffin mix. Mix well. Add sauteed onion, stirring to mix. Spread corn bread batter into a greased 9 x 13-inch pan. Sprinkle with cheese. Bake at 425° (400° for glass pan) for 35 minutes or until puffed and golden. Let stand 10 minutes before cutting into squares. May be refrigerated or frozen and reheated.

Yield: 16 servings

Kay Love-Caskey

"A great accompaniment to go with chili."

LITE CORN BREAD

1 cup yellow cornmeal
1 cup flour
¼ cup sugar
4 teaspoons baking powder
½ teaspoon salt
1 cup milk
3 extra large egg whites
¼ cup sweet, unsalted corn
  oil margarine

Grease a 10-inch cast-iron skillet and place in preheated 425° oven. Combine cornmeal, flour, sugar, baking powder and salt; mix well. Add milk, egg whites and margarine. Stir with a few rapid strokes, until dry ingredients are just moistened. Pour batter into hot skillet. Bake at 425° for 20 to 25 minutes or until edges are light brown and bread is firm.

Yield: 1 (10-inch) round bread

Cherie Miles

KENTUCKY SPOON BREAD

2 cups cold water
1 cup white cornmeal
1 teaspoon salt
1 cup milk
3 eggs, well beaten
3 tablespoons corn oil

Mix cold water, cornmeal and salt in a large saucepan. Place over medium-high heat. Bring to a boil. Boil for 5 minutes, stirring constantly. Remove from heat. Stir in milk, eggs and oil. Pour into well-greased 8 x 12-inch glass baking dish. Bake at 400° for 25 minutes, until bread is firm and well browned.

Serves: 6

Almyra Whitehead

"This bread freezes well in a resealable plastic bag."

DATE BRAN BREAD

1 (16-ounce) package date
  quick bread mix
¾ cup shreds of whole bran
  cereal
1 cup buttermilk
2 tablespoons honey
1 egg
1 tablespoon wheat germ

Cream cheese
Orange marmalade or
  preserves

In a large bowl, combine quick bread mix, bran cereal, buttermilk, honey and egg. Stir by hand until dry particles are moistened. Pour into a greased and floured (bottom only) 9 x 5-inch loaf pan. Sprinkle wheat germ over batter. Bake at 375° for 45 to 55 minutes, until done. Cool 15 minutes and then remove from pan. Slice and serve with cream cheese and orange marmalade.

Yield: 1 loaf

Dan Hurley

"Wonderful for brunch or just a mid-morning snack."

ENGLISH COCONUT TEA LOAF

1 egg
1 ½ cups milk
½ teaspoon vanilla
¼ teaspoon almond extract
1 cup shredded coconut
3 cups flour
1 tablespoon baking
    powder
½ teaspoon salt
1 cup sugar

Combine egg, milk, vanilla, almond extract and coconut in a blender or food processor for 30 seconds. In a bowl, sift dry ingredients together. Pour liquid mixture over dry ingredients. Stir just until combined. Turn batter into a greased and floured 9 x 5-inch loaf pan. Bake at 350° for 60 to 70 minutes. Chill before slicing.

Yield: 1 loaf

Zola Vantaggi

GRANDMA'S FRUIT BREAD

1 cup dried apricots,
    snipped
1 ½ cups sugar
½ cup shortening
4 eggs
4 cups flour
2 tablespoons baking
    powder
1 teaspoon salt
2 cups milk
1 cup pitted prunes,
    snipped
½ cup walnuts, chopped

In a small bowl, cover apricots with warm water. Let stand for 5 minutes to soften. Drain; set aside. In mixer bowl, cream sugar and shortening together. Add eggs, beating until light. Sift together flour, baking powder and salt. Add alternately to creamed mixture with milk, beating well after each addition. Stir in apricots, prunes and nuts. Pour into 2 greased and floured 9 x 5-inch loaf pans. Bake at 350° for 60 to 65 minutes or until done. Remove from oven and cool in pans for 10 minutes. Remove bread from pans and let cool completely. Wrap and store overnight for best slicing.

Yield: 2 loaves

Nancy Brubaker

"Delicious!"

Hawaiian Bread

2 ¾ cups flour
2 cups sugar
1 teaspoon salt
1 teaspoon baking soda
1 cup chopped nuts
1 cup oil
½ cup shredded coconut
1 cup mashed bananas
3 eggs
1 teaspoon vanilla
1 (8-ounce) can crushed
    pineapple, with juice

Combine flour, sugar, salt and baking soda. Add nuts and set aside. In another bowl, combine remaining ingredients, mixing thoroughly. Add to dry ingredients, stirring carefully by hand just until blended. Pour into 2 well-greased and floured 9 x 5-inch loaf pans. Bake at 350° for 1 hour.

Yield: 2 loaves

Zola Vantaggi

Orange-Scented Pumpkin Spice Bread

2 eggs
¼ cup oil
1 cup pumpkin (canned or
    fresh)
½ cup milk
¼ cup orange marmalade
1 teaspoon vanilla
½ cup sugar
2 cups flour
2 teaspoons baking powder
½ teaspoon baking soda
1 teaspoon salt
¼ teaspoon black pepper
½ teaspoon ground
    cinnamon
½ teaspoon ground cloves
½ teaspoon nutmeg
½ teaspoon ground
    cardamom (optional)
½ cup chopped walnuts

In a medium mixing bowl, beat eggs and oil. Add pumpkin, milk, marmalade and vanilla; mix well. In a large bowl, combine sugar, flour, baking powder, baking soda, salt and spices. Make a well in the center. Pour liquid mixture in; stir just until moistened. Lightly stir in walnuts. Turn batter into a greased and floured 9 x 5-inch loaf pan. Bake at 350° for 55 to 60 minutes, or until a toothpick in center comes out clean. Cool in pan for 10 minutes, then turn out on wire rack to cool completely. To enhance flavor, wrap completely-cooled bread tightly in plastic and let sit overnight before slicing.

Yield: 1 loaf

Margo Stich

AUNT ADDA'S SODA BREAD

2 cups flour
1 tablespoon shortening
½ teaspoon baking soda
¼ teaspoon baking powder
¼ cup sugar
1 teaspoon salt
1 cup buttermilk
1 cup currants

Combine dry ingredients. Add buttermilk and mix well. Stir in currants. On a floured surface form into a flat, round loaf. Bake in a heavily greased and floured 9 x 5-inch pan. Cut an X on top of formed dough. Bake at 450° for 20 minutes covered, then 20 minutes uncovered.

Yield: 1 loaf

Mona Price

CRUSTY ROLLS WITH ITALIAN HERBS

Butter, softened
Fresh herbs (such as basil,
   Italian parsley, oregano
   or dried Italian herbs)
1 package pre-baked crusty
   rolls

Combine butter and herbs together, to taste. (Use oregano sparingly.) Bake rolls as package directs, for minimum time. Remove from oven. Split rolls slightly; spread herbed butter inside. Return rolls to oven until butter is melted and rolls are lightly browned.

Kay Love-Caskey

"The herbed butter will keep in the refrigerater for up to two weeks."

ROSEMARY FOCCACIA

1 tablespoon yeast
1 ¼ cups hot water, divided
2 tablespoons butter
½ cup instant potatoes
1 cup minced fresh parsley,
    loosely packed
2 tablespoons minced garlic
2 tablespoons minced fresh
    resemary
2 ½ to 3 cups flour
1 teaspoon salt
¼ to ⅓ cup olive oil
½ teaspoon coarse salt

Dissolve yeast in ¾ cup hot (115°-120°) water. Let sit for 10 minutes or until mixture is foamy. In a large bowl, combine ½ cup water, butter and instant potatoes, stirring to make mashed potatoes. Add remaining ingredients, except for olive oil and coarse salt, mixing thoroughly. Add yeast mixture. Knead into a soft pliable dough, adding more flour as needed. Knead dough for 10 minutes. Form dough into a ball. Place in a greased bowl, turning to coat top of dough; cover with plastic. Let dough rise until almost double. Punch dough down and form into a 10-inch disk. Pour olive oil into a 10-inch round pan, turning pan to coat bottom evenly. Place dough in pan, turning over once to coat both sides. Push dough to the sides of the pan and poke dough all over with your fingertips. Sprinkle with coarse salt sparingly over the top. Let dough rise to double in size. Bake at 350° for 20 to 25 minutes, or until golden brown. Remove from oven and cool in pan.

Yield: 1 loaf

Diane Nippoldt

"This Italian bread is wonderful with Olive Pesto, Winter Minestrone Soup, or just by itself."

No-Knead Crescent Rolls

1 cup scalded milk
½ cup (1 stick) butter or
    margarine
½ cup sugar
1 tablespoon salt
2 packages dry yeast
½ cup lukewarm water
4 eggs
6 cups flour, divided

Combine milk, butter, sugar and salt, mixing well. Allow to cool. Dissolve yeast in water and add to milk mixture. Add 2 cups flour. Beat 2 minutes at medium speed. Add eggs and beat another 2 minutes. Gradually stir in the remaining 4 cups of flour. Cover and refrigerate at least 2 hours or up to one week. Roll out dough on well-floured surface into three 14-inch circles. Cut each circle into 12 wedges and roll up tightly. Place on greased baking sheets. Cover and let rise in a warm place until double. Bake at 400° for 8 to 10 minutes.

Yields: 36 rolls

Georgia Hurley

Oatmeal Buns

1 cup oatmeal
¼ cup shortening
½ cup brown sugar
2 teaspoons salt
2 cups boiling water
1 package yeast dissolved in
    ⅓ cup lukewarm water
4 or more cups flour

Mix oatmeal, shortening, sugar and salt. Pour boiling water over, stirring to mix; let stand until lukewarm. Add yeast dissolved in ⅓ cup lukewarm water. Add 4 cups flour or more until dough is easy to handle and not sticky. Place dough in a large greased bowl; turn dough to grease top. Cover and let rise in a warm place. Punch dough down and let rise again about 3 times. Divide dough into 24 rolls and place in a greased 9 x 13-inch pan. Let rise once more and bake at 350° for 25 minutes.

Yields: 24 rolls

Georgia Hurley

POPOVERS

3 eggs
1 cup milk
3 tablespoons butter, melted
1 cup flour
½ teaspoon salt

Beat eggs until frothy. Beat in milk and melted butter. Beat in flour and salt until batter is smooth. Pour batter into well-greased popover or muffin tins. Bake at 375° for 50 minutes. Cut a slit in the top of each popover to let out steam. Bake 10 minutes longer.

Yield: 12

Mona Price

APPLE COFFEE CAKE

2 cups sugar
1 cup oil
2 eggs, well beaten
4 cups chopped fresh
    apples, peeled and cored
2 ½ cups flour
1 teaspoon salt
2 teaspoons baking soda
1 teaspoon cinnamon
1 teaspoon vanilla
½ cup chopped nuts

Powdered sugar

Combine sugar, oil, eggs and apples. Let stand for 20 minutes. Add remaining ingredients and stir well. Pour batter into a well-greased and lightly-floured bundt pan. Bake at 350° for 60 to 70 minutes. Let cool in pan for 10 minutes, then turn out on rack to cool completely. Sprinkle with powdered sugar.

Serves: 16

Mona Price

SOUR CREAM COFFEE CAKE

2 cups flour
1 teaspoon baking soda
1 teaspoon baking powder
½ cup (1 stick) butter,
    softened
1 cup sugar
2 eggs, room temperature
1 cup sour cream
1 teaspoon vanilla

Filling:
½ cup sugar
½ cup chopped nuts
2 teaspoons cinnamon
4 to 6 tablespoons butter,
    chilled

Sift flour, baking soda and baking powder together in a bowl; set aside. In a large bowl, cream butter and sugar together. Add eggs, mixing well. Gradually add flour mixture. Stir in sour cream and vanilla, mixing thoroughly. *For filling,* combine sugar, nuts and cinnamon in a small bowl, mixing well. Pour half of the batter into a greased and floured tube pan. Sprinkle half of the filling on top. Dot with butter. Pour remaining batter over filling. Sprinkle remaining filling on top; dot with butter. Bake at 375° for 35 to 40 minutes, or until toothpick inserted in center comes out clean.

Serves: 10 to 12

Karen Porayko

NORTHWOODS APPLESAUCE MUFFINS

½ cup chopped pecans
¾ cup applesauce
½ cup cooked wild rice
½ cup safflower or corn oil
½ cup light brown sugar
2 egg whites
½ teaspoon vanilla
2 cups flour
1 ½ teaspoons baking powder
¾ teaspoon baking soda
½ teaspoon allspice
¼ teaspoon salt

Spray 12 muffin cups with non-stick coating or line with paper liners; set aside. Place pecans in an ungreased pie plate. Toast at 375° for about 8 minutes or until lightly browned. Remove from oven and set aside to cool. Stir together applesauce and wild rice; set aside. In a medium bowl, beat together oil, brown sugar, egg whites and vanilla. Stir in applesauce and wild rice. Combine flour, baking powder, baking soda, allspice and salt. Stir into rice mixture just until blended. Fold in pecans. Spoon into prepared muffin cups. Bake at 375° for 20 to 25 minutes or until muffins are lightly browned and toothpick comes out clean.

Yield: 1 dozen.

Margo Stich

OAT AND BLUEBERRY MUFFINS

2 ½ cups old-fashioned or quick oats
½ cup brown sugar
2 teaspoons baking powder
¼ teaspoon salt
½ teaspoon cinnamon
1 cup fresh or frozen blueberries
⅔ cup skim milk
3 tablespoons oil
2 egg whites, slightly beaten

Combine dry ingredients. Add blueberries, milk, oil and egg whites. Stir just until combined. Spoon batter into greased muffin cups, filling each ¾ full. Bake at 400° for 20 to 22 minutes.

Yield: 12 muffins

Zola Vantaggi

STRAWBERRY MUFFINS

1 egg
¼ cup melted butter
2 tablespoons water
2 tablespoons lemon juice
1 cup flour
½ cup sugar
¼ teaspoon baking soda
¼ teaspoon baking powder
Dash of salt
½ teaspoon ground ginger
½ teaspoon cinnamon
1 cup sliced fresh
    strawberries

Beat together egg, butter, water and lemon juice. Combine flour, sugar, baking soda, baking powder, salt, ginger and cinnamon. Fold dry ingredients into egg mixture. Fold in strawberries just until combined. Spoon batter into greased muffin cups, filling each ¾ full. Bake at 400° for 25 minutes.

Yield: 12 muffins

Zola Vantaggi

SENSATIONAL SWEET POTATO MUFFINS

¾ cup sugar
1 cup mashed canned sweet
    potatoes (or yams)
½ cup butter or margarine
2 eggs
½ cup unbleached white
    flour
1 cup whole wheat flour
2 teaspoons baking powder
1 teaspoon baking soda
1 ½ teaspoons pumpkin pie
    spice
½ teaspoon cinnamon
1 cup buttermilk or sour
    milk
4 teaspoons grated orange
    peel
1 apple, peeled, cored and
    grated
⅓ cup golden raisins
⅓ cup chopped dates
⅔ cup chopped walnuts

Cream together sugar, sweet potatoes and butter until light and fluffy. Stir together flours, baking powder, baking soda and spices. Add alternately with milk to creamed mixture. Fold in remaining ingredients. Divide batter among 24 paper-lined muffin cups. Bake at 375° for 35 minutes, or until a toothpick inserted in center comes out clean and tops are slightly browned.

Yield: 2 dozen

Margo Stich

KITTY'S RHUBARB MUFFINS

1 ¼ cups brown sugar
½ cup oil
1 egg
2 teaspoons vanilla
1 cup buttermilk
2 ½ cups flour
1 teaspoon soda
1 teaspoon baking powder
1 teaspoon salt
½ cup chopped pecans
1 ½ cups finely chopped
   rhubarb

Topping:
⅓ cup quick oats
⅓ cup flour
⅓ cup brown sugar
1 teaspoon cinnamon
⅓ cup margarine, chilled

In a large bowl, combine brown sugar and oil. Add egg, vanilla and buttermilk, mixing well. Sift flour, soda, baking powder and salt together in a bowl; gradually add to sugar mixture, mixing thoroughly. Gently fold in rhubarb and pecans. Fill greased and floured muffin tins or paper muffin cups ¾ full. *For topping*, combine all ingredients together in a bowl; mix well. Sprinkle on top of each muffin. Bake at 350° for 20 to 25 minutes.

Yield: 20 to 24 muffins

Kathleen (Kitty) Tomjack

CREAM CHEESE STUFFED CINNAMON FRENCH TOAST

1 (8-ounce) package cream
   cheese, softened
1 teaspoon vanilla
½ teaspoon grated orange
   rind
½ cup chopped pecans
8 (1-inch thick) slices
   cinnamon-raisin bread
4 eggs
½ to 1 cup half and half (or
   2% milk)
½ teaspoon almond extract
½ teaspoon nutmeg
Butter
1 (12-ounce) jar thick orange
   marmalade
½ cup orange juice

Beat cream cheese, vanilla and orange rind together until fluffy. Stir in pecans; set aside. Make a deep slit in each bread slice to form a pocket. Fill with cream cheese mixture; squeeze gently together. Beat eggs, half and half, almond extract and nutmeg together. With tongs, quickly dip filled bread slices into egg mixture, stirring mixture to distribute nutmeg. Cook on lightly buttered griddle over medium-low heat until both sides are browned. Heat marmalade and orange juice together; serve hot over stuffed toast slices.

Serves: 4 to 8

Margo Stich

OATMEAL PANCAKES

2 cups buttermilk
1 ¼ cups quick oatmeal
2 eggs, separated
⅓ cup cooking oil
¾ cup white or whole
   wheat flour
2 tablespoons sugar
1 teaspoon baking powder
1 teaspoon baking soda
1 teaspoon salt

In a large bowl, combine buttermilk and oatmeal; let soak for 20 minutes. In another bowl, beat the egg whites until stiff; set aside. To the buttermilk-oatmeal mixture add the slightly beaten egg yolks, oil, flour, sugar, baking powder, baking soda and salt. Mix thoroughly. Fold in the beaten egg whites. Pour batter by scant ¼ cupfuls onto hot griddle, making a few pancakes at a time; cook until bubbly and bubbles begin to burst. With pancake turner, turn and cook until underside is golden. Serve at once.

Serves: 3 to 4

Janet Engels

DESSERTS

BETTER THAN KISSES CAKE

1 (18.25-ounce) package
   German chocolate cake
   mix
1 (14-ounce) can sweetened
   condensed milk
1 (17-ounce) jar butterscotch
   caramel fudge topping
1 (8-ounce) carton whipped
   topping
8 English toffee candy bars,
   crushed (they are easier
   to crush if frozen first)

Prepare cake as directed and bake
in a greased 9 x 13-inch pan. After
removing cake from oven, poke
holes over entire surface of cake.
Drizzle sweetened condensed milk
over top. Then drizzle caramel
sauce over top. Cool cake completely. Spread whipped topping on
cake. Sprinkle crushed candy bars
over topping. Refrigerate before
serving.

Serves: 12 to 15

Sonia Gisvold

BUTTERSCOTCH TOFFEE HEAVENLY DELIGHT CAKE

2 cups heavy cream
1 (5 ½ -ounce) can (⅔ cup)
   butterscotch syrup
   topping
½ teaspoon vanilla extract
1 unfrosted (9 ½ -inch)
   round angelfood cake
¾ pound English toffee
   candy bars, crushed

Whip cream until it starts to
thicken. Add syrup and vanilla
slowly and continue beating until
cream is thick and firm peaks form.
Cut cake horizontally into three
layers. Spread mixture on layers
and sprinkle each layer generously
with toffee bits. Frost top and sides.
Sprinkle top (and sides) with toffee.
Refrigerate at least 6 hours.

Serves: 8 to 10

Ann Jost

*"This recipe was given to me by Jean Bezoier
Hanson, a good friend and good cook!"*

CARROT CAKE WITH RUM SAUCE

1 (8 ¾-ounce) can crushed
  pineapple, drained,
  reserving syrup
3 cups flour
2 cups sugar
1 ½ teaspoons baking soda
1 teaspoon baking powder
2 teaspoons cinnamon
½ teaspoon salt
3 large eggs
1 ½ cups oil
2 teaspoons vanilla
2 cups coarsely shredded
  carrots, lightly packed
1 ½ cups chopped pecans

Rum Sauce:
1 cup dark brown sugar
½ cup dark corn syrup
½ cup light cream
¼ cup butter
¼ cup light rum
1 teaspoon vanilla

Drain pineapple, reserving syrup. In a large bowl, combine flour, sugar, baking soda, baking powder, salt and cinnamon. Make a well in the center and add eggs, oil, reserved pineapple syrup and vanilla. Beat at medium speed until well blended. With a spoon, stir in pineapple, carrots and pecans. Pour into a greased and floured 10-inch tube pan. Bake at 325° for 1 ½ hours. Place pan on a wire rack to cool for 10 minutes. Loosen edges, turn out onto rack and cool completely. Serve warm or cold with rum sauce. *For rum sauce,* combine brown sugar, corn syrup, cream and butter in a 2-quart saucepan. Heat over low heat, stirring constantly, until boiling. Remove from heat and cool slightly. Stir in rum and vanilla. Serve warm with carrot cake. (Rum sauce may be made ahead of time and refrigerated. Reheat gently before serving.)

Yield: 16 servings
        2 cups rum sauce

Faye Waldo

CHOCOLATE POUND CAKE

1 cup unsweetened cocoa
  powder
2 cups flour
½ teaspoon baking powder
1 teaspoon salt
2 tablespoons instant coffee
  powder
1 ½ cups (3 sticks) sweet
  unsalted corn oil
  margarine
3 cups sugar
2 teaspoons vanilla
8 extra large egg whites
1 cup buttermilk
¼ cup water

In a medium bowl, sift together cocoa, flour, baking powder, salt and coffee powder; set aside. In a large bowl with electric mixer, cream margarine until fluffy. Continue beating while adding sugar in a slow stream. Beat at high speed for 5 minutes. Slow mixer; add vanilla. Add egg whites, one at a time, beating briefly after each addition. Add dry ingredients alternating with buttermilk and water. Mix well, scraping bowl as necessary. Pour batter into a greased and floured 10-inch tube pan. Bake at 325° for 1 hour 20 minutes, until cake tests done. Let cake rest in the pan for 20 minutes, then unmold onto a cake rack. Cool completely before serving.

Serves: 12 to 15

Cherie Miles

"Use a dark rich cocoa for a wonderfully chocolate, moist cake. I prefer to use Williams-Sonoma's Pernigotti or a Dark Jersey cocoa."

CHOCOLATE HAZELNUT CAKE

1 cup skinned, toasted
   hazelnuts, ground
   semifine
1 cup sugar
¼ cup water
1 tablespoon instant coffee
   powder
6 ounces semisweet
   chocolate, in pieces
1 teaspoon almond extract
½ cup unsalted butter,
   room temperature
8 eggs, separated, room
   temperature
2 tablespoons graham
   cracker crumbs

Frosting:
6 ounces semisweet
   chocolate, in pieces
¼ cup water
1 tablespoon instant coffee
   powder
1 cup unsalted butter, room
   temperature
3 egg yolks
1 cup powdered sugar
¼ cup skinned, toasted
   hazelnuts, ground

Toast nuts in a shallow baking pan at 350° until skins begin to split, about 10 to 15 minutes. Transfer to strainer. Rub nuts against strainer with terrycloth towel to remove most of the skins (nuts do not need to be totally free of skins). Cool completely. Butter and flour two 9-inch round cake pans. Simmer sugar, water and coffee powder in a small saucepan over medium high heat for 3 to 4 minutes, stirring constantly. Remove from heat; stir in chocolate pieces and almond extract. Stir until chocolate is melted and mixture is smooth. Set aside to cool. Beat butter in a large mixing bowl until light and fluffy. Add egg yolks, one at a time, beating well after each addition. Stir in cooled chocolate mixture. Stir in hazelnuts and graham cracker crumbs. Set aside. Beat egg whites in a separate bowl with clean beaters, until stiff, not dry. Fold a quarter of the egg whites into chocolate mixture and then gently fold in remaining whites. Pour batter into prepared pans, dividing evenly. Bake at 350° for 25 to 30 minutes, until cake springs back when lightly touched in center. Cool in pans 5 minutes and then invert layers onto wire racks to cool completely. *For frosting,* heat chocolate, water and coffee powder in a small saucepan over very low heat until smooth, stirring constantly. Set aside to cool. Cream butter until light and fluffy. Beat in egg yolks, one at a time. Beat in cooled chocolate mixture, then powdered sugar. Refrigerate until thick enough to spread. Frost top of one cake layer. Place second layer on top and spread top and side of cake with frosting. Press ground hazelnuts around side of cake. Pipe any remaining frosting decoratively on top of cake.

Serves: 10 to 12

Cathy Tiegs

Note: This recipe calls for uncooked egg yolks.

LAURA'S CHOCOLATE CAKE

6 ounces fine quality
  bittersweet or semisweet
  chocolate, coarsely
  chopped
¾ cup water
2 ½ cups sifted cake flour
2 teaspoons baking soda
1 teaspoon salt
1 cup (2 sticks) unsalted
  sweet butter, softened
2 cups sugar
4 large eggs, room
  temperature
2 teaspoons vanilla
1 ½ cups sour cream

Frosting:
1 (16-ounce) package
  powdered sugar
6 tablespoons butter,
  softened
½ cup unsweetened cocoa
  powder
⅓ cup hot coffee, or more
  for desired consistency
½ teaspoon vanilla
⅛ teaspoon salt

Line the bottoms of three 8-inch cake pans with rounds of parchment or waxed paper (do not grease the paper or pans). Melt chocolate with water in the top of a double boiler set over barely-simmering water, stirring occasionally. Sift together flour, baking soda and salt; set aside. In a large bowl with an electric mixer, cream butter. Beat in sugar gradually and continue beating until mixture is light and fluffy. Add eggs, one at a time, beating well after each addition. Stir in chocolate mixture and vanilla. Alternately add flour mixture and sour cream, beginning and ending with flour mixture. Stir until batter is smooth. Divide batter among prepared pans, smoothing tops. Rap each pan on a hard surface to expel any air bubbles. Bake at 350° for 30 to 45 minutes. Let the layers cool in pans for 8 minutes. Run a thin knife around the edge of each pan, then invert the layers onto cooling racks. Remove the parchment or waxed paper and let the layers cool completely. *For frosting*, combine all ingredients in a large bowl. Beat until smooth. Frost layers, top and sides of cooled cake.
Serves: 10 to 12

Renda Meloy

"This cake is so good you may not even want to frost it!"

HEAVENLY CAKE

3 cups flour
1 teaspoon salt
2 teaspoons baking soda
2 cups sugar
4 tablespoons unsweetened
  cocoa powder
¾ cup oil
2 tablespoons cider vinegar
2 teaspoons vanilla
2 cups warm water

Frosting:
6 tablespoons butter
4 tablespoons milk
3 to 4 tablespoons
  unsweetened cocoa
  powder
2 ⅔ cups powdered sugar

In an ungreased 9 x 13-inch pan, combine flour, salt, baking soda, sugar and cocoa. Mix with a fork until thoroughly blended. Make 3 holes in the dry ingredients. Add oil in one hole, vinegar in one hole and vanilla in one hole. Pour warm, not hot, water over ingredients. Mix well with a fork. Bake at 350° for 35 to 40 minutes. Remove from oven and top with frosting immediately. *For frosting,* melt butter in a small saucepan. Add milk and cocoa. Bring to a boil and remove from heat. Gradually add powdered sugar, mixing thoroughly. When smooth, pour and spread over warm cake. Let cake cool completely before serving.

Serves: 16 to 20

Judi Bolander

"It's a crazy cake, but the frosting makes it heavenly! Note: the pan is not to be greased."

HAZELNUT CAKE

1 ½ cups (about
  6 ½ ounces) hazelnuts
¾ cup plus 3 tablespoons
  sugar, divided
3 tablespoons plus 2
  teaspoons flour
5 eggs, separated, room
  temperature
¼ teaspoon cream of tartar
3 tablespoons unsalted
  butter, melted and cooled
  slightly

Coffee Buttercream
Frosting:
3 teaspoons freeze-dried
  coffee crystals
1 ½ tablespoons boiling
  water
3 eggs, room temperature
1 ⅛ cups sugar
1 ½ cups plus 3 tablespoons
  unsalted butter, room
  temperature
Toasted hazelnuts, chopped

Toast nuts in shallow baking pan at 350° until skins begin to split, about 10 to 15 minutes. Transfer to strainer. Rub nuts against strainer with terrycloth towel to remove most of the skins (nuts do not need to be totally free of skins). Cool completely. Butter two 9-inch round cake pans. Line bottoms of pans with parchment or foil and butter the lining. Dust pans with flour. Grind 1 ½ cups nuts with ¼ cup sugar in food processor, as finely as possible. Transfer to a small bowl. Thoroughly blend in flour; set aside. Beat egg yolks with ½ cup sugar in a large bowl until they are pale yellow and a ribbon forms when beaters are lifted, about 5 minutes; set aside. In another large bowl, beat egg whites with cream of tartar until soft peaks form. Beat in remaining 3 tablespoons sugar, a tablespoon at a time. Continue beating until whites are stiff but not dry. Fold ⅓ of nut and sugar mixture into yolks. Gently fold in ⅓ of whites. Repeat with remaining nuts and whites in 2 batches, folding just until blended. Drizzle in melted butter just before final addition of whites is incorporated. Spread batter evenly in prepared pans. Bake at 350° in the center of the oven, about 17 minutes, or until tester inserted in centers comes out clean. Run thin knife around sides of each cake; turn out onto plates and remove paper. Invert again onto racks and cool completely. *For buttercream frosting,* dissolve coffee in boiling water in a small bowl.

Cool completely. Beat eggs in a large heatproof bowl. Beat in coffee mixture and sugar. Set bowl in a pan of hot water over very low heat. Using portable electric mixer, beat at medium speed for 5 minutes, then at high speed until ribbon forms when beaters are lifted, about 3 minutes. Remove bowl from water and beat egg mixture until cool. Set aside. Cream butter in a large bowl until soft and smooth. Beat in 1/2 cup of egg mixture. Slowly beat in remaining egg mixture, stopping occasionally to scrape down sides of bowl. Use buttercream frosting immediately. *To assemble cake,* invert one cake layer, smooth side up, onto a serving platter. Spread with 1/3 of buttercream. Place second layer smooth side up on top. Spread remaining buttercream on sides and top of cake, swirling top decoratively. Sprinkle top with chopped nuts. Refrigerate at least 2 hours before serving to set frosting. (Can be prepared 2 days ahead.) Serve at room temperature.

Variation: Reserve some buttercream and refrigerate to firm. Spoon into pastry bag fitted with medium star tip. Pipe rosettes along top edge of cake and one large rosette in center. Top each with whole hazelnut.

Serves: 10 to 12

Diane Nippoldt

Note: This recipe calls for uncooked eggs.

ITALIAN CREAM CAKE

½ cup butter or margarine,
   softened
½ cup shortening
2 cups sugar
5 large eggs
2 cups flour
1 teaspoon baking soda
1 cup buttermilk
1 teaspoon vanilla
1 (3 ½-ounce) can flaked
   coconut
1 cup chopped pecans

Frosting:
1 (8-ounce) package cream
   cheese, softened
1 (3-ounce) package cream
   cheese, softened
⅓ cup butter or margarine,
   softened
6 ½ cups powdered sugar
1 ½ teaspoons vanilla

Grease three 9-inch round cake pans. Line bottoms of pans with parchment paper. Grease and flour paper and sides; set aside. Beat butter and shortening at medium speed, until soft and creamy. Gradually add sugar, beating well. Add eggs, one at a time, beating after each addition. Combine flour and soda. Add to butter mixture alternating with buttermilk, beginning and ending with flour mixture, mixing after each addition. Stir in vanilla, coconut and pecans. Pour batter into prepared pans. Bake at 350° for 25 to 30 minutes. Remove from oven and cool in pans on wire racks for 10 minutes. Remove from pans and remove paper. Cool completely. *For frosting,* beat cream cheese and butter at medium speed until soft and creamy. Gradually add powdered sugar, beating until smooth. Stir in vanilla. Spread cream cheese frosting between layers and on top and sides of cake.

Serves: 12

Kay Love-Caskey

ITALIAN PARTY CAKE

1 (15-ounce) container
  ricotta cheese
2 tablespoons heavy cream
¼ cup sugar
3 tablespoons orange-
  flavored liqueur
3 tablespoons chopped
  candied fruit
⅓ cup semisweet chocolate
  chips
1 (10 ¾ -ounce) loaf frozen
  pound cake

Frosting:
1 (12-ounce) package
  semisweet chocolate
¾ cup strong coffee
1 cup (2 sticks) butter

Combine cheese, cream and sugar in a large bowl; mix until smooth. Add liqueur, fruit and chocolate chips; mix gently. Cut pound cake horizontally in ½ to ¾ -inch layers. Spread cheese mixture evenly between layers. Chill for two hours. *For frosting,* combine all ingredients together in a saucepan. Melt over medium-low heat, stirring constantly, until smooth. Cool slightly. Pour over cake, allowing frosting to drizzle down the sides. Chill until serving time.

Serves: 6 to 8

Margo Stich

LEMON-GLAZED BUTTER CAKE

1 cup (2 sticks) butter or
    margarine, softened
1 ¼ cups sugar
3 large eggs
2 teaspoons baking powder
2 teaspoons grated lemon
    peel
¾ teaspoon almond extract
3 cups flour
1 cup milk

Glaze:
¾ cup lemon juice
1 (16-ounce) box
    (approximately 3 ½ cups)
    unsifted powdered sugar

Lemon slices (optional)
Citrus leaves, washed and
    dried (optional)

In large bowl of electric mixer, combine butter and sugar. Beat on high speed until fluffy (about 5 minutes). Beat in eggs, one at a time. Mix in baking powder, lemon peel and almond extract. Add flour and milk alternately, beating well on low speed after each addition. Pour batter into a well-buttered and floured 10-cup tube or bundt pan. Tap pan on counter several times to level batter and eliminate any air pockets. Bake at 325° for about 1 hour or until cake begins to pull away from sides of pan. Set cake pan on cooling rack and let stand for 5 minutes. Run a sharp knife around edge of tube to loosen cake. Place rack on pan and invert gently to release cake. Return cake to pan. With thin skewer, pierce cake at 1-inch intervals. *For glaze,* blend lemon juice and powdered sugar until smooth. Pour all but ½ cup of glaze over hot cake. Let cake cool completely (at least 6 hours) in pan. Invert onto serving plate. Stir reserved glaze and spoon evenly over top. To serve, garnish with lemon slices and citrus leaves, if desired. Cake can be covered and store at room temperature for up to 1 day, then refrigerate or freeze.

Yield: 10 to 12 servings

Jane Aughenbaugh

"This is a favorite cake recipe. I always try to serve it at least once during the summer."

LEMON PUNCH CAKE

1 (18-ounce) package lemon-
   flavored cake mix
1 (3-ounce) package lemon
   jello
¾ cup oil
¾ cup water
4 eggs

Glaze:
2 cups powdered sugar
Juice of 2 lemons
Zest of 1 lemon
Few drops yellow food
   coloring

Combine cake mix, jello, oil and water in a large bowl. Beat 2 minutes at medium speed. Add eggs, one at a time, beating after each addition. Pour batter into a greased and floured 10-inch tube or bundt pan. Bake at 350° for 35 minutes. When done, invert onto a cake plate and punch holes in the cake with a meat fork. *For glaze,* blend powdered sugar with lemon juice. Stir in lemon zest and food coloring. Spoon glaze over cake while it is still hot.

Serves: 14 to 16

Dorothy Hartman

ORANGE POPPY SEED CAKE

1 ½ cups cake flour
¾ teaspoon salt
1 teaspoon baking soda
½ teaspoon baking powder
¼ cup poppy seed
¾ cup unsalted butter,
    softened
1 ¼ cups sugar, divided
2 teaspoons freshly grated
    orange zest
4 large eggs, separated
⅔ cup sour cream
2 teaspoons vanilla
Pinch of salt
¼ teaspoon cream of tartar

Syrup:
½ cup fresh orange juice
3 tablespoons orange-
    flavored liqueur
1 ½ tablespoons sugar

Powdered sugar
Fresh raspberries and
    blackberries
Creme fraiche or whipped
    cream

In a large bowl, sift together flour, salt, baking soda and baking powder. Stir in poppy seeds. With an electric mixer, cream butter with 1 cup sugar and orange zest until mixture is light and fluffy. In a small bowl, whisk together egg yolks, sour cream and vanilla until well combined. Alternately beat flour mixture and yolk mixture into butter mixture, beginning and ending with flour. Beat well after each addition. In another bowl, with clean beaters, beat egg whites with a pinch of salt until they are foamy. Add cream of tartar and beat until whites hold soft peaks. Beat in remaining ¼ cup sugar, a little at a time until meringue holds stiff peaks. Stir about one third of the meringue into the batter to lighten it. Fold in remaining meringue gently but thoroughly. Pour batter into a buttered and floured 10-inch springform pan, smoothing the top. Bake at 350°, in the middle of the oven, for 35 to 40 minutes, or until a tester comes out clean. *For syrup,* combine juice, liqueur and sugar in a small saucepan. Heat mixture over moderately high heat, stirring, until sugar is dissolved. Remove pan from heat. When cake is done, remove from the oven, and place on a rack. Poke entire cake top immediately with a skewer. Brush the top of the cake generously with half of the syrup, letting some of it run down between the cake and the side of the pan. Let the cake stand for ten minutes. Run a thin knife around the edge of the pan, remove the side of the pan, and invert the cake onto the rack. Poke bottom of cake all over with the skewer and brush it generously with the remaining syrup. Re-invert the cake onto another rack and let it cool completely. Just before serving, sift powdered sugar over the top of the cake. Serve with berries and cream.

Serves: 12

Renda Meloy

RHUBARB CHERRY CAKE

1 cup quick oatmeal
1 cup brown sugar
1 cup flour
Pinch of salt
½ cup butter or margarine
4 to 5 cups diced rhubarb
1 cup sugar
1 cup water
2 rounded tablespoons
    cornstarch
1 (21-ounce) can cherry pie
    filling
1 teaspoon almond
    flavoring
½ cup chopped nuts

Sweetened whipped cream
    (optional)

Combine oatmeal, brown sugar, flour, salt and butter in a large bowl; mix well. Press half of the mixture into the bottom of a 9 x 13-inch pan. Spread rhubarb over crust. In a small saucepan, bring sugar, water and cornstarch to a boil. Boil until thickened. Remove from heat. Add pie filling and almond flavoring; mix well. Spoon filling mixture over rhubarb. Sprinkle remaining crumb mixture over filling. Sprinkle nuts over top. Bake at 350° for 45 to 60 minutes or until rhubarb is tender. Remove from oven and cool in pan on rack. Top individual servings with sweetened whipped cream, if desired.

Serves: 12

Zola Vantaggi

NOODLE CAKE

2 ½ cups flour
1 teaspoon baking powder
1 teaspoon yeast
Water
5 eggs
3 teaspoons lemon juice
1 teaspoon vanilla
4 to 5 tablespoons sesame
    seeds
1 cup honey
Oil for frying

Sift flour and baking powder together; set aside. Dissolve yeast in a very small amount of warm water; set aside. In a large bowl, add eggs, one at a time, beating until light. Add flour mixture, lemon juice, vanilla and yeast to form soft dough. Cover the bowl with a wet cloth; let dough stand for a couple of hours at room temperature to allow dough to rise to approximately double in size. Knead dough for a few minutes, then divide into several pieces. Roll each piece out into a ⅛ -inch thick sheet. Cut sheet into small pieces approximately ⅓ x ½ -inch. Fry pieces in oil heated to 350°, until light brown. Drain browned noodles on paper towels. Brown sesame seeds in skillet. Put fried noodles in an 8 x 8-inch or 9 x 9-inch baking pan. Add honey and sesame seeds until the noodles are moist and stick together. Pack the noodles tight and keep in freezer. Cut cake into 2-inch or larger square pieces to serve with tea or coffee for dessert.

Serves: 12 to 16

Lily Weinshilboum

Rum Cream Cake

1 (18 ½ -ounce) package
    yellow cake mix
2 eggs
⅔ cup light rum
⅔ cup water

Frosting:
2 cups heavy cream
Pinch of salt
¼ cup light rum
1 cup powdered sugar

Fresh sliced strawberries for
    garnish
                or
1 quart fresh strawberries
1 tablespoon sugar

In large bowl of electic mixer, combine cake mix, eggs, rum and water. Beat at medium speed for 2 to 4 minutes. Pour batter into two greased and floured 9-inch round cake pans. Bake at 350° for 25 to 30 minutes. Cool thoroughly. Split each layer in half horizontally. *For frosting,* beat cream and salt together in a large bowl until slightly thickened. Slowly add rum alternating with powdered sugar. Continue to beat until stiff. Spread between layers and over the top of the cake. Chill. Garnish with fresh sliced strawberries. Or clean and hull one quart strawberries and sweeten with sugar; set aside. Before serving, crush strawberries with fork or masher. Spoon crushed strawberries and juice over each cut piece of cake.

Serves: 10 to 12

Nancy Brubaker

KATHRYN'S CHEESECAKE

Crust:
2 cups cinnamon graham
  cracker, crumbs
6 tablespoons sugar
6 tablespoons butter, melted

Filling:
3 (8-ounce) packages cream
  cheese, room temperature
4 extra large egg whites,
  room temperature
1 cup sugar
1 teaspoon vanilla

Topping:
1 (16-ounce) carton sour
  cream
½ teaspoon vanilla
2 tablespoons sugar

**Strawberries for garnish
  (optional)**

For crust, mix together graham cracker crumbs, sugar and butter. Pat into the bottom of a 10-inch springform pan. Place in refrigerator. *For filling*, beat cream cheese until smooth with an electric mixer. In a separate bowl, beat egg whites until soft peaks form. Gradually add 1 cup sugar. Continue beating until mixture looks like an uncooked meringue. Add cream cheese and 1 teaspoon vanilla; mix well. Turn into prepared pan. Bake at 325° for 25 to 30 minutes. Remove from oven and raise temperature to 475°. *For topping*, mix ingredients together and spread carefully on top of cheesecake. Return to oven for 5 minutes. Remove and cool to room temperature. Refrigerate for 6 hours before serving. Garnish individual servings with a strawberry if desired.

Serves: 8 to 10

Cheri Miles

"This is a favorite cheesecake. The lack of egg yolks gives it a lovely texture."

CHEESECAKE WINDYKNOWE

Crust:
1 tablespoon cinnamon
2 tablespoons sugar
2 cups crushed graham
   crackers
5 tablespoons butter,
   melted

Filling:
3 eggs, beaten
1 cup sugar
3 (8-ounce) packages cream
   cheese, softened
1 ½ pints sour cream
1 teaspoon lemon juice
Rind of one lemon, grated
1 tablespoon vanilla
1 tablespoon melted butter

For crust, mix cinnamon and sugar together. Add crushed graham crackers, stirring to mix. Add melted butter and mix thoroughly. Press into a greased 9-inch springform pan. Chill while preparing filling. *For filling,* beat sugar into the eggs. Stir in cream cheese, sour cream and lemon juice. Add lemon rind to mixture. Add vanilla and beat until smooth. Fold in melted butter. Pour filling into the prepared crust. Bake at 350° for 60 to 70 minutes. Cool completely. Refrigerate at least 4 hours or overnight before serving.

Variation: To sweeten, add 2 more tablespoons sugar to crust and ¼ cup more sugar to filling.

Serves: 12

Betsy Ogle Weitz

"An old Washington Post *article called this recipe a 'collector's item.' It's a favorite of ours because it is not a sweet cheesecake."*

FROZEN RASPBERRY CHEESECAKE

Crust:
24 chocolate wafers, crushed
¼ cup butter or margarine, melted

Filling:
1 egg, separated
1 cup heavy cream
1 (8-ounce) package cream cheese
⅔ cup powdered sugar
¾ cup frozen concentrated raspberry juice or frozen raspberry-cranberry juice cocktail, thawed
1 teaspoon lemon juice

Sauce:
1 (10-ounce) package unsweetened frozen raspberries, thawed
2 tablespoons kirsch or creme de cassis
2 tablespoons powdered sugar, or to taste (leave out if berries are sweetened)

Garnish:
Kiwi slices

Combine crushed chocolate wafers and melted butter together in a bowl, mixing thoroughly. Press on the bottom only of a 9-inch springform pan. Place in freezer. *For filling,* beat egg white until stiff. Beat heavy cream in a separate bowl until quite thick, but still smooth; set aside. In a large bowl, beat cream cheese. Gradually add sugar, beating until smooth. Beat in egg yolk. Blend in juices. Fold in whipped cream. Fold in egg white until well blended. Pour mixture over crust and freeze for at least 3 hours. *For sauce,* puree raspberries. Strain to remove seeds. Add kirsch and sugar, if needed. To serve, remove cheesecake from freezer. Remove side of pan and let cheesecake sit for a couple of minutes before cutting into slices. Spoon sauce over slices. Garnish with kiwi.

Serves: 8 to 10

Cindy Ullman

"Can be made a few days before serving. Note: this recipe calls for an uncooked egg."

PEACH CREAM CHEESE CAKE

¾ cup flour
1 (3.4-ounce) package
   regular vanilla pudding
   mix (not instant)
1 teaspoon baking powder
½ teaspoon salt
3 tablespoons butter, melted
1 egg
½ cup milk
1 (16-ounce) can sliced
   peaches, drained,
   reserving juice
1 (8-ounce) package cream
   cheese, softened
½ cup plus 1 tablespoon
   sugar, divided
3 tablespoons reserved
   peach juice
½ teaspoon cinnamon

Combine flour, pudding mix, baking powder, salt, butter, egg and milk in mixing bowl and stir until smooth. Pour into a greased 9 ½-inch pie plate. Arrange peaches on top in a single layer, centering 1 inch from edges. Combine cream cheese, ½ cup sugar and peach juice in a bowl; mix until smooth. Spread cream cheese mixture over top of peaches. Sprinkle 1 tablespoon sugar mixed with cinnamon over the top. Bake at 350° for 30 minutes. Cool completely, then refrigerate until ready to serve. Serve chilled.

Serves: 6 to 8

Julie Larson

APPLE TORTE

1 egg
¾ cup sugar
¾ cup apples, peeled and
   sliced
1 teaspoon baking powder
½ cup flour
Pinch of salt
¼ teaspoon almond
   flavoring
¼ cup chopped walnuts

Whipped cream or vanilla
   ice cream

In a medium bowl, beat egg slightly. Stir in remaining ingredients, except whipped cream, mixing well. Pour into a greased 9-inch pie plate. Bake at 325° for 25 minutes. Serve warm, topped with whipped cream or vanilla ice cream.

Serves: 8

Janet Engels

"This was a favorite dessert at the old Carroll's White House restaurant located in Oronoco."

BETE NOIRE

1 cup (2 sticks) unsalted
    butter, room temperature
8 ounces unsweetened
    chocolate
4 ounces bittersweet
    chocolate
½ cup water
1 ⅓ cups sugar, divided
5 extra large eggs, room
    temperature

Whipped cream with
    amaretto for garnish

Grease a 9-inch round cake pan. Cut parchment paper to fit bottom and sides; set aside. Cut butter and chocolate into small pieces; set aside. In a heavy 1½-quart saucepan, combine water with 1 cup sugar. Bring to a rapid boil over high heat. Boil for 2 minutes, stirring constantly. Remove from heat and add chocolate pieces immediately; stir until melted. Add butter, stirring until melted completely. In a mixing bowl, place eggs and ⅓ cup sugar. Beat until triple in volume. Add chocolate mixture and mix until completely incorporated. Spoon into prepared pan. Place a larger pan on the center rack in the oven. Set cake pan in larger pan. Pour boiling water into larger pan for a water bath (bain marie). Bake at 350° for 20 to 25 minutes. Remove from oven and cool 10 minutes in pan. Invert to remove cake from pan. Serve warm or at room temperature with whipped cream garnish.

Serves: 8

Julie Huettner
Peggy King

BLUEBERRY AND BUTTERMILK TART

Crust:
1 ⅓ cups flour
¼ cup sugar
¼ teaspoon salt
½ cup (1 stick) cold
  unsalted butter, cut into
  bits
1 large egg yolk
2 tablespoons ice water
Pie weights, dried beans, or
  rice to weight the shell

Filling:
1 cup buttermilk
3 large egg yolks
½ cup sugar
1 tablespoon freshly grated
  lemon zest
1 tablespoon fresh lemon
  juice
4 tablespoons unsalted
  butter, melted and cooled
1 teaspoon vanilla
½ teaspoon salt
2 tablespoons flour
2 cups blueberries

Powdered sugar (optional)

In a bowl or food processor, mix together flour, sugar and salt. Cut in butter and process until it resembles coarse meal. In a small bowl, beat egg yolk and water. Add to flour mixture and blend until well combined. Form dough into a ball, flatten slightly and dust with flour. Wrap dough in plastic wrap; chill for 1 hour. On a floured surface, roll out dough, about ⅛ -inch thick. Carefully line a 10-inch tart pan that has a removable rim. Chill the crust for 1 hour. Cover crust with aluminum foil, then fill with the pie weights. Bake at 350° for 25 minutes in the middle of oven. Carefully remove the foil and weights. Bake until crust is light brown, about 5 to 10 minutes more. Set pan on rack to cool. *For filling,* combine all ingredients except blueberries. Process or blend until the mixture is smooth. Spread blueberries over the bottom of the crust and pour filling over them. Bake at 350° for 30 to 35 minutes or until the filling is set. Let cool completely. Serve at room temperature. If desired, sprinkle some powdered sugar over the top just before serving.

Serves: 8

Sally Duffy

"The tart may be made one day ahead and kept covered and chilled. Allow to return to room temperature before serving."

CARAMEL CUSTARD

Caramel:
½ cup sugar

Custard:
5 eggs
½ cup sugar
¼ teaspoon salt
1 teaspoon vanilla
3 ½ cups hot milk

Sprinkle sugar evenly in a heavy 8-inch skillet. Cook over medium heat (do not stir) until sugar begins to melt, shaking skillet occasionally. Reduce heat to low. Cook about 5 minutes more until sugar is golden brown, stirring frequently. Pour hot liquid sugar into an ungreased 4-cup metal mold. Holding mold with potholder, quickly rotate mold to coat bottom and sides. Set aside to harden. *For custard,* beat eggs in a large bowl. Add sugar, salt and vanilla, mixing well. Gradually add hot milk and beat until smooth. Pour mixture over hardened caramel in mold. Place mold in a 9 x 13-inch pan. Pour boiling or hottest tap water into the pan around the mold to a depth of 1 inch. Bake at 325° for 60 minutes or until knife inserted comes out clean. Cool completely on wire rack. Cover and refrigerate for at least 4 hours until ready to serve. *To serve,* unmold custard onto a rimmed serving plate. Spoon any sugar that remains in mold on top of custard.

Serves: 6 to 8

Eleni George

CHOCOLATE ROLL WITH SAUCE

6 eggs, separated
½ teaspoon cream of tartar
1 cup sugar, divided
4 tablespoons unsweetened
  cocoa powder
4 tablespoons flour
¼ teaspoon salt
1 teaspoon vanilla

Powdered sugar

Filling:
1 cup heavy cream
1 tablespoon sugar
1 teaspoon vanilla

Chocolate Sauce:
1 cup sugar
2 tablespoons flour
2 tablespoons unsweetened
  cocoa powder
1 cup boiling water
1 teaspoon vanilla
1 heaping teaspoon butter

Line a 15 ½ x 10-inch jelly roll pan with wax paper and grease well. Separate eggs, reserving both yolks and whites. In a large bowl, beat egg whites and cream of tartar until stiff. Gradually add ½ cup sugar. Continue beating until whites are very stiff and glossy; set aside. In a medium bowl, beat egg yolks until thick and lemon colored. Add remaining ½ cup sugar, mixing well. Sift together cocoa, flour and salt. Fold dry ingredients into egg yolk mixture. Stir in vanilla. Carefully fold egg yolk mixture into beaten egg whites. Spread batter evenly in the prepared pan. Bake at 325° for 20 to 25 minutes or until cake springs back when touched lightly in center. Remove from oven. Immediately invert pan onto a dish towel that has been sprinkled with powdered sugar. Peel off wax paper. Starting at the short end, roll the cake up with the towel and place it on a rack to cool. *For filling,* beat heavy cream until thickened. Gradually add sugar and vanilla. Beat until stiff. When cake is cool, unroll and remove the towel. Spread filling evenly over cake. Reroll and chill for 1 hour. *For chocolate sauce,* combine sugar, flour and cocoa in a small saucepan. Stir in boiling water. Cook over medium heat until thick. Remove from heat. Stir in vanilla and butter, mixing well. Cool slightly. To serve, cut in 1-inch thick slices and top with the warm chocolate sauce.

Serves: 8 to 10

Phyllis Tracy

CHOCOLATE AND GRAND MARNIER MOUSSE

20 ounces bittersweet (not
   unsweetened) or
   semisweet chocolate,
   chopped
½ cup (1 stick) unsalted
   butter
6 tablespoons Grand
   Marnier (or other orange
   liqueur)
½ cup sugar
2 tablespoons water
6 large egg whites
1 cup chilled heavy cream

Melt chopped chocolate and butter in top of a double boiler over simmering water, stirring occasionally until smooth. Remove top pan from hot water. Stir in Grand Marnier. Cool chocolate mixture to room temperature. Stir sugar and water together in a heavy saucepan over low heat until sugar dissolves. Increase heat and boil until candy thermometer registers 238°, tilting saucepan if necessary to submerge thermometer tip. Meanwhile, using electric mixer, beat egg whites in a large bowl until very soft peaks form. Gradually beat boiling sugar syrup into egg whites. Continue beating until soft peaks form. Fold into chocolate mixture. Beat chilled whipping cream to soft peaks in a medium bowl. Fold whipped cream into chocolate mixture. Spoon or pipe mousse into small bowls or dessert cups. Cover and refrigerate until firm, about 4 hours. (Can be prepared 1 day ahead).

Yield: 10 to 12 servings

Julie Larson
Rebecca Torgerson

Note: This recipe calls for uncooked egg whites.

CHOCOLATE TORTE

2 ⅔ cups flour, divided
2 cups sugar
1 ½ cups unsalted butter,
  room temperature
2 eggs, room temperature
1 tablespoon cinnamon

Filling:
4 cups heavy cream
¾ cup unsweetened cocoa
  powder
½ cup powdered sugar

3 ounces semisweet
  chocolate, grated

Tear fourteen 9 ½ -inch long sheets of waxed paper. Stack sheets and, using a 9-inch pie pan as a guide, cut into circles. Combine 2 cups flour with sugar, butter, eggs and cinnamon in a large bowl. Mix at low speed until well blended. Increase speed to medium and beat until very light and fluffy, about 3 minutes. Stir in remaining ⅔ cup flour to form a soft dough. Dampen a large baking sheet with a moist cloth. Arrange 2 circles of waxed paper on baking sheet. Spread about ⅓ cup dough in very thin layer over each waxed paper circle, almost covering entire surface. Bake at 375° until edges are lightly browned, about 8 to 10 minutes. Set baking sheet on wire racks. Cool 5 minutes, then carefully transfer baked layers (with waxed paper circles attached) to another wire rack to cool completely. Repeat with remaining dough. Stack cooled layers on a flat plate, leaving paper as dividers. (Torte can be prepared up to 3 days ahead to this point. Wrap layers tightly with plastic wrap. Store in cool, dry place.) *For filling*, combine cream, cocoa and sugar in a large bowl. Beat at medium speed until soft peaks form. Arrange 1 baked chocolate layer on a flat platter and carefully peel off waxed paper. Spread about ½ cup filling over entire surface. Repeat layering, ending with filling. Sprinkle with grated chocolate. Chill torte about 30 minutes before serving to facilitate slicing. Slice with a sharp, thin-bladed knife.

Serves: 16

TRIPLE CHOCOLATE TORTE

2 eggs, separated
1 ½ cups sugar, divided
1 ¼ cups flour
½ cup unsweetened cocoa
  powder
¾ teaspoon baking soda
½ teaspoon salt
½ cup oil
1 cup buttermilk

Cream Filling:
⅔ cup sugar
⅓ cup unsweetened cocoa
  powder
1 ½ cups heavy cream,
  chilled
1 ½ teaspoons vanilla

Chocolate Glaze:
3 tablespoons butter
3 tablespoons light corn
  syrup
1 tablespoon water
1 cup semisweet chocolate
  chips

In a small mixer bowl, beat egg whites until foamy; gradually beat in ½ cup sugar until stiff peaks form. In a large mixer bowl, combine remaining 1 cup sugar, flour, cocoa powder, baking soda and salt. Add oil, buttermilk and egg yolks. Beat until smooth. Gently fold egg whites into batter. Pour batter into two greased and floured 9-inch round cake pans. Bake at 350° for 25 to 30 minutes. Let cool 5 minutes; remove from pans onto wire rack. Let cool completely. *For cream filling,* combine sugar and cocoa powder in a large bowl. Add cream and vanilla. Mix thoroughly on low speed, then increase speed to medium and beat until stiff. Cut cakes in half, horizontally. Place one half cake on serving plate. Spread ⅓ of the cream filling on top. Repeat layers, ending with cake layer on top. *For chocolate glaze,* combine butter, corn syrup and water in a small saucepan. Cook over medium heat, stirring constantly, until mixture begins to boil. Remove from heat; stir in chocolate morsels until melted. Let cool to room temperature. Spread glaze over top and sides of cake. Refrigerate cake until ready to serve. Remove from refrigerator 30 minutes before serving.

Serves: 12 to 16

Laurie Fulgham

"Easy to make, but allow yourself time. Best if made the day of serving, although can be made a day ahead. Rich and delicious!"

CREME DE MENTHE MOUSSE

60 large marshmallows (2
  10-ounce packages)
4 tablespoons butter
⅔ cup green creme de
  menthe
2 cups heavy cream
Few drops of green food
  coloring
2 dozen ladyfingers or 1
  prepared angel food cake

Fresh fruit

Melt marshmallows and butter in the top of an uncovered double boiler, or in microwave. Remove from heat. Stir in creme de menthe until smooth. Cool to room temperature. Beat cream to stiff peaks. Fold whipped cream into marshmallow mixture. Add green food coloring as desired, mixing well. Line a large springform pan or tube pan with lady fingers or strips of angel food cake. Cover with mousse. Chill until set, then unmold. Serve with seasonal fresh fruit.

Serves: 8 to 10

Almyra Whitehead

"Serve with frozen strawberries for a colorful Christmas dessert."

LEMON SOUFFLÉ

1 cup sugar, divided
2 tablespoons flour
2 tablespoons butter
4 eggs, separated
1 cup milk
Rind of 1 lemon, grated
¼ cup fresh lemon juice
½ teaspoon cream of tartar

Whipped cream

Grease the bottom of a 6 x 9-inch oven proof dish (do not grease sides). In a medium bowl, cream together ½ cup sugar, flour and butter. Add 4 beaten egg yolks, milk, lemon rind and lemon juice; set aside. Beat egg whites in a large bowl until foamy. Add cream of tartar; beat until stiff and dry. Add remaining ½ cup sugar. Fold lemon mixture into egg whites; pour into prepared dish. Set dish in a pan of hot water and bake at 350° for 45 min. Cool to room temperature (may be refrigerated at this point). May be served at room temperature or chilled. Top individual servings with whipped cream.

Serves: 6 to 8

Kristina Lantz

"This naturally separates into 2 layers-bottom is pudding, top is fluffy. I highly encourage making a double recipe because it goes so fast! "

LINZER TORTE

Butter
Dried bread crumbs, finely
   ground
1 cup sugar
2 cups ground almonds
   (about 8 ounces)
1 ½ cups plus 2 tablespoons
   flour
1 rounded teaspoon
   unsweetened cocoa
   powder
1 teaspoon cinnamon
1 package vanilla sugar (or 2
   teaspoons sugar plus
   ½ teaspoon vanilla)
⅛ teaspoon ground cloves
2 eggs, divided
4 teaspoons kirschwasser
1 cup (2 sticks) plus 2
   tablespoons butter,
   chilled
1 to 1 ½ cups raspberry jam

Powdered sugar (optional)

Prepare a 10-inch springform pan by greasing with butter and sprinkling with bread crumbs. In a large bowl, mix sugar, almonds, flour, cocoa, cinnamon, vanilla sugar and cloves together. Make a well in the middle. Add 1 egg and kirschwasser, mixing thoroughly. Add small pieces of butter and blend in using a pastry blender or fork. Mix until a dough has formed (do not overwork). Form into a ball and flatten; wrap in plastic wrap and refrigerator for 1 hour. Using ⅔ of the dough, roll out (or press with fingers) dough into prepared pan. Make an edge that is about one inch high. Fill pastry bottom with jam. Roll out remaining dough and cut into strips with pastry cutter. Lay strips over the top, making a diamond pattern. Thin strips can also be put around the edge of the torte. Brush a beaten egg or egg yolk over the lattice and rim of the torte. Bake torte at 350° for 50 to 60 minutes or until lightly browned. Remove from oven and let cool completely. Remove sides of pan to serve. Sprinkle with powdered sugar as desired.

Serves: 8 to 10

Diane Nippoldt

"A classic Austrian dessert featuring a raspberry filling."

MERINGUE TORTE

4 egg whites
Pinch of salt
¼ teaspoon cream of tartar
1 cup sugar

Filling:
6 ounces semisweet
   chocolate chips
3 tablespoons water
3 cups heavy cream
⅓ cup sugar

1 pint strawberries, hulled
   and sliced

Line 2 baking sheets with non-stick parchment paper. Trace three circles 8 inches in diameter. In a large bowl, beat egg whites until frothy. Add salt and cream of tartar. Beat until stiff peaks form. Gradually add 1 cup sugar, continuing to beat until meringue is stiff and glossy. Spread meringue evenly over circles. Bake slowly at 250° for 45 to 55 minutes. (Meringue should be lightly colored but still pliable.) Remove from oven. Carefully peel paper from bottom. Place meringues on rack to cool. *For filling,* melt chocolate chips with water in top of double boiler. Whip cream until stiff peaks form. Gradually add ⅓ cup sugar. Beat until very stiff peaks form. Place one meringue layer on a serving plate. Spread with thin layer of melted chocolate. Spread ¾ -inch layer of whipped cream over chocolate. Top with layer of fruit. Place second layer of meringue on top and repeat procedure. Top with third meringue layer. Frost sides and top with whipped cream. Decorate with fruit as desired. Refrigerate for 2 hours before serving.

Serves: 12

Renda Meloy

MARGARITA CHARLOTTE

Two dozen lady fingers

Filling:
1 (8-ounce) package cream
   cheese, softened
1 (14-ounce) can sweetened
   condensed milk
1 (6-ounce) can limeade
   concentrate, thawed
1 (3 ¾ -ounce) package
   instant lemon pudding
   mix
6 tablespoons tequila
1 tablespoon finely
   shredded lemon peel
1 tablespoon finely
   shredded lime peel
1 (8-ounce) container frozen
   whipped dessert topping,
   thawed

Citrus glaze:
⅔ cup sugar
1 tablespoon cornstarch
⅔ cup water
1 egg yolk, slightly beaten
½ teaspoon vanilla
2 tablespoons lemon juice
½ tablespoon butter
1 ½ teaspoons finely
   shredded lemon peel

Fresh raspberries for
   garnish

Line the bottom and sides of a 9-inch springform pan with lady fingers. *For filling,* beat cream cheese with an electric mixer until light and fluffy. Add condensed milk, limeade concentrate, pudding mix, tequila, lemon and lime peel, beating until smooth and blended. Fold in whipped topping. Turn into lined springform pan. Cover with plastic wrap and chill for several hours until firm. *For glaze,* combine sugar and cornstarch in a saucepan. Gradually add water, stirring until smooth. Bring to a boil, then boil 1 minute, stirring constantly. Remove from heat. Add a bit of the hot mixture to the egg yolk. Return all to saucepan, blending well. Cook over medium heat until thick and bubbly. Remove from heat. Add vanilla, lemon juice, butter and peel, stirring to mix thoroughly. Cover surface with waxed paper. Refrigerate until completely cooled. Unmold charlotte. Spoon glaze over the surface to cover before cutting and serving. Garnish with fresh raspberries as desired.

Serves: 12 to 16.

"This was an original endeavor of the cookbook committee. Enjoy!"

OBSTTORTE (FRUIT TORTE)

Butter
Dried breadcrumbs, finely
    ground
2 eggs, separated
2 tablespoons cold water
⅔ cup sugar
¼ teaspoon vanilla
1 cup sifted flour
½ teaspoon baking powder

Filling:
Canned or fresh fruits
1 rounded tablespoon sugar
    (if fresh fruits are used,
    use 3 rounded
    tablespoons sugar)
1 tablespoon cornstarch
1 ¼ cups fruit juice from
    the canned fruits, or
    1 ¼ cups water if fresh
    fruits are used

Whipped cream for garnish
Toasted almonds, grated, for
    garnish

Prepare a 10 ½ -inch tart pan with raised rim by greasing with butter; coat with breadcrumbs. In a large bowl, beat egg whites and water to stiff peaks. Add sugar and vanilla gradually, mixing thoroughly. Beat egg yolks with a fork; fold into sugar mixture. Sieve and simultaneously fold in flour and baking powder. Spoon batter into prepared pan and smooth out. Bake at 375° for 10 to 15 minutes. Remove from oven and let cool for 5 minutes. Loosen edges and invert on rack; let cool completely. *For filling,* arrange fruits decoratively in the center of the torte. (It should be practically covered.) In a small saucepan, stir together sugar and cornstarch. Add fruit juice or water slowly and stir well so that there will be no lumps. Bring to a boil, stirring constantly. Cook 1 to 2 minutes, until mixture clears. Remove from heat. Spoon immediately over the fruits, making sure all fruits are covered. Set aside to cool. Decorate with whipped cream and grated toasted almonds, if desired. Refrigerate until ready to serve.

Serves: 8

Diane Nippoldt

Ricotta Tart

1¾ cups flour
½ cup sugar
Grated zest of ½ lemon
⅓ cup butter, softened
1 egg

Filling:
1¼ cups ricotta cheese
3 eggs, separated
¼ cup sugar
½ tablespoon unsalted
    butter, softened

Sifted powdered sugar for
    garnish (optional)
Blueberries for garnish
    (optional)

Combine flour, sugar, lemon zest, butter and egg in the bowl of a food processor. Process with brief pulses until dough begins to come together in a ball. Gather dough into a ball, wrap in plastic wrap and refrigerate for about 1 hour. Meanwhile, *for filling*, combine ricotta cheese, egg yolks and sugar in a large mixing bowl; blend well. In a separate bowl, beat egg whites until stiff, moist peaks form. Gently fold egg whites into ricotta mixture. Grease a 9-inch flat tart pan with a removable bottom. On a lightly floured surface, roll out dough into a 10½-inch diameter circle. Transfer to prepared pan and press gently against bottom and sides. Trim dough even with the rim of the tart pan. Spoon filling into pastry shell and smooth out surface. Bake at 350° for 45 minutes, until just golden. Remove from oven. Let tart cool completely on wire rack. Remove rim and transfer tart to platter. Serve at room temperature. Sift powdered sugar on top and garnish with blueberries in the center of the tart, if desired.

Serves: 6

RUSSIAN DESSERT

3 egg yolks, slightly beaten
½ cup sugar
⅓ to ½ cup fresh orange
   juice
1 tablespoon grated orange
   rind
1 cup heavy cream, whipped
   stiff

1 chiffon, angelfood, or
   sponge cake
Sliced almonds for garnish

In the top of a double boiler, combine slightly beaten egg yolks, sugar and orange juice. Cook over hot water, stirring constantly until thickened, about 15 to 20 minutes. Remove from heat. Stir in grated orange rind. Cool and then chill completely. Fold in whipped cream and chill another hour so flavors can blend. Serve over slices of chiffon, angelfood, or sponge cake. Garnish with sliced almonds.

**Yield: 4 cups orange topping
        8 servings**

Phyllis Tracy

"This is an easy but delicious dessert to serve to your bridge club or any time!"

SACHERTORTE

½ cup (1 stick) unsalted
    butter
½ cup oil
1 cup water
2 cups sugar
2 cups flour
½ cup unsweetened cocoa
    powder
2 large eggs
½ cup buttermilk
2 teaspoons baking soda

2 cups seedless raspberry
    jam, pureed

Glaze:
1 cup heavy cream
16 ounces fine quality
    semisweet or bittersweet
    chocolate, chopped fine

Lightly sweetened whipped
    cream for garnish

In a small saucepan, combine butter, oil and water. Bring to a boil. In a bowl with an electric mixer, beat together sugar, flour and cocoa powder for 30 seconds, or until the mixture is well combined. Add butter mixture in a stream while beating. Beat just until thoroughly combined. Pour into a greased and floured 9-inch pan (2 inches deep). Bake torte in the middle of oven at 350° for 55 to 60 minutes, or until tester comes out clean. Remove from oven and cool pan on rack for 5 minutes. Turn torte onto rack and let cool completely. With a long serrated knife carefully cut the torte horizontally into 3 even layers. Invert the top layer onto a small rack, and spread it with about ½ cup of jam. Top the first layer with the middle layer. Spread it with about ½ cup of jam. Invert the third layer onto the middle layer. Spread the top and sides of the torte with the remaining jam. Chill the torte for at least 2 hours, or until it is very cold. *For glaze,* bring cream to a boil in a small saucepan. Put chocolate in a bowl and pour hot cream over it. Stir mixture until chocolate is melted and it forms a smooth glaze. Let cool until lukewarm and thickened but still pourable. Put the torte on a rack over a jelly-roll pan and pour glaze over it, spreading glaze to coat the top and sides evenly. Chill for 1 hour or until glaze is set. Garnish with whipped cream as desired.

Serves: 8

VIENNA SACHERTORTE

¾ cup cake flour
2 teaspoons baking powder
6 (1-ounce) squares
   semisweet chocolate
¾ cup unsalted butter,
   softened
¾ cup plus 2 tablespoons
   sugar
6 eggs, separated

1 (12-ounce) jar apricot
   preserves or jam

Chocolate Glaze:
1 cup heavy cream, divided
9 ounces bittersweet or
   semisweet chocolate,
   chopped finely or in the
   form of chips
1 tablespoon cognac
   (optional)

Sift flour and baking powder together; set aside. Melt chocolate in the top of a double boiler over barely simmering water, or in microwave. Set melted chocolate aside to cool slightly. In a large bowl, beat butter and ¾ cup sugar together until well blended. Add egg yolks one at a time; continue beating until mixture is fluffy and light. Stir in melted chocolate. Stir half of the flour mixture into the butter mixture. Beat egg whites in a separate bowl, until foamy. Add 2 tablespoons sugar and beat until soft peaks form. Gently fold half of the egg whites into the butter mixture. Fold in remaining flour mixture, then remaining egg whites, until completely blended. Pour batter into a greased and floured 9-inch springform pan, smoothing it well to the edges. Bake slowly at 250° for 40 minutes. Increase heat to 350° and bake for 40 minutes longer, or until toothpick inserted in center of cake comes out clean. Remove from oven and cool cake in the pan on wire rack for 20 minutes. (It will sink slightly in the center but that is because of its richness.) Carefully loosen cake around edge; release spring and remove side of pan. Cool cake for several hours. (It is very delicate when warm.) Carefully remove pan bottom. Heat apricot preserves in a small saucepan until softened and somewhat runny; press through a sieve into a small bowl. Halve cake horizontally with a long-bladed serrated knife. Put bottom layer on serving plate, or for easy handling, cut a cardboard round to fit and put cake layer on cardboard. Spread with two-thirds of sieved apricot preserves. Set top layer in place. Apply a thin layer of preserves to top and sides of cake to seal in any loose crumbs. Let dry several hours before glazing. *For chocolate glaze,* heat ¾ cup cream in a small, heavy saucepan to boiling point. Remove from heat and add chocolate. Cover for 5 minutes to allow chocolate to melt, then gently stir until smooth. Pass through a fine strainer, stir in cognac and allow to cool just until tepid. The glaze should mound a bit when dropped from a spoon before smoothly disappearing. If the glaze is too thick, add some of the remaining cream by teaspoon-fuls. Place the cake on a rack set on a baking sheet to catch excess glaze. Pour glaze onto the center of the cake, allowing the excess to flow down the sides. Smooth quickly and evenly with a large spatula. If any spots on the sides remain unglazed, use a spatula to lift up some glaze from the baking sheet to cover unglazed areas. Allow cake to set at room temperature for at least 2 hours. (Refrigerating the cake will speed up the process, but will dull the glaze.) Transfer to serving plate. **Serves: 12**

Diane Nippoldt

"Vienna's most famous gift to good eating is, perhaps, this dense, apricot-jam-filled chocolate cake, created in 1832 by 'master sugar baker' Franz Sacher to salve the sweet tooth of Prince von Metternich. It is still served in Vienna's venerable Hotel Sacher and shipped around the world to hundreds of thousands of fans. The original recipe is a well-guarded secret, but this one comes very close to the one on the hotel menu."

SHORTBREAD WITH RASPBERRY COULIS AND LEMON CREAM

Shortbread:
1 pound butter, softened
1 cup sugar
3 cups flour
¾ cup cornstarch

Raspberry Coulis:
1 (10-ounce) package frozen raspberries with syrup, thawed
1 (12-ounce) bag frozen raspberries without syrup, thawed

Lemon Cream:
4 eggs, separated
½ cup sugar
¼ cup lemon juice, strained
Rind of ½ lemon, grated
1 cup heavy cream

Fresh raspberries for garnish (optional)

For shortbread, cream together butter and sugar. Sift together flour and cornstarch; stir into creamed butter mixture, just until blended. Turn onto a floured surface; knead slightly. Divide into two equal parts. Grease two 9-inch round cake pans. Pat dough evenly into each pan. Pierce dough with fork or skewer. Bake at 375° for 5 minutes. Reduce heat to 300° and bake an additional 45 to 55 minutes until golden brown. Cut one shortbread into eight wedges while still warm. Sprinkle with granulated sugar. *For raspberry coulis,* blend both packages of raspberries together. Strain raspberries and discard seeds. Refrigerate. *For lemon cream,* place egg yolks in a bowl. Beat thoroughly, adding sugar a little at a time. When pale and fluffy, beat in strained lemon juice and grated lemon peel. Cook slowly in the top of a double boiler over simmering water, stirring constantly until mixture thickens somewhat. Take great care not to overheat or it will curdle. Remove from heat and cool. Beat whipping cream and egg whites in separate bowls until stiff and fold first the cream, then the egg whites gently but thoroughly into the cooled lemon mixture. Transfer to a glass serving bowl and chill for at least 2 hours. *To assemble,* ladle raspberry coulis onto dessert plate. Place a shortbread wedge on top of coulis. Spoon lemon cream onto shortbread. Garnish with fresh raspberries.

Serves: 8

Marilee Wood
Margaret O'Sullivan

"This makes a colorful and fresh tasting dessert. Only one pan of shortbread is necessary for this recipe. Cut second pan into sixteenths while still warm and enjoy small wedges the next day. Store in an air tight tin."

SCHWARZWALDER KIRSCHTORTE
(BLACK FOREST CHERRY TORTE)

2 eggs, separated
1 ½ cups sugar, divided
1 ¾ cups cake flour
¾ teaspoon baking soda
1 teaspoon salt
⅓ cup oil
1 cup milk, divided
2 ounces unsweetened
   chocolate, melted and
   cooled

Cherry Filling:
2 (16-ounce) cans pitted tart
   red cherries, plus juice
⅔ cup sugar
¼ cup cornstarch
1 teaspoon vanilla

Chocolate Buttercream
Frosting:
3 tablespoons butter or
   margarine
2 cups sifted powdered
   sugar, divided
1 ounce unsweetened
   chocolate, melted and
   cooled
2 tablespoons half and half
1 teaspoon vanilla

Topping:
1 teaspoon unflavored
   gelatin
2 tablespoons cold water
3 cups heavy cream
⅛ cup kirsch or cherry
   liqueur
¾ cup sliced almonds,
   toasted

1 ounce semisweet or milk
   chocolate, shaved
Maraschino cherries

In a small bowl, beat egg whites until soft peaks form. Gradually add ½ cup sugar, beating until stiff peaks form. Set aside. In a large bowl, sift together cake flour, 1 cup sugar, baking soda and salt. Add oil and ½ cup milk. Beat for 1 minute at medium speed, scraping bowl often. Add remaining milk and egg yolks; beat 1 minute more. Fold in egg whites, mixing well. Pour a third of the batter into a greased and lightly floured 9-inch round cake pan. (You may also use waxed paper or parchment on the bottom of the pan. Be sure to grease and flour.) Set aside. Add cooled, melted chocolate to remaining mixture in bowl; fold until well blended. Pour chocolate batter into two more prepared 9-inch cake pans. Bake all three layers at 350° for 20 to 25 minutes, or until they test done. Remove from oven. Cool in pans for 10 minutes, then remove and cool on wire racks. *For cherry filling,* drain cherries, reserving ⅔ cup juice. In a 2-quart saucepan, combine sugar and cornstarch. Stir in reserved juice. Cook over medium heat, stirring constantly, until mixture is thickened and bubbly. Add cherries; cook two minutes more. Remove from heat. Stir in vanilla. Set aside to cool. *For chocolate buttercream frosting,* cream butter in a medium bowl. Add 1 cup sifted powdered sugar, mixing well. Beat in melted and cooled chocolate, cream and vanilla. Gradually beat in remaining cup of sifted powdered sugar until fluffy. Add a teaspoon or two more of light cream, if necessary, to make of piping consistency. Set aside. *For topping,* combine gelatin and water in a small heatproof cup. Place over low heat, stirring just until dissolved. Set aside but do not cool. In a large bowl, whip cream until slightly thickened. Add gelatin all at once; continue beating until soft peaks form. *To assemble cake,* place one chocolate cake layer on a serving plate. (If you find cakes have become rounded on top during baking, use a serrated knife or cake slicer to cut a thin slice off the top so cakes will lie flat.) Fit pastry bag with medium rose point (no. 2F); fill with chocolate butter cream. Starting a third of the way out from the center of the cake, pipe a ring of buttercream frosting. Pipe a second ring ⅔ of the way from the center. Pipe a third ring around outer edge of cake. Fill in area between buttercream with some of the cherry filling. Spread a thin layer (1 cup) of whipped cream over top. Place yellow cake layer on top. Drizzle or brush kirsch or cherry liqueur over cake. Put about 2 cups of the whipped cream in pastry bag with large rosette tip (no. 1C); pipe a band of whipped cream about 2 inches wide around outer edge of cake layer (save enough cream for rosette garnish). Fill center with cherry filling (there will be some left over). Place second chocolate cake layer over cherries. Frost cake with remaining whipped cream. Press almonds onto side of cake. Pipe rosettes evenly around top of cake. Sprinkle shaved chocolate in center. Garnish rosettes with cherries. Chill until ready to serve.

Serves: 12 to 16

Diane Nippoldt

"This cake takes some time, but it is an elegant dessert."

WHITE CHOCOLATE ALMOND POUNDCAKE WITH AMARETTO CREME ANGLAISE

3 ounces white chocolate, coarsely chopped
9 tablespoons butter
1 cup plus 2 tablespoons sugar
3 large eggs
2 ⅓ cups flour
¾ teaspoon baking powder
¼ teaspoon salt
½ cup sour cream
2 tablespoons amaretto
⅓ cup sliced almonds, toasted*

Amaretto Creme Sauce:
1 cup heavy cream
2 eggs, beaten
2 tablespoons amaretto
2 tablespoons sugar

or

Melt chocolate with butter in a small saucepan, over low heat, or in a microwave proof container, with microwave set on partial power. Stir frequently while melting, until ingredients have melted and mixture is smooth. Set aside to cool until barely warm. Beat sugar and eggs in a large bowl until well mixed. Beat in chocolate-butter mixture. Stir together flour, baking powder and salt. Add alternately to creamed mixture with sour cream and amaretto. Stir in sliced almonds. Turn the batter into a greased and floured 9 x 5-inch loaf pan. Bake at 350° for 55 minutes, or until a toothpick inserted into the center of the cake comes out clean. Remove from oven and set pan on a rack to cool for 5 minutes. Loosen cake by running a knife around the edge of the pan. Invert pan to remove cake. Cool completely, then wrap tightly in plastic wrap. Flavors will improve overnight with cake tightly wrapped. *For amaretto creme sauce*, combine cream, eggs, amaretto and sugar in

Amaretto Chocolate Sauce:
½ cup butter or margarine
1 cup plus 2 tablespoons
   sugar
¹⁄₁₆ teaspoon salt
½ cup unsweetened cocoa
   powder
¾ cup light or heavy cream
1 ½ teaspoon vanilla
¼ cup amaretto

the top of a double boiler. Whisk until well blended. Cook, stirring constantly, over low heat until thickened (do not boil). Pour sauce into a serving bowl; cool. Serve at room temperature or chilled. Store sauce, tightly covered, in refrigerator. To reheat, return sauce to a saucepan and place over low heat, stirring frequently, until just warmed. *For amaretto chocolate sauce,* melt butter in a quart saucepan, over medium heat. Blend in sugar, salt, cocoa and cream using a whisk or rotary beater. Heat, stirring occasionally, until sugar is dissolved. Remove from heat. Stir in vanilla and amaretto. Serve warm or cold.

*To toast almonds, spread them on a shallow baking pan. Set in 350° oven for 7 to 10 minutes, stirring frequently until golden brown. Set aside to cool before adding to the batter.

Serves: 8 to 10

Margo Stich

"Chocolate lovers may prefer the intensity of a dark chocolate amaretto sauce on this poundcake. For an alternate sauce, try heavenly Amaretto Chocolate Sauce."

ZUCCOTTO

¾ cup chopped pecans
1 teaspoon oil
Salt
1 (12-ounce) pound cake
⅓ cup amaretto liqueur
3 tablespoons Cointreau
⅔ cup miniature semisweet
    chocolate bits, divided
2 cups heavy cream
⅓ cup plus 2 tablespoons
    powdered sugar, divided
4 teaspoons light corn syrup
2 teaspoons vanilla
2 tablespoons unsweetened
    cocoa powder

Place pecans in a shallow pan. Drizzle with oil and sprinkle lightly with salt; toss to mix. Toast pecans in oven at 375° until golden brown, about 5 minutes, stirring occasionally. Remove from oven and set aside to cool. Cut pound cake into ⅛-inch slices and cut each slice in half diagonally. Place cake triangles close together on a jelly roll pan. Combine liqueurs in a measuring cup and drizzle evenly over cake. Line a 1½-quart round-bottomed bowl with plastic wrap. Place a triangle of cake against the inside of the bowl and repeat until the inside of the bowl is completely lined with cake. If there are gaps, fill in with pieces of moistened cake (reserve some for top). Coarsely chop ⅓ cup plus 1 tablespoon chocolate bits; set aside. In a chilled bowl, combine cream, ⅓ cup powdered sugar, corn syrup and vanilla. Beat until cream is very stiff. Fold in ½ cup toasted pecans and chopped chocolate bits. Divide mixture into 2 equal parts. Spoon half of the whipped cream mixture into the cake-lined bowl, spreading it evenly over entire cake surface. Leave a well in the center. Melt the remaining chocolate bits. Cool slightly and fold into remaining half of whipped cream mixture. Spoon into cavity, completely filling the center. Even top, trimming pieces of cake. Top mixture with remaining cake pieces and cover bowl with plastic wrap. Refrigerate overnight. *To serve,* remove top layer of plastic wrap. Cover bowl with a flat serving dish and invert dessert onto the plate. Lift off bowl, and carefully remove plastic wrap. Refrigerate until serving time. Combine 2 tablespoons powdered sugar and cocoa in a jar with a shaker top. Sprinkle mixture over top and sides of unmolded dessert just before serving. Sprinkle with remaining chopped pecans. Cut into wedges and serve.

Serves: 8 to 10

Kay Love-Caskey

APPLE AND PEAR SAUTÉ

1 large golden delicious apple
2 small Bosc pears
1 tablespoon butter
¼ teaspoon ground allspice
¼ teaspoon finely grated lemon peel

Core apple and cut into ⅓-inch thick slices. Core pear and cut into ¾-inch thick slices. Melt butter in a heavy skillet over medium-high heat. Add apple and stir gently for 2 minutes. Add pears and stir gently for 2 more minutes. Add remaining ingredients and stir until fruit is just tender, about 2 more minutes. Serve immediately.

Serves: 2

Diane Nippoldt

"This is a nice, low calorie alternative for dessert, and can easily be doubled or tripled to serve more. May also be served as a side dish accompaniment to pork chops or a pork roast."

TRIPLE BERRY TART

1 ¾ cups flour
⅓ cup sugar
1 tablespoon grated lemon
  peel
½ teaspoon salt
¾ cup chilled unsalted
  butter, cut into pieces
2 large egg yolks
1 tablespoon fresh lemon
  juice
1 teaspoon vanilla
1 tablespoon water

Filling:
⅓ cup red currant jelly
¼ cup raspberry jam
2 tablespoons framboise
  eau-de-vie (clear
  raspberry brandy), kirsch
  (clear cherry brandy) or
  orange juice
½ pint blackberries or
  boysenberries
1 pint strawberries, hulled
½ cup fresh blueberries

Combine flour, sugar, lemon peel and salt in a large bowl. Add butter pieces and blend until mixture resembles coarse meal. Whisk egg yolks, lemon juice and vanilla in small bowl to blend. Add to flour mixture and stir until moist clumps form, adding water by tablespoons if mixture is dry. Roll dough into a ball and flatten. Wrap dough tightly in plastic and refrigerate for 3 hours. Roll dough out on a lightly floured surface to 13-inch round. Transfer dough to a 9-inch tart pan with removable bottom. Press dough onto bottom and up sides; trim edges. Pierce bottom of dough all over with fork. Refrigerate for 2 hours. Line crust with aluminum foil. Fill with dried beans, rice or pie weights. Bake at 425° for 20 minutes or until golden brown. Remove from oven to rack to cool. *For filling*, cook jelly, jam and brandy in a small heavy saucepan over medium-high heat for about 3 minutes, until thick; stir frequently. Brush some of the jam glaze over bottom of tart. Arrange a circle of blackberries in the ring just inside of tart edge. Arrange strawberries in ring, pointed end up, inside ring of blackberries. Fill center of tart with blueberries. Brush remaining jam glaze over all the berries. (Tart can be prepared 2 hours ahead; let stand at room temperature.) Cut into wedges to serve. Serve at room temperature.

Serves: 6

Julie Roenigk

BUTTERSCOTCH APPLE DESSERT

Filling:
1 (12-ounce) package
  butterscotch morsels
⅓ cup brown sugar
⅓ cup flour
¾ teaspoon cinnamon

2 ½ pounds tart apples,
  cored, peeled and diced

Topping:
½ cup flour
¼ cup brown sugar
¼ cup butter
1 cup pecans, chopped
¾ cup quick or old-
  fashioned oats, uncooked

Whipped cream, vanilla ice
  cream or frozen vanilla
  yogurt

For filling, in small bowl, combine butterscotch morsels, brown sugar, flour and cinnamon; set aside. Place apples in an ungreased 9 x 13-inch baking pan. Sprinkle filling mixture over apples. Bake at 375° for 20 minutes. *For topping,* combine flour and brown sugar in a small bowl. With a pastry blender cut in butter until crumbly. Stir in pecans and oats. Sprinkle over hot apple mixture. Return dessert to oven and bake 30 to 40 minutes longer, until apples are tender. Cool slightly. Serve warm with whipped cream, vanilla ice cream or frozen vanilla yogurt.

Serves: 8 to 10

Connie Gambini

FRUIT COMPOTE

2 cups peach slices
2 cups strawberries
2 cups blueberries, frozen
  and well drained
2 cups grapes or fresh
  pineapple
1 (8-ounce) package cream
  cheese, softened
2 tablespoons lemon juice
1 teaspoon grated lemon
  peel
½ cup heavy cream
½ cup powdered sugar
Lemon rind for garnish

Layer fruit in a trifle bowl or serving bowl; set aside. In a medium mixer bowl, combine cream cheese, lemon juice and lemon peel. Beat until smooth and fluffy. In a small mixer bowl, combine heavy cream and powdered sugar. Beat until thickened and smooth. Fold into cream cheese mixture, blending thoroughly. Pour over fruit. Garnish with lemon rind. Refrigerate until ready to serve.

Serves: 8 to 10

Sheila Kramer

ORANGE-GLAZED BANANAS

6 bananas, halved
  lengthwise
¾ cup orange juice
¼ cup orange liqueur
  (Grand Marnier
  preferred)
3 tablespoons unsalted
  butter
⅓ cup chopped walnuts
⅓ cup brown sugar

Vanilla ice cream or sour
  cream

Arrange bananas in a shallow baking dish. Combine orange juice and liqueur; pour over bananas. Dot with butter. Bake at 450° for 10 minutes, basting occasionally. Sprinkle with nuts and brown sugar. Continue baking until sugar is melted and nuts are glazed and toasted, about 5 minutes more. Serve warm with ice cream or sour cream.

Serves: 6

Diane Nippoldt

POACHED WINTER PEARS

6 medium Bosc winter pears
3 tablespoons lemon juice
1 ½ cups sugar
1 teaspoon vanilla
3 cups water
1 cup crushed almond
  macaroons
3 to 4 tablespoons Grand
  Marnier

Chocolate sauce (optional)
Mint leaves for garnish

Wash pears. Core each from bottom, leaving stem attached. Pare. Brush each pear with lemon juice. In a large kettle or skillet, combine sugar, vanilla and water. Bring to a boil over medium heat, stirring until sugar is dissolved. Add pears. Reduce heat, and simmer covered until pears are tender, but not soft, about 15 minutes. Turn into a large bowl, cover and chill for 3 hours. Combine crushed macaroons and Grand Marnier; mix well. Carefully remove pears from the syrup to drain on paper towels. Fill center of each pear with macaroon mixture, about 1 tablespoon for each. Brush pears with Grand Marnier. Refrigerate. *To serve,* place one pear on individual serving dish and top with 1 or 2 tablespoons of chocolate sauce, if desired. Garnish with a mint leaf.

Serves: 6

Nina Sudor

"My mother made this recipe using orange juice mixed with the macaroons. I changed to Grand Marnier when I became of age."

RHUBARB CRUNCH

Crust:
1 cup flour
5 tablespoons powdered sugar
½ cup butter, softened

Topping:
2 eggs
1 ½ cups sugar
¼ cup flour
¾ teaspoon baking powder
¼ teaspoon salt
2 to 3 cups diced rhubarb

Mix flour, powdered sugar and butter together. Press into a 9-inch square pan. Bake at 350° for 15 minutes. *For topping*, beat eggs in a large bowl. Gradually add sugar, flour, baking powder and salt. Stir in rhubarb. Pour over crust. Bake for 35 minutes more.

Serves: 8 to 9

Ann Groover

STRAWBERRY BRULEE

1 quart fresh strawberries
1 (3-ounce) package cream cheese, softened
¾ cup sour cream
¼ cup plus 1 ½ tablespoons brown sugar, divided

Slice strawberries and place in a 9 x 9-inch ovenproof glass pan. Combine cream cheese, sour cream and 1 ½ tablespoons brown sugar. Beat well with a whisk. Spoon evenly over sliced strawberries. Sieve ¼ cup brown sugar over top. Broil 4 to 5 inches from heat for 2 to 3 minutes until golden and bubbly. Serve immediately.

Serves: 8

Sally Hanson

STRAWBERRIES WITH RASPBERRY SAUCE

4 cups strawberries, hulled
3 cups raspberries
1 ½ tablespoons lemon
  juice
Powdered sugar to taste
½ cup crumbled macaroons
  or amaretti (Italian
  macaroons)

Arrange strawberries in a one-quart jar. Puree raspberries in blender or food processor with lemon juice and powdered sugar to taste. Press through fine sieve into jar with strawberries. Seal tightly and refrigerate until well chilled. Spoon strawberries with sauce into bowls to serve. Top with macaroons.

Serves: 4

Diane Nippoldt

COCOA SORBET

1 ½ cups water
1 ½ cups sugar
1 ¼ cups unsweetened
  alkalized cocoa powder
½ cup freshly brewed
  espresso
2 teaspoons vanilla

Combine water and sugar in a medium saucepan. Cook over medium heat, stirring constantly, until sugar is dissolved. Increase heat to medium-high and bring the mixture to a gentle boil. Remove pan from heat. Gradually whisk in cocoa until combined. Whisk in espresso and vanilla. Strain the mixture through a fine-meshed sieve into a medium metal bowl. Fill a large bowl with iced water. Set metal bowl into water bath. Stir chocolate mixture occasionally for 10 to 15 minutes, or until completely cool. Cover surface of the mixture with plastic wrap. Refrigerate for 4 to 6 hours or overnight, until very cold. Pour chocolate mixture into the container of an ice cream maker and freeze according to manufacturer's instructions. Transfer sorbet to a chilled bowl or loaf pan and cover the surface with plastic wrap. Freeze overnight or until ready to serve.

Serves: 6

Cherie Miles

"A heart-healthy dessert, and chocolate too!"

OLD-FASHIONED RICE PUDDING

4 eggs
¾ cup sugar
2 cups non-fat dairy milk
1 ½ cups cooked rice
1 ½ teaspoons lemon juice
1 ½ teaspoons vanilla
1 tablespoon melted butter
1 teaspoon nutmeg
Raisins (optional)

Raspberry sauce (optional)
Whipped cream (optional)
Dash of nutmeg (optional)

Grease a 2-quart casserole dish. Beat together eggs, sugar and milk. Stir in rice, lemon juice, vanilla, melted butter, nutmeg and raisins. Pour into casserole dish and set in a larger pan of hot water. Bake at 350° for 45 minutes or until knife comes out clean. Serve warm or cold. Top with raspberry sauce or whipped cream with a dash of nutmeg, if desired.

Serves: 4

Nan Douglas

"Use any pureed fruit for sauce, or try strained baby fruit with a splash of Grand Marnier."

STEAMED PERSIMMON PUDDING

1 cup flour
1 cup sugar
1 teaspoon baking powder
Pinch of salt
½ teaspoon cinnamon
1 teaspoon baking soda
1 egg, beaten
½ cup whole milk
1 cup persimmon pulp,
  (peeled and diced)
1 teaspoon margarine, melted
½ cup walnuts, chopped
  (optional)

Whipped cream or ice cream

Combine dry ingredients; set aside. Combine egg, milk, persimmon and margarine, mixing well. Add to dry ingredients, stirring until blended. Add walnuts. Place in top of double boiler over simmering water. Cover and steam for 2 hours. Do not remove the cover while steaming. Serve with whipped cream or ice cream.

Serves: 6 to 8

Dorothy Hartman

CHOCOLATE SAUCE SUPREME

4 (1-ounce) squares
   unsweetened chocolate
1 ½ cups sugar
1 cup sweetened condensed
   milk
4 tablespoons butter
1 teaspoon vanilla

Vanilla ice cream

In a small heavy saucepan, melt chocolate and sugar. Slowly stir in milk. Cook 6 minutes, stirring constantly. Remove from heat. Add butter and vanilla, stirring until melted and smooth. Serve warm over ice cream. Refrigerate leftovers.

Yield: 1 ½ cups sauce

Janet Engels

ENGLISH APPLE PIE

1 cup flour
1 teaspoon baking soda
1 teaspoon cinnamon
¾ teaspoon mace or nutmeg
¼ teaspoon salt
¼ cup butter
1 cup sugar
1 egg
2 cups grated unpeeled
   apples

Sauce:
½ cup butter
1 cup sugar
½ cup half and half
1 teaspoon vanilla
2 to 3 tablespoons rum

Sift together first five ingredients; set aside. Cream together butter, sugar, and egg until light and fluffy. Add apples to creamed mixture and stir. Add dry ingredients, mixing thoroughly. Pour into a 9-inch pie pan. Bake at 400° for 20 to 30 minutes, until baked through. *For sauce*, combine butter, sugar and half and half in a saucepan. Cook and stir until sugar is dissolved and mixture has thickened slightly. (If made a day ahead, refrigerate and reheat.) Just before serving, add vanilla and rum. Serve pie at room temperature and ladle warm sauce over slices.

Yield: 6 to 8

Cindy Ullman

RHUBARB AND APPLE PIE

2 prepared pastry crusts, unbaked, or 1 (15-ounce) package of 2 all-ready refrigerated pie crusts
2 Granny Smith apples, cored, peeled and thinly sliced
2 cups cubed rhubarb
1 cup plus 1 teaspoon sugar, divided
2 eggs
2 tablespoons minute tapioca
3 tablespoons flour, divided
1 to 2 tablespoons butter

Put bottom crust into a 9 or 10-inch pie pan. Place one layer of apples to cover bottom and sprinkle with 1 teaspoon sugar. Reserving 4 slices of apple, combine the remaining apples, rhubarb, 1 cup sugar, eggs, tapioca and 2 tablespoons flour. Mix thoroughly. Pour mixture over layer of apples. Arrange reserved apple slices on top. Sprinkle with a little sugar. Dot the filling with butter. Sprinkle a thin row of flour around edge of the filling to absorb the juices. Cover pie with top crust. Seal edges of crust with a little water on your finger. Cut slits in top crust to allow steam to escape. Bake at 400° for 1 hour or until golden brown.

Serves: 8

Celia Weitz

"This is an original recipe. Everyone thinks the pie is really delicious."

SOUR CREAM APPLE PIE

Crust:
1 cup flour
¼ teaspoon salt
¼ cup light margarine
3 to 4 tablespoons cold milk

Filling:
2 tablespoons flour
⅛ teaspoon salt
¾ cup sugar
1 egg
**1 cup non-fat dairy sour
   cream**
1 teaspoon vanilla
¼ teaspoon nutmeg
**2 cups sliced, peeled baking
   apples**

In a medium mixing bowl, stir together flour and salt. Using a pastry blender, cut in margarine until pieces are the size of small peas. Sprinkle 1 tablespoon milk; gently toss with a fork. Repeat, using 1 tablespoon milk at a time until all is moistened. Form dough into a ball. On a lightly floured surface, use your hands to slightly flatten dough. Roll dough from center to edges, forming a 12-inch circle. Wrap pastry around the rolling pin. Unroll onto a 9-inch pie plate. Trim pastry to ½ inch beyond edge of plate. Fold under extra pastry and crimp edge. *For filling,* combine flour, salt and sugar in a medium bowl; blend with a fork. Add egg, sour cream, vanilla and nutmeg. Beat well with a fork until batter is smooth and thin. Place sliced apples into unbaked pie shell. Pour batter over apples. Bake at 400° for 15 minutes. Reduce heat to 350° and continue baking for 25 to 30 minutes, or until filling is set. Cool completely on rack. Refrigerate until ready to serve.

Serves: 8

Cherie Miles

Best Ever Pecan Pie

1 cup sugar
1 cup pecans
1 cup dark maple-flavored
    pancake syrup
3 eggs
1 teaspoon vanilla
4 tablespoons butter, melted
Dash of salt
1 (9-inch) pie crust, unbaked

Combine all ingredients except pie crust. Mix well. Pour into prepared crust. Bake at 300° for 1 hour.

Serves: 6 to 8

Almyra Whitehead

Praline Pumpkin Pie

3 tablespoons margarine,
    melted
⅓ cup brown sugar
⅓ cup pecans, chopped
1 (9-inch) pie shell, unbaked

Pumpkin Pie Filling:
1 (16-ounce) can pumpkin
⅔ cup sugar
1 teaspoon ground cinnamon
½ teaspoon ground ginger
½ teaspoon ground nutmeg
3 eggs
1 (5-ounce) can evaporated
    milk
½ cup milk

Whipped cream for garnish
    (optional)

Combine margarine, sugar and pecans. Spread over pie shell. Bake at 450° for 10 minutes. Remove from oven and cool for 10 minutes. *For pumpkin pie filling* (or use your own favorite), stir together pumpkin, sugar, cinnamon, ginger and nutmeg in a large mixing bowl. Add eggs. Beat until thoroughly combined. Gradually stir in evaporated milk and milk. Mix well. Pour over praline layer. Bake at 350° for 35 minutes or until filling is set. Remove from oven and cool. Serve with whipped cream as desired.

Serves: 6 to 8

Dorothy Hartman

Fresh Strawberry Pie

1 frozen pie crust
1 (3-ounce) package cream
  cheese, softened
Milk, as needed
1 to 1 ½ quarts fresh
  strawberries, cleaned and
  hulled

Glaze:
1 cup sugar
3 tablespoons cornstarch
1 tablespoon lemon juice
Red food coloring (optional)

Whipped cream (optional)

Bake pie crust according to package directions. Soften cream cheese and add just enough milk so it will spread easily on the bottom of baked pie shell. Halve the nicest strawberries and place them open side down on the cream cheese to make one layer. *For glaze,* mash the rest of the strawberries and add water to make 2 cups (or use more strawberries). Bring to a boil in a saucepan. Boil for 1 minute. Remove from heat. Mix together sugar and cornstarch. Add to strawberry mixture. Add lemon juice and red food coloring, if desired. Bring to second boil and boil until thick and clear, about 5 to 6 minutes. Let cool about half an hour. Pour glaze over strawberries. Refrigerate for at least 2 hours. Serve with whipped cream.

Variation: Increase cream cheese to 6 ounces. Omit milk. Add ½ cup sugar, mixing well. In a small bowl, whip ½ cup heavy cream until stiff. Combine with cream cheese mixture. Spread in cooled pie shell. Place 8 to 12 whole berries bottom up, on cheese mixture. Mash remaining strawberries, adding enough water to make 1 ½ cups. Continue as above. Pour cooled glaze over berries. Refrigerate.

Yield: 8

Ellen Cascino
Judy King
Sheila Kramer

"Great recipe! Looks pretty! Light!"

MOCHA ALMOND ICE CREAM PIE

2 ¾ cups (about 12 ounces) sliced, blanched almonds, divided
1 ¼ cups chocolate wafer crumbs
¼ cup unsalted butter, melted

Filling:
3 ½ tablespoons amaretto
2 pints coffee ice cream, softened
4 ounces bittersweet or semi-sweet chocolate, chopped fine
1 ounce bittersweet or semi-sweet chocolate, grated for garnish

Spread almonds on a baking sheet. Toast almonds at 350° for 10 to 15 minutes, stirring occasionally, just until they are light brown. Cool. Finely grind 1 cup toasted almonds in a food processor or blender. In a large bowl, combine ground almonds, chocolate wafer crumbs and melted butter; mix well. Pat mixture on the bottom and sides of a greased 10-inch tart pan with removable rim. Freeze crust for 30 minutes or until it is firm. *For filling,* grind 1 ½ cups of the almonds in a food processor or blender until it forms a nut butter. Blend in amaretto. Add ice cream and 4 ounces of chopped chocolate. Blend until the filling is smooth and well combined. (If using a blender, the ice cream and chocolate may be easier to add by hand). Pour filling into crust; spread evenly. Garnish with remaining ¼ cup almonds and grated chocolate. Freeze the pie for one hour. Cover with plastic wrap and freeze overnight.

Serves: 8

Sally Duffy

"Please note that the pie should be frozen overnight."

Banana Sour Cream Bars

1 ½ cups sugar
1 cup sour cream
½ cup butter or margarine,
  softened
2 eggs
1 ½ cups mashed ripe
  bananas (about 3 large
  bananas)
2 teaspoons vanilla
2 cups flour
1 teaspoon salt
1 teaspoon baking soda
½ cup nuts, chopped

Frosting:
¼ cup butter or margarine
2 cups powdered sugar
1 teaspoon vanilla
3 tablespoons milk

In a large mixing bowl, on low speed, cream together sugar, sour cream and butter. Add eggs, mixing well. Beat in bananas and vanilla. In another bowl, sift flour, salt and baking soda together. Add to banana mixture, mixing well. Stir in nuts. Pour into a greased 10 x 15-inch jelly roll pan. Bake at 375° for 20 to 25 minutes, until light brown. Remove from oven and cool completely. *For frosting,* heat butter in a medium saucepan, over medium heat, until light brown. Remove from heat. Stir in powdered sugar. Add vanilla and milk. Stir until frosting is of spreading consistency. Spread on slightly warm bars. Cool completely before cutting.

Yield: 3 to 4 dozen

Janet Engels

BUTTER PECAN TURTLE BARS

Crust:
2 cups flour
1 cup brown sugar
½ cup butter

Filling:
1 cup whole pecans
⅔ cup butter
½ cup brown sugar
**1 cup milk chocolate or
  semisweet chocolate
  chips**

Mix crust ingredients until well blended. Pat into an ungreased 9 x 13-inch pan. *For filling,* sprinkle pecans over crust. Heat butter and brown sugar over medium heat, stirring constantly, until it comes to a boil. Boil for 1 minute. Pour over pecans and crust. Bake at 350° for 18 to 20 minutes. Caramel layer should be bubbly and light golden brown. Remove from oven and sprinkle chocolate chips over top. Allow to melt for 2 to 3 minutes. Swirl chips as they melt. Cool completely and cut into squares to serve.

Yield: 3 to 4 dozen bars

Lisa Rodysill

CARROT BARS

Bars:
1 cup golden raisins
4 eggs
2 cups sugar
2 teaspoons baking soda
½ teaspoon salt
2 teaspoons cinnamon
1 ½ cups oil
3 small jars strained baby
    food carrots or 1 cup
    cooked sieved carrots
1 teaspoon vanilla
2 ½ cups flour
1 ½ cups walnut pieces

Frosting:
1 (8-ounce) package cream
    cheese, softened
6 tablespoons butter or
    margarine, softened
2 ¼ cups powdered sugar
1 ½ teaspoons vanilla

Grease and flour two 9 x 13-inch pans or one 11 x 17-inch pan. Place golden raisins in a jar or bowl and cover with hot tap water to soften. In a large mixing bowl, beat eggs well. Add sugar, mixing well. Add baking soda, salt, cinnamon, oil, carrots and vanilla. Blend well. Add flour and walnut pieces. Drain raisins and add to batter. Stir until mixed. Pour into prepared pan. Bake at 350° for 40 minutes or until done. Remove from oven and cool bars completely. *For frosting,* combine cream cheese and butter in mixer bowl. Add powdered sugar and vanilla; beat thoroughly until smooth. (You may need to add up to 1 tablespoon milk to reach a spreading consistency.) Spread generously over bars.

Serves: Lots!
    40 to 48 bars

Ellen Hurley

"These freeze well, if you can hide them long enough!"

BOURBON BARS

1 (18 ½ -ounce) box yellow
  cake mix
2 teaspoons nutmeg
½ cup corn oil
½ cup bourbon
3 eggs, separated
¼ cup sugar
1 cup chopped pecans

Reserve ⅓ cup dry cake mix. In a large bowl, combine remaining cake mix, nutmeg, corn oil, bourbon and egg yolks. Mix at low speed until moist, then increase to medium speed for one minute. In a small bowl, beat egg whites until frothy. Gradually add sugar and continue to beat until soft peaks form. Gently fold egg whites into cake mixture. Combine reserved cake mix with pecans. Fold into cake batter. Spread in a well-greased 15 x 10-inch jelly roll pan. Bake at 325° for 25 to 30 minutes, or until top springs back. Cool completely before cutting.

Yield: About 40 bars

Almyra Whitehead

S'MORES BARS

2 cups graham cracker
  crumbs
⅓ cup sugar
¼ teaspoon salt
½ cup (1 stick) unsalted
  butter, melted
1 pound milk chocolate
4 cups mini-marshmallows

Combine graham cracker crumbs, sugar, salt and butter in a bowl. Reserve one cup of mixture. Press remaining mixture into the bottom of a 9 x 13-inch flameproof baking dish. Bake the crust at 350° for 12 minutes, or until golden. Remove from oven to rack to cool. Melt chocolate in a double boiler or microwave. Pour chocolate over cooled crust, spreading evenly. Sprinkle with marshmallows, pressing them lightly into the chocolate. Top with reserved crumb mixture. Place under a preheated broiler, about 2 inches from the heat, for 30 seconds, or until the marshmallows are golden. Let pan cool completely before cutting into squares.

Yield: 24 bars

Renda Meloy

CREME DE MENTHE BROWNIES

Brownies:
1 cup sugar
½ cup margarine
4 eggs
1 cup flour
½ teaspoon salt
1 (16-ounce) can chocolate
  syrup
1 teaspoon vanilla

Frosting:
2 cups powdered sugar
2 tablespoons creme de
  menthe
½ cup margarine or butter

Chocolate glaze:
1 cup chocolate chips
6 tablespoons margarine or
  butter

Combine sugar, margarine, eggs, flour, salt, chocolate syrup and vanilla in a large bowl. Mix until ingredients are moistened. Pour into a greased 9 x 13-inch pan. Bake at 350° for 30 minutes. Remove from oven and cool completely. *For frosting,* cream powdered sugar, creme de menthe and margarine in a medium bowl. Spread over cooled brownies. Refrigerate while preparing chocolate glaze. *For chocolate glaze,* melt chocolate chips and butter together. Stir until smooth. Cool for 5 minutes. Pour over creme de menthe layer and spread evenly.

Serves: 24 to 36

Sheila Kramer

"These brownies just melt in your mouth!"

FROSTED CHOCOLATE BROWNIES

Brownies:
4 (1-ounce) squares
   unsweetened chocolate
1 cup margarine or butter
6 eggs
2 cups sugar
2 teaspoons vanilla
1 ½ cups flour
1 ½ teaspoons baking soda
½ teaspoon salt
1 cup chopped walnuts

Chocolate Frosting:
¼ cup butter
14 large marshmallows
2 (1-ounce) squares
   unsweetened chocolate
Dash of salt
1 box (1 pound) powdered
   sugar
⅓ cup milk

Melt chocolate and butter; set aside. Beat together eggs and sugar. Add vanilla. Add dry ingredients alternating with melted chocolate mixture. Stir in nuts. Spread in a greased 9 x 13-inch pan. Bake at 350° for 20 to 25 minutes. *For frosting*, melt butter, marshmallows and chocolate. Add salt and powdered sugar. Beat in milk. Spread on warm brownies. Cool and cut into squares.

Serves: 20 to 24

Lois Swanson

FUDGE BROWNIES

6 tablespoons unsweetened
   cocoa powder
2 ¼ cups dark brown sugar
1 cup margarine, melted
3 large eggs, slightly beaten
1 ½ cups flour
⅜ teaspoon salt
1 ½ teaspoons vanilla
1 to 1 ½ cups chopped
   pecans (optional)

Combine cocoa and brown sugar in a mixing bowl. Stir in margarine and eggs. Mix with a spoon until thoroughly blended. Sift together flour and salt. Mix into the batter. Add vanilla. Stir until well blended. Add chopped nuts and mix well. Pour batter into a greased 9 x 13-inch pan. Bake at 325° for 25 minutes, or until done.

Yield: 20 to 24 brownies

Cherie Miles

"I prefer to use Williams-Sonoma's Penigotti or Dark Jersey cocoa for a rich taste."

Peanut Butter Lover's Brownies

1 cup (2 sticks) butter or
  margarine, softened
2 cups sugar
2 eggs
1 cup milk
2 teaspoons vanilla
½ cup unsweetened cocoa
  powder
2 cups flour

Topping:
Peanut Butter

Frosting:
½ cup (1 stick) butter or
  margarine
4 tablespoons unsweetened
  cocoa powder
6 tablespoons milk
1 teaspoon vanilla
1 (1 pound) box powdered
  sugar

Cream together butter, sugar and eggs. Add milk and vanilla. Combine cocoa and flour together. Add to sugar mixture, mixing thoroughly. Spread in a 9 x 13-inch pan. Bake at 350° for 20 to 25 minutes. Remove from oven. Cool slightly. Carefully spread a layer of your favorite peanut butter over the brownies. *For frosting,* melt butter and cocoa together in a small saucepan. Remove from heat. In a medium heat-proof bowl, combine chocolate butter, milk, vanilla and powdered sugar. Beat until creamy. Pour over warm brownies.

Serves: 20

Alice Schiefen
Kathy Johnstone
Georgia Hurley

"A favorite!! The frosting will keep them coming back for more and more."

FALL FESTIVAL BROWNIES

1 (21 ½-ounce) package
   fudge brownie mix
1 teaspoon cinnamon
⅛ teaspoon nutmeg
   (optional)
½ cup water
½ cup oil
1 egg

1 (16-ounce) can chocolate
   fudge frosting
Fall candy mix (pumpkins,
   candy corn, other
   seasonal shapes)

In a large bowl, combine brownie
mix, cinnamon, nutmeg, water, oil
and egg. Beat by hand until
moistened. Spread in a greased 9 x
13-inch pan. Bake at 350° for 30 to
35 minutes. Do not overbake.
Remove from oven and cool. Frost
with chocolate fudge frosting. With
a knife, score frosting into 24 bars.
Garnish with a candy pumpkin or
other candy pieces on each bar.
Refrigerate until frosting is firm.
Cut into bars.

Yield: 24 bars

CHOCOLATE CHIP-OATMEAL COOKIES

1 cup margarine or butter,
   softened
1 ¼ cups brown sugar
½ cup granulated sugar
2 eggs
2 tablespoons milk
2 teaspoons vanilla
2 cups flour
1 teaspoon baking soda
2 ½ cups quick or old-
   fashioned oatmeal
1 (12-ounce) package
   chocolate chips

Beat margarine and sugars until
creamy. Add eggs, milk and vanilla,
mixing well. Add flour and baking
soda; mix well. Stir in oatmeal and
chocolate chips. Drop rounded
tablespoonfuls onto a greased
baking sheet. Bake at 350° for 8
minutes for a chewy cookie or 9 to
10 minutes for a crisp cookie.

Yield: 3 to 4 dozen cookies

Jeanette Howe

CHOCOLATE MOUNTAIN COOKIES

½ cup corn oil
4 (1-ounce) squares
   unsweetened chocolate,
   melted
2 cups sugar
4 eggs
2 teaspoons vanilla
½ teaspoon salt
2 cups flour
2 teaspoons baking powder
1 cup powdered sugar

Combine oil, chocolate and sugar in large mixer bowl. Beat in one egg at a time until well mixed. Add vanilla. Mix salt, flour and baking powder together. Stir into chocolate mixture. Chill several hours or overnight. Roll small balls (about 1 teaspoon) of dough in powdered sugar. Place 2 inches apart on a greased baking sheet. Bake at 350° for 10 to 12 minutes. Do not overbake.

Yield: 50 cookies

Lois Kennel

DUSSELDORF COOKIES

4 cups flour
¼ teaspoon salt
1 pound (4 sticks) butter
1 cup sugar
2 tablespoons vanilla
1 (8-ounce) package pecans,
   ground

Seedless raspberry
   preserves
Granulated sugar

Sift flour and salt together in a bowl; set aside. Cream butter and sugar together in a large bowl. Add vanilla and nuts. Add sifted flour and salt, mixing well. Shape into rolls about ¾-inch in diameter. Wrap in waxed paper and refrigerate at least 8 hours. Slice thin with sharp knife. Bake on an ungreased cookie sheet at 350° for 6 to 8 minutes. While cookies are still warm, put 2 cookies together with seedless raspberry preserves and roll in granulated sugar.

Yield: 6 to 8 dozen

Bev Olander

LISA'S KILLER COOKIES

1 (18-ounce) box yellow
  cake mix with pudding
¼ cup brown sugar
1 egg
¾ cup oil
1 cup pecans, chopped
1 (4.67-ounce) box creme de
  menthe chocolate mints,
  broken into pieces

Combine cake mix and brown sugar in medium size bowl. Stir in egg and oil with a fork. Mix well. Add nuts and chocolate pieces; mix well. Drop heaping tablespoons of dough, 2 inches apart, onto an ungreased baking sheet. With your fingers, shape each into a 2 ½ x ½-inch thick disk. Bake at 375° for 10 to 15 minutes, or until golden. Cool cookies on a rack.

Yield: 2 dozen

Sonia Gisvold

MACAROONS

2 egg whites
1 cup sugar
½ teaspoon vanilla
1 cup flaked coconut
2 cups corn flakes

Beat egg whites until foamy. Add sugar gradually, beating until stiff. Add vanilla. Fold in flaked coconut. Add corn flakes, mixing well. Drop by teaspoonful onto a greased baking sheet. Bake at 350° for 20 minutes, until golden brown.

Yield: About 4 dozen

Margaret McVay

OATMEAL CRISPS

½ cup butter
1 tablespoon white corn
   syrup
½ cup brown sugar
1 teaspoon vanilla
1 ¾ cups old-fashioned or
   quick oats, uncooked
¼ teaspoon baking powder
¼ teaspoon salt
⅓ cup coconut

Melt butter. Add corn syrup, brown sugar and vanilla. Mix oats, baking powder, salt and coconut. Combine with butter-sugar mixture. Divide mixture in half and pat evenly, about ¼-inch thick, into two greased 8-inch square baking pans. Bake at 325° for 15 to 20 minutes. Watch carefully! Cut into finger-shaped pieces.

Yield: 3 dozen

Mrs. George B. Logan

"These are crunchy and good with tea."

OATMEAL-CARROT COOKIES

1 cup butter or margarine
¾ cup granulated sugar
¾ cup brown sugar
2 eggs
1 teaspoon vanilla
2 ½ cups flour
1 teaspoon baking soda
1 teaspoon salt
½ teaspoon nutmeg
1 teaspoon cinnamon
¼ teaspoon cloves
½ teaspoon cardamon
1 ½ cups quick oats
1 cup finely shredded
   carrots
½ cup raisins

In a large mixing bowl, cream butter and sugars until fluffy. Beat in eggs and vanilla. In a small bowl, combine flour, soda and spices. Stir well with a fork. Gradually add to butter and sugar mixture, mixing well. Stir in oats, carrots and raisins, blending well. Drop by teaspoon onto ungreased baking sheets. Bake at 375° for 8 to 10 minutes. Transfer baked cookies to racks to cool.

Yield: About 5 dozen

Nina Sudor

"An easy way to get children to eat their carrots!"

ORANGE CARROT COOKIES

¾ cup margarine, melted
2 teaspoons baking powder
½ teaspoon vanilla
¾ cup sugar
1 egg
1 cup cooked, mashed
  carrots
2 cups flour

Frosting:
¼ cup butter or margarine,
  melted
3 tablespoons orange juice
2 cups powdered sugar
Rind of ½ orange, grated

Combine margarine, baking powder, vanilla and sugar in a large mixing bowl. Beat in egg. Add carrots, mixing thoroughly. Add flour gradually, mixing until smooth. Drop by tablespoonfuls onto greased baking sheets. Bake at 350° for 12 to 15 minutes. *For frosting,* combine butter and juice in a bowl. Add powdered sugar, mixing until smooth. Stir in orange rind. Frost cooled cookies.

Yield: 3 to 4 dozen cookies

Kathleen Lowery
Mary Urquhart

EASY OLD-FASHIONED FUDGE

1 (5-ounce) can evaporated
  milk
2 cups sugar
½ cup (1 stick) butter
1 (6-ounce) package
  semisweet chocolate
  chips
1 teaspoon vanilla
Chopped nuts (optional)

In a small heavy saucepan, boil milk and sugar together for 6 minutes, stirring constantly. Remove from heat. Add remaining ingredients, except nuts. Stir until combined. Beat with an electric mixer for 5 minutes, until it starts to thicken. Chopped nuts may be added at this point, if desired. Pour onto a buttered plate or pan and allow to cool. Cut into 1-inch pieces.

Yield: 24 to 36 pieces

Maren Stocke

"This has the taste and texture of good old-fashioned fudge."

CAPPUCCINO CARAMELS

1 cup butter or margarine
1 (16-ounce) package
   (2 ¼ cups packed)
   brown sugar
1 (14-ounce) can sweetened
   condensed milk
1 cup light corn syrup
3 tablespoons instant coffee
   crystals
1 teaspoon finely shredded
   orange peel
1 cup chopped walnuts or
   pecans
1 teaspoon vanilla

In a heavy 3-quart saucepan, melt butter over low heat. Stir in brown sugar, sweetened condensed milk, corn syrup, coffee crystals and orange peel. Carefully clip candy thermometer to the side of the saucepan. Cook over medium heat, stirring frequently, about 15 to 20 minutes, until thermometer registers 248° (firm-ball stage). Mixture should boil at a moderate, steady rate over the entire surface. Remove saucepan from heat; remove candy thermometer from saucepan. Immediately stir in nuts and vanilla. Quickly pour mixture into a foil-lined and buttered 9 x 9-inch pan. When caramel is firm, use foil to lift it out of the pan. With a buttered knife, cut candy into ¾ to 1-inch squares. Wrap each piece in clear plastic wrap.

**Yields: Approximately 100 — ¾-inch
pieces, or about 3 pounds**

Ann Jost

"These are wonderful for gift-giving!"

YULE-FEST
SPECIALTIES

WINTER CIDER

1 (12-ounce) can frozen
   apple juice concentrate,
   thawed
1 (12-ounce) can frozen
   cranberry-apple juice
   concentrate, thawed
1 (6-ounce) can frozen
   cranberry juice cocktail
   concentrate, thawed
9 (12-ounce) cans or
   13 ½ cups of water
1 (12-ounce) can frozen
   lemonade concentrate,
   thawed
5 sticks cinnamon
¾ teaspoon ground nutmeg
7 whole cloves, tied in
   cheesecloth or placed in
   teaball
⅓ cup rum or cinnamon
   schnapps (optional), or
   rum flavoring to taste
Additional cinnamon sticks
   (optional)

In a 6-quart Dutch oven or large kettle, combine first three concentrates and water. Stir in lemonade concentrate, cinnamon sticks, nutmeg and cloves. Bring to a boil. Reduce heat, cover and simmer for 15 minutes. Remove cloves and cinnamon sticks before serving and discard. Stir in rum, cinnamon schnapps or rum flavoring. Pour into mugs or glasses. Serve warm with a cinnamon stick in each mug.

Yield: About 4 ½ quarts

Jeannette Hansen

Swedish Christmas Glogg

Peel of one orange
12 whole cardamom, peeled
  and crushed with mortar
  and pestle
10 whole cloves
1 (2-inch) piece of fresh
  ginger, peeled
1 cinnamon stick
4 quarts dry red wine
2 tablespoons Angostura
  bitters
2 cups raisins
1 cup sugar, or to taste
2 cups whole almonds,
  blanched and peeled
1 ½ cups aquavit or vodka
  (optional)

Place orange peel, cardamom, cloves, ginger and cinnamon stick on a piece of cheesecloth; tie securely with string to form a bag. In an 8-quart kettle, combine red wine, bitters, raisins and spice bag. Cover and let stand for 12 hours at room temperature. Stir well to mix. Bring to boil over medium-high heat. Stir in sugar. Add almonds. Reduce heat to low and keep hot for serving. Stir in aquavit or vodka just before serving. Spoon almonds and raisins into each cup before adding hot glogg.

Yield: 20 to 25 servings

Nan Douglas

"The aroma and spiciness of the warm drink makes it perfect for a cold winter's night party around the fire."

Wassail

2 quarts apple cider
2 cups cranberry juice
  cocktail
¾ cup sugar
1 teaspoon aromatic bitters
2 sticks cinnamon
1 teaspoon whole allspice
1 small orange, studded
  with whole cloves
1 cup rum

Mix all the ingredients in a large crockpot. Cover and cook on high for 1 hour. Reduce heat to low and simmer for 4 to 8 hours.

Yield: 12 cups

Margo Stich

CHRISTMAS MORNING FRITTATA

1 to 2 potatoes, sliced
⅜-inch thick
2 tablespoons olive oil
1 large red bell pepper,
chopped, divided
¾ cup chopped green
onions, divided
8 ounces feta cheese, broken
into small pieces, divided
8 eggs, beaten
1 cup milk
1 teaspoon tarragon

In a 12-inch cast-iron frying pan over medium heat, sauté sliced potatoes in olive oil until golden brown. Combine half of the chopped red pepper, ¼ cup green onion, and 2 ounces feta cheese in a small bowl; set aside. In a large bowl, combine remaining red pepper, ½ cup green onions, 6 ounces feta cheese, beaten eggs, milk and tarragon; mix well. Pour egg mixture over the browned potatoes. Continue to cook on stove top for 4 to 6 minutes. Top with the pepper-onion-cheese mixture that had been set aside. Place frying pan in a preheated oven and bake at 350° for 20 to 30 minutes, until set.

Serves: 6 to 8

Jane Aughenbaugh

TOASTED ENGLISH MUFFINS WITH SPICED HONEY

1 cup honey
¼ teaspoon ground cloves
¼ teaspoon cinnamon
English muffins

Combine honey, cloves and cinnamon in a bowl, mixing thoroughly. Let stand for at least 30 minutes before serving. Serve on toasted English muffins.

Jane Aughenbaugh

Avocado and Mozzarella with Vinaigrette

½ cup olive oil
3 tablespoons red wine
  vinegar
1 clove garlic, minced
3 ripe avocados, halved,
  pitted, peeled and cubed
15 ounces fresh mozzarella
  in milk, drained and
  cubed
¼ cup fresh basil, chopped
Salt and pepper to taste
Raddichio for garnish

Whisk olive oil, vinegar and garlic together in a large bowl, blending well. Add avocados, mozzarella and basil; toss together. Season with salt and pepper. Refrigerate until ready to serve. Serve on a plate, on a leaf of raddichio for color.

Serves: 8

Lois Martin

Baked Cheddar Olives

1 cup grated sharp Cheddar
  cheese
2 tablespoons unsalted
  butter, softened
½ cup flour
⅛ teaspoon cayenne
  pepper, or less to taste
1 (3-ounce) jar small
  pimiento-stuffed green
  olives, drained and
  patted dry

In a medium-size bowl, combine Cheddar cheese and butter. Add flour and cayenne. Blend dough until well combined. Wrap or mold one tablespoon of dough around each olive, covering completely. Place Cheddar olives on a baking sheet. Bake at 400° for 15 minutes, or until pastry is golden. Serve warm.

Yield: 24 Cheddar olives

Renda Meloy

"Easy to make. Prepare early in the day and bake just before serving. Be sure the olives are thoroughly patted dry."

STUFFED CORNETS WITH GINGER CREAM

Ginger Cream:
3 ounces cream cheese,
    softened
1 teaspoon grated peeled
    fresh ginger root
1 teaspoon milk
1 teaspoon dry mustard
Pepper to taste

2 firm-ripe pears
Juice of 1 lemon
20 thin slices of prosciutto
    ham
40 fresh chives, cut into
    3-inch lengths

In a small bowl, beat together cream cheese, ginger root, milk, mustard and pepper until smooth; set aside. Halve, core and cut each pear lengthwise into 20 slices. Gently toss pear slices with lemon juice, coating them thoroughly. Spread ¼ teaspoon ginger cream on 1 piece of prosciutto. Arrange 1 pear slice and 3 pieces of chives in the center, and fold the side of prosciutto to enclose in a cone shape. Repeat with remaining ginger cream, prosciutto, pears and chives. Arrange decoratively on a platter.

Yield: 40 cornets

CRANBERRY-CHEESE CRACKER SPREAD

1 pound fresh or frozen
    cranberries
1 large apple, peeled, cored
    and diced
1 pear, peeled, cored and
    diced
⅓ cup golden raisins
⅓ cup dark raisins
½ cup fresh orange juice
¾ cup sugar
1 tablespoon grated orange
    peel
1 teaspoon cinnamon or
    apple pie spice
¼ cup tawny port

1 (8-ounce) package cream
    cheese
Wheat crackers

In a large kettle or pan, heat first nine ingredients to boiling. Reduce heat and simmer, uncovered, stirring frequently, about 40 to 50 minutes. Remove from heat. (Taste at this point for sweetness, adding more sugar if desired.) Stir in port. Refrigerate overnight. *To serve,* unwrap cream cheese. Place on a serving plate with a rim. Pour cranberry relish over. Serve with crackers.

Margo Stich

"This is an adaptation of the recipe 'Cranberries to be Relished', which was so popular in the first cookbook 'Recipes of Note'. The original recipe calls for Grand Marnier and nutmeg."

VEAL PATÉ

Patés:
6 tablespoons unsalted
  butter
1 cup minced onions
½ cup minced shallots
4 large cloves garlic, minced
1 ½ pounds mushrooms,
  finely chopped
2 pounds ground veal
1 cup Madeira wine
1 ½ cups pimiento-stuffed
  green olives, drained
  (juices reserved) and
  chopped
4 teaspoons salt
2 teaspoons freshly ground
  pepper
2 teaspoons dried thyme,
  crumbled
2 pounds sweet Italian
  sausage, casings removed
4 eggs, beaten to blend
½ cup chopped fresh
  parsley
¼ cup drained green
  peppercorns in brine,
  rinsed

Aspic:
4 envelopes unflavored
  gelatin
2 cups veal or beef stock,
  divided
¼ cup Madeira wine
Fresh thyme or parsley
  sprigs for garnish
Mushroom slices for
  garnish

Purple cabbage for garnish
French bread baguettes,
  sliced

Grease two 8-cup terrine molds. Melt butter in a large heavy skillet over medium-low heat. Add onions, shallots and garlic; cook until soft, stirring occasionally, about 10 minutes. Increase heat to high and add mushrooms. Stir until mushrooms exude juices, about 3 minutes. Reduce heat and simmer until juices reduce slightly, about 5 minutes. Remove from heat and cool. Regrind veal finely in a food processor. Add Madeira, 6 tablespoons reserved olive juice, salt, pepper and thyme. Blend until smooth. Add sausage and pulse to blend just until incorporated. Transfer mixture to a large bowl. Stir in mushroom mixture, olives, eggs, parsley and green peppercorns. Press meat into prepared terrine molds. Cover tightly with foil. Place in a large baking pan. Add enough boiling water to pan to come halfway up sides of terrines. Bake at 350° for 1 hour 15 minutes, until patés pull from sides of terrines, juices run clear and thermometer inserted in center registers 160°. Remove terrines from oven and water bath. Cool for 1 hour on a rack. Weight each with about 3 pounds and refrigerate for 3 hours. Remove weights and refrigerate overnight. (Can be prepared up to 5 days ahead of time.) *For aspic,* sprinkle gelatin over ½ cup stock. Let stand until softened, about 5 minutes. Bring remaining stock to a simmer in a small saucepan. Add gelatin mixture and stir until dissolved. Remove from heat and stir in Madeira. Cool until mixture is just syrupy. Meanwhile, remove patés from terrines. Scrape fat away. Place each on a plate. Wrap foil securely around edges of patés , extending at least 1 inch above top, forming collars. Spoon a thin layer of aspic over each and refrigerate until set. Spoon another thin layer of aspic over each, gently warming aspic in saucepan if jelling. Garnish with thyme and mushrooms; refrigerate until set. Spoon another layer of aspic over; refrigerate until set. Spoon one more layer of aspic over; refrigerate until aspic sets. (Patés can be prepared 1 day ahead of time.) Remove collars from patés. Arrange on a platter. Garnish with purple cabbage. Serve with baguette slices.

Yield: Two 8-cup terrines

Julie Larson
Julie Roenigk

APPLE SOUP WITH ROQUEFORT CROUTONS

6 tablespoons unsalted butter, divided

1 ¼ pounds Red Delicious apples (about 3 large apples), peeled, cored and sliced

1 ¼ pounds Granny Smith apples (about 3 large apples), peeled, cored and sliced

1 cup chopped onion

1 teaspoon minced garlic

5 cups chicken stock or canned chicken broth

1 ½ cups whipping cream

¼ cup Calvados (apple brandy)

Salt and freshly ground pepper to taste

½ Red Delicious apple, cored (unpeeled)

½ Granny Smith apple, cored (unpeeled)

1 tablespoon fresh lemon juice

2 tablespoons snipped fresh chives

Roquefort Croutons:

4 bacon slices

18 (¼-inch-thick) slices French bread baguette

4 ounces Roquefort cheese, crumbled

¼ cup unsalted butter, room temperature

Melt 4 tablespoons butter in a large heavy saucepan or Dutch oven over medium heat. Add apples, onion and garlic. Cook for 5 minutes, stirring occasionally. Add stock and simmer until apples are very tender, about 25 minutes. Puree mixture in batches in a blender or food processor. Return puree to pan. Add cream and Calvados. Bring to a simmer. Season with salt and pepper. (Can be prepared 1 day ahead. Cool, cover and refrigerate.) Cut each apple half into 12 thin slices. Gently mix with lemon juice; set aside. Melt 2 tablespoons butter in a large skillet over medium-high heat. Add apples and sauté until golden brown, about 10 minutes. *For croutons,* cook bacon until crisp. Transfer to paper towels and drain. Crumble bacon. Arrange bread slices on a large baking sheet. Bake in the center of the oven at 350° until bread begins to look crisp, about 10 minutes. Remove from oven. Mix cheese and butter in a food processor until smooth. Spread one side of each crouton with cheese mixture. (Can be prepared 4 hours ahead. Cover croutons and store at room temperature.) Broil croutons 5 inches from heat source until cheese bubbles, about 2 minutes. Remove from oven and sprinkle with bacon. *To serve,* bring soup to a simmer over medium heat. Ladle into bowls. Top each bowl with 2 red apple slices and 2 Granny Smith

apple slices. Sprinkle with chives.
Serve with warm croutons.

Serves: 6

Julie Roenigk

"Delicious!"

CRANBERRY GLAZED BRIE

3 cups cranberries
¾ cup brown sugar
⅓ cup dried currants
⅓ cup water
⅛ teaspoon dry mustard
⅛ teaspoon ground allspice
⅛ teaspoon cardamom
⅛ teaspoon cloves
⅛ teaspoon ginger

**1 (2.2-pound) Brie cheese
   wheel**

Apple slices
Pear slices
Crackers

In a saucepan, combine cranberries, brown sugar, currants, water and spices. Cook over high heat for 5 minutes. Remove from heat to cool. Cover and refrigerate. (This may be made up to 3 days in advance.) Set Brie on a heat-proof platter. Using a sharp knife, cut a circular top off rind, leaving ½-inch border. Spread cranberry marmalade over brie and refrigerate for 6 hours. Remove from refrigerator 2 hours before serving and bring to room temperature. Bake at 300° for 12 minutes. Serve with fresh fruit slices and/or crackers.

Serves: 12

Julie Larson

CURRIED CARROT AND PARSNIP SOUP

¼ cup unsalted butter
1 ½ cups chopped leeks,
   white part only (about 2
   large)
1 pound carrots, peeled and
   coarsely chopped
¾ pound parsnips, peeled
   and coarsely chopped
8 cups chicken stock or
   canned chicken broth
1 ¾ teaspoons curry
   powder
½ cup whipping cream
Salt and freshly ground
   pepper
2 tablespoons chopped
   fresh parsley

Melt butter in large heavy pot over medium-high heat. Add leeks and sauté until just softened, about 4 minutes. Add carrots and parsnips and sauté 3 minutes. Add stock and curry and bring to boil. Reduce heat and simmer until vegetables are very tender, stirring occasionally, about 30 minutes. Cool slightly. Puree soup in blender in batches. (Can be prepared 1 day ahead and refrigerated.) Return puree to pot. Add cream and bring to simmer. Season with salt and pepper. Ladle soup into bowls. Sprinkle with parsley and serve.

Serves: 8

Renda Meloy

OVEN-BAKED SPLIT PEA SOUP

1 pound split peas
8 cups water
1 ½ cups diced carrots
1 ½ cups diced celery
¾ cup diced onion
2 cloves garlic, minced
½ cup parsley sprigs,
   chopped
2 teaspoons dried thyme
1 teaspoon celery seeds
1 teaspoon salt
¼ teaspoon freshly ground
   pepper
1 bay leaf
1 pound fully cooked
   smoked sausage
   (kielbasa), coarsely
   chopped
1 teaspoon aromatic bitters

Rinse split peas in cold water. Place peas in a large kettle with remaining ingredients, except sausage and bitters. Bake, covered, at 350° for 2 hours. Remove from oven and cool. Discard bay leaf. Puree soup in a food processor or blender, working in batches, until smooth. Return pureed soup to the kettle. Add sausage and bitters. Bake 30 minutes longer, or until sausage is heated through.

Serves: 8

Barbara Young

"After trimming the tree, this hearty soup is easy and delicious. Turkey kielbasa can be substituted for regular sausage if desired."

GRAPEFRUIT POMEGRANATE MEDLEY

4 grapefruit
6 oranges
1 avocado
1 pomegranate

Lettuce

Peel outside of grapefruits and oranges with a knife, as if peeling an apple. Remove as much membrane as possible. Separate fruit into sections, following section lines, retaining as much juice as possible (best to separate into sections over the bowl in which you are mixing salad). Place fruit sections in bowl. Peel avocado, cut into slices and then into chunks; combine with fruit sections. Open pomegranate, removing only seeds. Add seeds to fruit-avocado mixture. Toss gently and chill. Serve on a bed of lettuce in a large bowl or in individual servings.

Serves: 6 to 8

Lisa Rodysill

"A colorful winter salad with green avocado, red pomegranate and orange citrus fruits. Pomegranates are usually in season during November and December. If unavailable, add chunks of red apple with peel left on."

BEEF CREPES

½ cup chopped onion
¼ cup butter or margarine
1 pound cooked beef roast,
    ground fine
2 tablespoons flour
1 teaspoon salt
1 clove garlic, minced
¼ teaspoon pepper
1 (4-ounce) jar sliced
    mushrooms, drained
2 ounces slivered almonds
¼ cup sherry
1 (10 ¾-ounce) can cream of
    chicken soup
1 cup sour cream

Crepes:
⅔ cup flour
½ teaspoon salt
3 eggs
1 ½ cups milk
About ¼ cup melted butter
    or margarine, divided

Sliced almonds for garnish
Strawberries for garnish

In a large skillet, sauté onions in butter until tender. Stir in ground meat, flour, salt, garlic, pepper and mushrooms. Cook for 5 minutes, stirring constantly. Stir in almonds, sherry and soup; heat to boiling, stirring constantly. Reduce heat; simmer, uncovered, for 10 minutes. Stir in sour cream and heat through; do not boil. *For crepes,* combine flour, salt and eggs in a medium bowl; beat with a wire whisk until smooth. Gradually beat in milk and 1 ½ tablespoons melted butter until well blended. Cover and refrigerate at least 2 hours. Brush bottom and sides of a 7-inch skillet generously with melted butter. Heat skillet over low heat. Pour in a scant ¼ cup batter; tip pan to coat bottom with batter. Over low heat, cook batter until top is set and underside lightly browned, about 3 minutes. With a spatula, turn crepe and cook the other side until golden, about 1 minute. Slip crepe onto waxed paper. Repeat until all batter is used, stacking with waxed paper between crepes. (Crepes can be made early in the day or up to 2 months ahead. Wrap in foil and refrigerate or freeze. Thaw, wrapped, at room temperature for about 1 hour.) *To make beef crepes,* spread ⅓ cup beef mixture along the center of each crepe; fold one side over and roll up. Place two crepes on a plate. Spread 1 tablespoon of beef mixture across crepes. Sprinkle scant amount of sliced almonds over beef. Garnish with strawberries. Serve immediately.

Serves: 4 to 6

Georgia Hurley

"My grandmother started serving crepes on Christmas Eve. It became a tradition for our family."

MIXED GREENS WITH RASPBERRY VINAIGRETTE AND ROASTED PECANS

6 cups mixed salad greens
1 small red onion, sliced
4 slices bacon, cooked and crumbled

Raspberry Vinaigrette:
¼ cup olive oil
2 tablespoons raspberry vinegar
1 ½ teaspoons sugar
⅛ teaspoon salt
Dash of white pepper

Roasted Pecans:
2 tablespoons sugar
1 tablespoon butter or margarine
1 tablespoon orange juice
¼ teaspoon ground cinnamon
⅛ teaspoon red pepper
1 cup pecan halves

Combine mixed greens, onion and bacon in a large salad bowl; cover and refrigerate until ready to serve. *For raspberry vinaigrette,* combine all ingredients in a jar; cover tightly and shake vigorously. Store at room temperature until ready to mix with greens. *For roasted pecans,* combine all ingredients in a large heavy skillet; cook over medium heat, stirring constantly, until sugar dissolves. Spread pecans on a lightly greased baking sheet; bake at 200° for 1 hour, stirring every 15 minutes. Let cool completely; store in an airtight container until ready to serve. *To serve,* pour vinaigrette over greens, tossing to coat. Sprinkle pecans over top. Serve immediately.

Yield: 6 servings
      1 cup roasted pecans

Georgia Hurley

BEEF TENDERLOIN

¼ cup minced fresh parsley
3 tablespoons Dijon
mustard with seeds
½ teaspoon dried basil
1 (3-pound) beef tenderloin
roast

In a cup, mix parsley, mustard, and basil; set aside. Place beef tenderloin on a rack in broiling pan. Broil for 15 to 20 minutes. Turn tenderloin; broil 15 minutes longer. Remove pan from oven. Spread parsley mixture over tenderloin; broil 5 minutes longer for rare or until desired doneness. Remove from oven. Place on cutting board and let stand for 10 minutes for easier slicing. Serve beef thinly sliced. Or, to serve cold, place beef on a platter; cover and refrigerate until ready to serve. May be served as an appetizer or entree.

**Yield: 24 appetizer servings
6 main dish servings**

Georgia Hurley

BEETS AND PINEAPPLE

2 (16-ounce) cans sliced or
chunk beets
1 (20-ounce) can pineapple
chunks
4 tablespoons cornstarch
2 tablespoons brown sugar
2 tablespoons vinegar
Salt to taste
Butter to taste

Drain liquid from beets and pineapple into a saucepan. In a small cup, dissolve cornstarch with a bit of the liquid. Return to saucepan. Heat over medium-high heat, stirring constantly, until mixture thickens. Add brown sugar and vinegar. Add beets and pineapple chunks; heat through before serving. Add salt and butter to taste.

Serves: 10 to 12

Almyra Whitehead

"A beautiful Christmas dish, but good anytime, especially with green beans and slivered almonds."

CROWN ROAST OF PORK WITH SPICED FRUIT CHUTNEY

1 (8-pound) crown roast of
    pork
Salt and freshly ground
    pepper
1 teaspoon dried thyme,
    crumbled
½ cup dark unsulphured
    molasses
½ cup light soy sauce

Spiced Fruit Chutney:
2 cups cider vinegar
1 medium onion, finely
    chopped
½ cup water
1 tablespoon ground ginger
2 teaspoons grated orange
    peel
1 ½ teaspoons salt
½ teaspoon cinnamon
1 clove garlic, minced
¼ teaspoon dried red
    pepper flakes
3 cups brown sugar
2 small pears, cored and
    diced
1 large Granny Smith apple,
    cored and diced
2 cups fresh cranberries
½ cup dried currants

Red and green grapes for
    garnish

Season pork inside and out with salt and pepper. Rub with thyme. Place roast on a rack set in a large roasting pan. Mix molasses and soy sauce in a small bowl. Brush some of the mixture over roast. Bake at 350° for 2 hours, basting occasionally with molasses mixture. *For chutney,* combine vinegar, onion, water, ginger, orange peel, salt, cinnamon, garlic and red pepper flakes in a heavy medium saucepan over medium-high heat. Bring to a boil, stirring frequently. Reduce heat to low and simmer for 15 minutes, stirring occasionally. Add remaining ingredients, stirring until sugar dissolves. Cook until fruits are soft and liquid thickens slightly, stirring occasionally, for about 1 hour. Cool to room temperature. Chutney will thicken as it cools. (Chutney can be prepared up to 4 days in advance. Cover and refrigerate. Bring to room temperature before serving.) Remove roast from oven when done and transfer to a platter. Tent with foil and let stand for 20 minutes at room temperature. Pour any juices accumulated on platter into a sauceboat. Remove any string from roast. Fill center with grapes. Cut roast into chops when ready to serve. Spoon juices over meat and serve with chutney.

Serves: 8

Renda Meloy

CARROT RING WITH FRENCH PEAS AND CAULIFLOWER FLORETS

1 ½ cups (3 sticks) butter,
  room temperature
1 cup brown sugar
4 eggs, separated
3 cups finely grated raw
  carrots
2 tablespoons cold water
2 tablespoons lemon juice
2 cups flour
1 teaspoon baking soda
2 teaspoons baking powder
1 teaspoon salt
¼ cup breadcrumbs

French Peas:
6 tablespoons butter
¼ cup finely chopped
  lettuce
1 ½ pounds tiny frozen
  peas
¼ cup minced shallots or
  white part of green onion
1 large whole sprig parsley
2 to 4 teaspoons sugar
1 teaspoon salt
⅛ teaspoon white pepper

Cauliflower Florets:
1 large head cauliflower
1 teaspoon salt
Paprika

Parsley for garnish

Cream butter and brown sugar together in a large mixer bowl. Add yolks, beating until thick. Add carrots, water, lemon juice, flour, baking soda, baking powder and salt; mix thoroughly. In a separate bowl, beat egg whites until stiff peaks form; fold into carrot mixture. Generously oil a 3-quart ring mold; dust with breadcrumbs. Turn mixture into mold. (Carrot ring may be prepared the day before and refrigerated. Bring to room temperature and bake just before serving.) Bake at 350° for 1 hour. *For French peas*, melt butter in a 3-quart saucepan. Place lettuce on top of butter. Add remaining ingredients. Simmer covered, stirring occasionally, about 10 to 15 minutes, or until peas are just tender. *For cauliflower florets*, trim heavy outside leaves from cauliflower. Cut cauliflower into florets. Place in steamer or colander over boiling salted water; steam until crisp tender. *To serve*, remove carrot ring from oven and allow to cool for 3 minutes before loosening edges with a dull-edged knife. Turn onto a heated round serving platter. Carefully drain French peas, and remove parsley sprig. Pour into center of carrot ring. Place steamed cauliflower florets around the outer edge of carrot ring. Lightly sprinkle florets with paprika. Garnish with fresh parsley and serve.
Serves: 6 to 8

Renda Meloy

SCALLOPED OYSTERS AND CORN

½ cup (1 stick) butter or margarine
3 cups saltine cracker crumbs
16 canned oysters (reserve 1 cup of liquid)
4 cups cream style corn
½ cup half and half
1 teaspoon salt
¼ teaspoon pepper

Melt butter in a large skillet over medium-low heat. Stir in cracker crumbs until well combined. Remove from heat; set aside. In a large bowl, combine corn, half and half, oyster liquid, salt and pepper; mix well. In a greased casserole dish, spoon in a layer of corn mixture, 4 to 5 oysters, and then cracker crumbs. Repeat layers, ending with crumbs. Bake at 350° for 40 to 45 minutes or until liquid bubbles up through cracker crumb top.

Serves: 6 to 8

Lorene Geidel

CHOCOLATE NUT LOAF

2 cups flour
¾ cup sugar
1 teaspoon baking soda
1 teaspoon salt
¼ teaspoon nutmeg
1 cup mini chocolate chips
¾ cup chopped nuts
1 egg
½ cup buttermilk
½ cup orange juice
¼ cup butter, melted
1 teaspoon grated orange rind

In a large bowl, combine flour, sugar, baking soda, salt and nutmeg. Stir in chocolate chips and nuts. In a small bowl, combine egg, buttermilk, orange juice, butter and grated orange rind; mix well. Make a well in the flour mixture. Add egg mixture; stir just until flour mixture is moistened. Spoon into a greased and floured 9 x 5-inch loaf pan. Bake at 350° for 50 to 55 minutes, or until wooden pick inserted near center comes out clean. Cool in pan for 10 minutes. Remove from pan and cool on a wire rack.

Yield: 1 loaf

HOLIDAY ZUCCHINI BREAD

3 eggs
2 cups sugar
1 cup oil
2 cups peeled and grated
   zucchini
2 teaspoons vanilla
3 cups flour
½ teaspoon baking powder
1 teaspoon salt
1 teaspoon soda
3 teaspoons cinnamon
½ to ¾ cup chopped nuts
½ cup candied fruit
6 maraschino cherries,
   minced
Whole pecans for garnish
   (optional)
Sliced maraschino cherries
   for garnish (optional)

In a large bowl, beat eggs until
frothy. Add sugar, oil and zucchini.
Add vanilla, mixing lightly. Sift
flour, baking powder, salt, soda and
cinnamon together. Gradually add
to egg mixture, mixing well. Fold in
nuts, candied fruit and cherries.
Divide batter among six greased
and floured 6 x 3-inch loaf pans.
Decorate with whole pecans and
sliced maraschino cherries as
desired. Bake at 350° for 30 to 45
minutes, or until toothpick inserted
in the center comes out clean.
Remove from oven and cool
completely. Wrap in foil, then
plastic wrap. Freezes well.

Yield: 6 mini-loaves

Alice Schiefen

*"The pecans and cherries arranged decoratively
on top add a nice touch when giving the bread as
gifts."*

BRANDIED SWEDISH FRUIT SOUP

2 cups water
6 ounces pitted prunes
½ cup golden raisins
½ cup dried apricots
2 small Golden Delicious apples (peeled, if desired), cored and cut into ¼-inch slices
½ cup sugar
1 cinnamon stick
1 (16-ounce) can pitted sweet cherries, juice reserved
4 teaspoons cornstarch
¼ cup brandy

Whipped cream (optional)

In a 2 to 3-quart pan, combine water, prunes, raisins, apricots, apples, sugar and cinnamon stick. Bring to a boil over high heat; reduce heat, cover and simmer until apples are tender, about 5 minutes. Add cherries, reserving juice. Stir cornstarch into juice; stir into fruit mixture. Cook, stirring constantly, until mixture boils and thickens. Remove from heat and stir in brandy. Serve hot with a dollop of whipped cream. Or let cool; cover, refrigerate until well chilled, and serve cold.

Serves: 6

Ina Chase Sherman

"Served either hot or chilled, this makes a wonderful winter dessert. Add a dollop of whipped cream to create a festive and crowning touch."

OLD-FASHIONED MINCEMEAT

1 pound lean beef (or
   venison)
½ pound suet
Water
About 3 cups chopped tart
   apples
1 cup brown sugar
½ cup molasses
2 cups apple cider
½ cup cider vinegar
½ tablespoon ground
   cinnamon
½ tablespoon salt
½ teaspoon ground allspice
½ teaspoon ground nutmeg
½ teaspoon ground cloves
1 pound raisins
1 pound currants

Cover meat and suet with water and cook until tender, about 1 ½ hours. Cool in cooking water, then refrigerate overnight. Remove fat that congeals on top. Remove meat, reserving liquid and suet. Chop or grind meat, mixing it with apples. (Amount of apples should be approximately twice the amount of meat.) Place apple-meat mixture in a large kettle or Dutch oven. Add sugar, molasses, cider, vinegar and spices. Bring to a boil, reduce heat and simmer for about one hour. Add currants, raisins, suet and 1 cup of reserved beef stock; cook one hour more. Pour into sterile jars and process in hot water bath for 1 ½ hours. Can also be packed in freezer containers and frozen. Thaw before using.

Yield: 2 ½ quarts

Dora Ann Chase

"I like to make the mincemeat late in the fall to have on hand for the holidays. Make mincemeat pie using a double crust. Fresh apples, additional raisins, or nuts may be added to the mincemeat just before baking. Flavor with brandy or rum as desired. Bake at 400° for about 1 hour, covering the crust to prevent burning. Serve warm with whipped cream or a buttered rum sauce."

BELGIAN APPLE PIE

Pastry:
½ cup butter
⅓ cup sugar
½ teaspoon vanilla
1 cup flour

Apples:
4 cups Haralson apples,
   peeled and sliced
⅓ cup sugar
½ teaspoon cinnamon

Filling:
1 (8-ounce) package cream
   cheese, softened
¼ cup sugar
1 egg
¼ teaspoon vanilla

Cream butter and sugar together. Add vanilla, blending well. Mix in flour and form into a ball. Press on the bottom of a 10-inch springform pan; set aside. In a large bowl, combine apples, sugar and cinnamon; set aside. *For filling,* mix cream cheese and sugar. Add egg and vanilla, beating until smooth and creamy. Pour filling into pastry shell. Sprinkle apple mixture over evenly. Bake at 450° for 30 minutes. Remove from oven and cool. Remove rim of pan to serve.

Serves: 8

Phyllis Hammes

BUCHE DE NOEL (CHOCOLATE YULE LOG)

Melted butter
¾ cup cake flour
¼ cup unsweetened cocoa
   powder
6 large eggs, separated,
   room temperature
1 teaspoon vanilla
1 teaspoon fresh lemon
   juice
¾ cup sugar, divided
Pinch of salt

Truffle Buttercream:
½ cup heavy cream
6 ounces fine-quality
   bittersweet chocolate,
   chopped fine
¾ cup (1 ½ sticks) unsalted
   butter, cut into pieces and
   softened
1 tablespoon finely chopped
   candied orange rind

Decoration:
Powdered sugar
Meringue mushrooms
   (recipe on page 318)

Ivy branches (optional)

Prepare a 15 x 10 ½-inch jelly roll pan by brushing it with melted butter. Chill for 15 minutes. Line pan with parchment paper. Brush paper with melted butter and chill for 15 minutes more. Dust pan with additional flour, knocking out the excess; chill while making cake batter. Sift flour and cocoa powder together on a sheet of wax paper; set aside. In a large bowl with an electric mixer, beat egg yolks with vanilla, lemon juice and half the sugar until mixture is thick and pale, and forms a ribbon when the beaters are lifted. In another bowl, with clean beaters, beat egg whites with salt at medium speed, until soft peaks form. Increase speed to high and add remaining sugar in a stream, beating the whites until they hold stiff glossy peaks. Stir one fourth of the whites into the yolk mixture. Fold in remaining whites while sifting flour mixture in. Spread batter evenly in prepared pan. Smooth top. Bake at 350° in the middle of the oven for 10 to 12 minutes, or until cake springs back when touched. Remove from oven and invert onto a dampened kitchen towel. Remove parchment paper. (You may wish to trim edges with a sharp serrated knife.) Beginning with a long side, roll up cake in a towel. Let cake cool in the towel. (The cake may be made 4 hours in advance and kept wrapped in the towel at room temperature.) *To make truffle buttercream*, bring cream to a boil in a saucepan. Remove from heat and add chocolate. Let mixture stand for 5 minutes and then stir until well blended. Transfer mixture to a bowl and chill, covered, for 15 to 30 minutes, or until cool to touch. With an electric mixer, beat mixture until it lightens in color and thickens. Add butter gradually, beating constantly until thick and well blended. Remove 1 cup of buttercream to a small bowl, stir in candied orange rind and set aside. *To assemble cake,* unroll cake partially, being careful not to open it so far that it cracks. Spread inside of roll with orange-flavored buttercream. Reroll cake carefully, removing towel, and transfer to a cake board or platter. Trim ends diagonally with a serrated knife and attach the ends to the log, cut sides down, with wooden picks to form "limbs". Spread the remaining buttercream over the cake roll. Run a fork through the buttercream to resemble bark. Chill for 1 hour or until buttercream is firm. (The cake roll may be made up to this point 2 days in advance. Keep chilled. Cover loosely.) *Just before serving,* dust the cake roll with powdered sugar to resemble snow. Arrange meringue mushrooms decoratively on and around the cake roll. Decorate the cake board with ivy branches if desired.

Serves: 12 to 16

Renda Meloy

"A traditional French Christmas dessert."

Meringue Mushrooms

4 egg whites, room temperature
½ teaspoon cream of tartar
1 cup plus 2 tablespoons superfine sugar
1 teaspoon vanilla

6 ounces semisweet chocolate chips

Unsweetened cocoa powder

Beat egg whites in a large bowl with an electric mixer until foamy. Add cream of tartar, beating until soft peaks form; do not overbeat. Sprinkle in 3 tablespoons sugar; beat well. Continue adding 3 tablespoons of sugar at a time, beating well after each addition, until half of the sugar has been incorporated. Beat in vanilla. Continue adding sugar, beating until it is all dissolved and stiff peaks form when beaters are lifted. Line 2 to 3 baking sheets with foil or parchment. Fit a large pastry bag with a wide tip. Fill bag with meringue and squeeze a dozen plump mounds (the size of medium mushroom caps) onto baking sheets. Use a finger or table knife dipped in water to smooth the tops of each mound to make the mushroom cap. To make the stems, hold the pastry bag straight up, perpendicular to baking sheet, and pipe into conical mounds. Vary the width and height of each cone, from ½ to 1-inch long, slicing them off with a wet knife. Repeat with the remaining meringue to make an equal number of caps and stems. Bake at 200 to 225° for at least 2 hours. Meringues should be dry and very lightly colored if at all. Turn off oven and let them continue drying for several hours or overnight. (Be sure not to turn on oven until meringue has been removed.) Cool pieces completely before assembling the mushrooms.

To assemble mushrooms, melt chocolate in the top of a double boiler over hot water; remove from heat. Put a small spoonful of chocolate on the underside of a mushroom cap and spread it slightly with the tip of a stem. Push the stem against the center of the cap to secure it. (Do not let chocolate drip or smear.) Place mushrooms, cap down, in an empty egg carton or mini-muffin pan until chocolate has set. Repeat using remaining pieces. If chocolate begins to harden, gently reheat it on the double boiler. After the mushrooms have set, lightly dust the tops of the caps with a bit of cocoa shaken through a sieve. Store in an airtight container until ready to serve. The meringue mushrooms will keep for 1 to 3 days depending on the humidity.

Yield: 35 to 45

CANDY CANE CHEESECAKE

Crust:
1 ⅓ cups chocolate cookie
  crumbs
2 tablespoons sugar
¼ cup butter or margarine,
  melted

Filling:
1 ½ cups sour cream
½ cup sugar
3 eggs
1 tablespoon flour
2 teaspoons vanilla
¼ teaspoon peppermint
  extract
3 (8-ounce) packages cream
  cheese, softened
2 tablespoons butter,
  softened
⅔ cup crushed candy canes

**Sweetened Whipped
Cream:**
½ cup heavy cream
¼ cup granulated sugar
¾ teaspoon vanilla extract

Round candy cane tied with
  red ribbon to decorate
  top of cake (optional)

Combine cookie crumbs, sugar and butter, mixing well. Press into the bottom of a 9-inch springform pan; set aside. *For filling,* combine sour cream, sugar, eggs, flour and flavorings in a blender or food processor, and blend until smooth. Add cream cheese and butter, blending until completely smooth. Stir in crushed candy. Pour into crust. Bake at 325° on the lowest rack of oven for 50 to 60 minutes, or until firm. Allow to cool completely (cheesecake may crack while cooling). Refrigerate overnight. *For sweetened whipped cream,* place all ingredients in a large mixing bowl. Beat at high speed until soft peaks form. Using a knife to loosen cheesecake, remove side of springform pan. Spread top of cheesecake with sweetened whipped cream. Garnish with round candy cane and ribbon.

Serves: 10 to 12

Georgia Hurley

CHOCOLATE BALLS

1 cup peanut butter
1 cup powdered sugar
1 cup chopped dates
1 cup chopped nuts
1 (12-ounce) package
    chocolate chips

Combine peanut butter, sugar, dates and nuts. With hands, mix ingredients until well blended. Roll into small balls and refrigerate for 4 to 5 hours. Melt chocolate chips in a double boiler. Dip cold balls in melted chocolate and place on wax paper. Refrigerate until set and ready to serve. Will keep for several weeks stored in an airtight container.

Yield: 30 to 36

Karen Petitt

SALTED PEANUT BRITTLE DELUXE

2 cups sugar
1 cup white corn syrup
¼ cup water
3 tablespoons butter
1 ¼ cups salted peanuts
1 teaspoon vanilla
2 teaspoons baking soda

Grease a large baking sheet generously with butter; set aside. Combine sugar, corn syrup and water in a 3-quart saucepan, mixing well. Cook over medium heat, stirring constantly until sugar dissolves. Continue cooking and stirring until mixture reaches 285° on a candy thermometer. Stir in butter and peanuts. Cook, stirring constantly, until mixture reaches 295°. Remove from heat. Add vanilla and baking soda, stirring to blend (mixture will foam). Pour onto prepared baking sheet, spreading thin. Cool completely. Break into pieces.

Yield: 1 ½ pounds

Lisa and Scott Stiving

"Stir constantly or this will burn!"

Santa's Swedish Gnomes in a Gingerbread Bowl

Gnome Cutouts:
1 cup dark molasses
1 cup light brown sugar
1 cup (2 sticks) butter, cut
  into ½-inch pieces
2 large eggs, lightly beaten
5 to 5 ½ cups flour
1 tablespoon ground ginger
1 ½ teaspoons baking soda
1 teaspoon cinnamon
½ teaspoon ground cloves

Ornamental Icing:
1 cup powdered sugar
2 to 3 teaspoons milk
1 to 2 drops cinnamon oil
  (optional)
Red food coloring - enough
  drops to make the icing a
  true red

Gingerbread Bowls:
8 ½ to 9 cups flour, divided
1 tablespoon ginger
2 teaspoons ground
  cinnamon
½ teaspoon salt
1 ¼ cups shortening
1 (16-ounce) bottle dark corn
  syrup
1 ½ cups dark brown sugar,
  firmly packed

Heat molasses and sugar to boiling in a small saucepan. Place butter in a large heat-proof bowl. Add hot molasses, stirring until butter melts and mixture is warm to the touch. Whisk in eggs until blended. In another bowl, sift 4 cups flour, ginger, baking soda, cinnamon and cloves together. Pour flour mixture over batter and stir until smooth. Gradually stir in remaining 1 to 1 ½ cups flour, until dough comes together. Shape dough into a thick disc with floured hands. Wrap in plastic wrap and refrigerate for 3 hours or overnight. Divide chilled dough into quarters and return 3 pieces to refrigerator. On a lightly floured pastry cloth, with a covered rolling pin, roll dough to a ⅛-inch thickness. Cut out shapes with a gnome-shaped cookie cutter. Place on a lightly greased sheet and bake at 350° for 8 to 10 minutes. Remove from oven, cool slightly on cookie sheets and transfer to racks; cool completely. Continue with remaining dough. *For icing,* combine all ingredients together in a bowl. Icing should be slightly runny. Add milk if needed, 1 teaspoon at a time. Dip caps of gnomes in icing and place on waxed paper to dry. *For gingerbread bowls,* mix together 4 cups flour, ginger, cinnamon and salt in a large bowl. Melt shortening in a medium saucepan over low heat. Stir in corn syrup and dark brown sugar until ingredients are well mixed. Remove from heat. With electric mixer, at low speed, gradually beat syrup mixture into flour mixture. Increase to medium speed and beat in 2 more cups flour. With a wooden spoon or hands, mix in remaining 2 ½ to 3 cups flour until stiff dough forms. Dough should be firm, not sticky. Divide dough in 4 parts. Shape into ½-inch thick discs. Wrap each disc in plastic wrap, and refrigerate for at least an hour, or up to 1 week. When ready to bake, cover the outside of inverted oven-proof bowls (metal mixing bowls work well) with aluminum foil, making it as smooth as possible. Place bowls on a baking sheet; spray lightly with non-stick cooking spray. Remove dough from refrigerator. On a lightly floured board, roll out a circle of dough ¼-inch thick and large enough to cover the inverted bowl. Center rolled dough on top of inverted bowl and press down sides to make as smooth as possible. Trim to just above edge of bowl if necessary. Using a 1 to 1 ½-inch cookie or canapé cutter, cut out a decorative design about 1 ½ inches from the edge of the dough. Place the inverted bowls on baking sheets. Chill for 2 to 3 hours in the refrigerator. Remove from refrigerator and place in a 350° oven for 20 to 30 minutes. Remove from oven and cool completely on wire racks. Gently remove gingerbread from bowls and turn upright. Peel away any foil that may remain. Fill the cooled gingerbread bowls with gnomes.

Yield: 6 dozen cookies
     3 to 4 gingerbread bowls

Nina Sudor

"If a gnome cookie cutter is unavailable, a small gingerbread man cookie cutter could be used. Decorate the gingerbread men as you please. When the cookies are all gone, you can eat the bowl!"

SPICED NUTS

1 egg white, slightly beaten
1 teaspoon water
1 ⅔ cups mixed nuts
¾ cup sugar
1 tablespoon pumpkin pie spice
½ teaspoon salt

Combine egg white and water in a small bowl. Add nuts and stir to coat. Combine dry ingredients and toss with nuts to coat evenly. Spread in a single layer on a greased baking sheet. Bake at 300° for 20 minutes. Remove from oven and immediately spread on waxed paper to cool.

Yield: 1 ⅔ cups

Sheila Kramer

"These are wonderful for gift giving! Be sure to include the recipe because they will want to make more!"

Santa's Surprise

½ cup butter
½ cup brown sugar
½ cup granulated sugar
½ cup peanut butter
1 egg
1 teaspoon vanilla
1 ½ cups flour
½ teaspoon salt
1 teaspoon baking soda

1 (14-ounce) bag miniature
    candy peanut butter cups
Non-pareils to decorate
    (optional)

Combine butter, sugars, peanut butter, egg, vanilla, flour, salt and baking soda together in a large bowl, mixing well. Roll dough into 1-inch balls and place in small muffin tins. Bake at 375° for 10 minutes. Remove from oven and immediately push one peanut butter cup into the center of each "muffin". Sprinkle with non-pareils to decorate as desired. Remove from pan to cool.

Yield: About 4 dozen

Dan and Philip Hurley

"Santa will love these! And the children will enjoy making, as well as eating, these rich treats."

Winter Wonderland Sugar Cookies

1 ½ cups sugar
1 cup butter, softened
2 eggs, beaten
1 cup sour cream
2 to 3 tablespoons boiling
    water
1 teaspoon soda
1 tablespoon vanilla
4 cups flour
1 teaspoon baking powder

Cream sugar and butter together in a large bowl. Add eggs, mixing well. Stir in sour cream, blending well. Stir water and soda together in sour cream container. Add to sugar mixture and mix thoroughly. Pour in vanilla. Sift flour and baking powder together. Add gradually to sugar mixture while continuing to beat. Cover with plastic wrap and refrigerate overnight. Roll out dough on a very lightly floured surface. Cut in circular shapes. Sprinkle with sugar. Place on baking sheets and bake at 350° for 8 minutes. Remove from oven and transfer to wire rack to cool.

Yield: 6 dozen cookies

GRANDMA JENSEN'S SPRITZ

1 cup butter, softened
¾ cup powdered sugar
Pinch of salt
1 teaspoon vanilla
1 ½ cups flour
½ cup cornstarch

German chocolate
Decorative sprinkles

Cream butter and sugar together in a large bowl. Add salt, vanilla, flour and cornstarch and beat until well mixed. Cover and refrigerate for 1 hour. Press dough through a cookie press, about 1 inch apart, down the length of an ungreased baking sheet. Bake at 275° for 25 to 35 minutes, until lightly golden on the bottom. (Be careful not to overbake!) Remove from oven and let cool for 3 to 5 minutes. Remove cookies to a wire rack to finish cooling. Melt chocolate and drizzle over cookies. Dip in sprinkles.

Yield: 6 to 7 dozen

Tom Meloy

MACAROON ALMOND CRUMB BARS

1 (18 ¼-ounce) box German chocolate cake mix
¼ cup vegetable oil
2 eggs, divided
1 (14-ounce) can sweetened condensed milk
½ to 1 teaspoon almond extract
1 ½ cups coconut macaroon crumbs, divided
1 cup chopped slivered almonds

In a large bowl, combine cake mix, oil and 1 egg. Beat on medium speed until crumbly. Press firmly on bottom of a greased 13 x 9-inch pan. In a medium bowl, combine sweetened condensed milk, remaining egg and almond extract, mixing well. Add 1 cup macaroon crumbs and almonds. Spread evenly over prepared crust. Sprinkle with remaining ½ cup macaroon crumbs. Bake at 350° for 30 to 35 minutes or until lightly browned. Cool thoroughly. Cut into bars. Store loosely covered at room temperature.

Yield: 36 bars

CHRISTMAS FRUITCAKE SQUARES

Crust:
¾ cup (1 ½ sticks) butter or margarine
1 (12-ounce) box vanilla wafers, finely crushed (3 ¼ cups) or 3 ¼ cups graham cracker crumbs plus ½ cup sugar

Filling:
1 (10-ounce) jar red maraschino cherries, drained, halved and wrapped in paper towels to dry thoroughly
1 ½ (6-ounce) jars green maraschino cherries, prepared as above
½ cup canned pineapple bits, drained thoroughly and wrapped in paper towels
1 cup pecan halves, plain or salted
1 (14-ounce) can sweetened condensed milk
¼ cup bourbon, rum, brandy or milk

Spray a 15 x 10 ½-inch baking pan with non-stick spray. Mix crust ingredients in a bowl or food processor; press evenly into prepared pan. Bake at 350° for 4 to 6 minutes, until slightly browned. Remove from oven. *For filling,* arrange fruits and nuts evenly over crust: begin with red and green cherry halves, cut side down, then pecan halves, then pineapple bits to fill in the spaces. Press down gently into crust. Combine sweetened condensed milk with liquor or milk, mixing well. Pour evenly over top. Return pan to oven and bake for 20 to 25 minutes, until set and lightly golden brown around edges. Cool and cut into squares.

Yield: 60 squares

Ann Jost

"The original recipe called for candied cherries and pineapple. We like this version better."

CHOCOLATE CHIPS

1 (6-ounce) package semi-
   sweet or milk chocolate
   chips
24 perfect ridge-style potato
   chips (such as Pringles)

Melt chocolate in double boiler over low heat or in microwave. Remove from heat. Carefully dip one half of each chip in chocolate. Place on waxed paper or foil. Let dry completely before storing in an airtight container.

Yield: 24 chips

Georgia Hurley

"Easy! A unique gift treat to give to friends."

INDEX

Skillet New Potatoes with Garlic,
200
Spatzle, 207
Spiced Rice, 205
Spinach Provencale, 201
Steamed Carrot and Zucchini
Julienne, 192
Supreme Candied Sweet Potatoes,
202
Swedish Green Potatoes, 200
Tennessee Summer Squash, 202
Tomatoes Baked with Spinach and
Feta, 203
Vegetables in Celery Seed Marinade,
116
VEGETARIAN
Cheddar Ramekin, 174
Fettuccine Alfredo, 179
Lasagna Primavera, 184
Spinach Artichoke Casserole, 177
Spinach Pie, 178
Three-Cheese Spinach Frittata, 174
Zippy Eggs, 179
Victorian Cheese Dainties, 42
VICTORIAN TEA
Apricot Sugar Plums, 52
Asparagus Whirls, 37
Assorted Tea Sandwiches, 38
Battenberg Cake, 54
Bonbons, 56
Cheese Dainties, 42
Cream Scones, 43
Cucumber-Shrimp Tea Sandwiches,
39
Cupid's Love Wells, 49
Curried Chicken and Chutney
Sandwiches, 42
Curried Tuna Hearts, 41
Gingerbread Husbands, 44
Homemade "Devonshire" Cream,
43
Lemon and Cherry Tarts, 53
Marzipan, 54
Miniature Chocolate Eclairs, 48
Petticoat Tails, 45
Pinwheel Sandwiches, 37
Potted Shrimp Sandwiches, 40
Ratafias, 46
Sparkling Catawba Punch, 36
Spiced Nuts , 36
Tea Cakes, 50
Tomato-Egg Sandwiches, 40
Trilbys, 45
Victorian Tea Cakes, 50
Vienna Sachertorte, 260
Vivaldi Cocktails, 81
Viva La Chicken Tortilla Casserole, 161

Vodka
Bloody Mary Soup, 102
Paddler's Passion, 81
Swedish Christmas Glogg, 296

W

Waldorf Salad Extraordinaire, 120
Wassail, 296
Watercress
Assorted Tea Sandwiches, 38
Bacon Chevre Chicken Sauté, 149
Pinwheel Sandwiches, 37
Seafood Stuffed Mushrooms, 66
Wontons, 141
White Chocolate Almond Poundcake
with Amaretto Creme Anglaise, 266
Whole Wheat Flour
Oatmeal Pancakes, 222
Sensational Sweet Potato Muffins,
220
Wild Rice
Casserole, 135
Cornish Game Hen with Sausage
and Wild Rice Stuffing, 163
"Creamless" Creamy Wild Rice
Soup, 101
Ham and Wild Rice Chowder, 102
Northwoods Applesauce Muffins,
219
Turkey Supreme, 167
Wild Rice Casserole, 135
Wine
Apricot Stuffed Chicken Breasts
with Sauce Supreme, 150
Barbecued Garlic Shrimp, 170
Chevre Stuffed Chicken, 152
Chicken Marbella, 156
Cranberry-Cheese Cracker Spread,
299
Cumberland Sauce, 145
Filet of Beef in Phyllo Pastry with
Madeira Sauce, 132
Game Hens with Honey-Sauternes
Sauce, Spinach and Pearl
Onions, 164
Giuseppi's Clam Chowder, 87
Grilled Swordfish with Ginger
Butter, 173
Imperial Grilled Chicken, 154
Italian Stuffed Beef Tenderloin with
Roasted Red Pepper and Garlic
Sauce, 128
Marinated Brisket of Beef, 130
Pineapple Sorbet, 70
Provencal Chicken Sauté, 159
Red Bell Pepper Terrine with
Asparagus Vinaigrette, 114
Rosé Sorbet, 70

RECIPES OF NOTE

FOR ENTERTAINING

ORDER YOUR COPY TODAY

Quantity		Price Each	Total
_____ Recipes of Note for Entertaining			
(NEW)		$18.00	_____
_____ Recipes of Note			
(first cookbook)		$12.00	_____

Minnesota residents add 6 1/2% sales tax
$12.00 + $0.78 $18.00 + $1.17
Rochester Residents add 7% sales tax
$12.00 + $0.84 $18.00 + $1.26
}   Tax   _____

Add shipping and handling $3.00 each   _____

TOTAL   _____

Mail this form and check to:

Rochester Civic Music Guild
P.O. Box 5802
Rochester, MN 55903

Ship to:

Name _____

Address _____

City _____State _____Zip _____

Daytime Telephone _____

Thank you for your order!